EMPOWERING WOMEN
With Words

LIFE-CHANGING CONVERSATIONS

EMPOWERING WOMEN ALLIANCE

FriesenPress

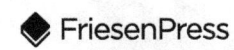

One Printers Way
Altona, MB R0G 0B0
Canada

www.friesenpress.com

Copyright © 2023 by Empowering Women Alliance
First Edition — 2023

Foreword by Sandra Yancey

All rights reserved.

No part of this publication may be reproduced in any form, or by any means, electronic or mechanical, including photocopying, recording, or any information browsing, storage, or retrieval system, without permission in writing from FriesenPress.

ISBN
978-1-03-916245-7 (Hardcover)
978-1-03-916244-0 (Paperback)
978-1-03-916246-4 (eBook)

1. SELF-HELP, SPIRITUAL

Distributed to the trade by The Ingram Book Company

A COMPASSIONATE HEADS UP

This book is about real life.

It is a collection of powerful stories written by brave women who unflinchingly tell the truth about their personal journeys and their healing, self-awareness, and empowerment. Authentic self-expression in writing requires tremendous courage. Reading a story written with absolute honesty may also require a bit of courage.

Some of the stories and conversations in this book may evoke unfamiliar or uncomfortable feelings in the moment. However, the authors' intent is to be transparent and straightforward. Each chapter moves through any difficult moments with the writer's promise of leaving the reader encouraged, enlightened, or uplifted.

As a result, each chapter offers the possibility of personal transformation through inspiration and empowerment.

TABLE OF CONTENTS

FOREWORD VII
SANDRA YANCEY

MY PAGE AND MY STORY 2
RHONDA PEOPLES

THE POWER OF PURPOSE 18
DEB ANDERSON

THE POWER OF POSSIBILITY 36
SUSAN JOHNSON

AN ODE TO ORDINARY WOMEN 52
SUE HARRIS-WILLIE

EMBRACING TRUTH 66
MING LOVEJOY

SELF-RESPECT 85
BECKY NOEL

FREEDOM COMES AT THE PACE OF GRACE 100
CHRISTY LEE

BEING CRUNCHY 116
DEBRA MUSE WOLFF

THE MOST BEAUTIFUL TAPESTRY EVER WOVEN 135
ADA IRIS JAIME

DIVINE AWAKENING 148
SUSAN JONES

WHAT I DIDN'T KNOW COST ME PLENTY! 166
KATHY PEAKE

THE WAY OF THE HEART 184
UTE VAUGHN

FEELING YOUR WAY TO FREEDOM 201
VERA KNIGHT

CULTIVATING WISDOM 217
KATHLEEN WESTWOOD

THE GIFT OF BEING SEEN 233
ANASUYA ISAACS

THE POWER OF CREATION 241
RHONDA PEOPLES

AN EMPOWERING INVITATION 258

FOREWORD

SANDRA YANCEY

Words convey power.

Without realizing it, the words that surround you leave lasting impressions. Sometimes you are bathed in words that nurture and soothe, and other times you are battered by words that prick and bruise. While some words buoy you like an ocean swell or hit you like a tsunami, all words that touch you gradually shape and change you, much like waves lapping at a shoreline. You are uniquely fashioned this way—tumbled, polished, and sculpted from your personal experience in the world of words.

You may have grown up armed with a children's rhyme as a defense against name-calling and verbal bullying: "Sticks and stones may break my bones, but words will never hurt me." That sentiment may have helped deter fistfights in the schoolyard, but it is also a lie. Words *can* hurt. They can injure, cripple, incapacitate, maim, and even kill.

Yet words can also give life. The right words at the right time can throw you a lifeline when you are drowning in despair. Positive words can brighten your moods and give you the heart to keep going when times are tough. Empathetic words can let you know you are not fighting your battles alone. Affirmative words can hold up an undistorted mirror, allowing you to focus on your strengths rather than your flaws. Encouraging words can lead the way, embolden you to stretch and grow, and give you permission to celebrate your triumphs instead of dwelling on your failures.

You live in the words you think and speak. In your mindset and speech, as in your listening, words can deceive or enlighten, dishearten or inspire, wound or heal. You alone are responsible for your choice of words, and the words you say to yourself are as important as those you say to others. Your words deserve watchful attention because, ultimately, they are judged—not by their coarseness or elegance, not by their simplicity or grandiosity, but by their destructive or beneficial effect.

The women who collaborated in writing this book have chosen their words carefully. In this labor of love, they came together to share their conversations and personal stories as well as their knowledge and experience. Each has written a separate chapter that contributes to a cohesive whole. Many of them were strangers when invited to join this project. In sharing their writing with one another, they became intimately acquainted.

Through their willingness to be vulnerable, they also deepened their understanding, compassion, and sense of community. They developed their own collaborative process while meeting together online, where they thoughtfully chose to review, rather than critique, each other's chapters. In that nurturing space, they influenced one another's writing by using words that validated and lifted every woman involved.

As CEO of eWomenNetwork, I also lift and validate women, and I choose my words carefully. I communicate with women all over the world, and I make far-reaching decisions daily with the intention of making a positive difference in the lives and businesses of women. I empower entrepreneurial women by sharing stories and expertise as well as education, networking, and opportunities. I encourage emerging female leaders of tomorrow to be unapologetic for their ambition, drive, and success. And I embolden today's businesswomen to own their greatness, to lift as they climb, and to give first, share always. My unwavering commitment to empowering women leads me to use this foreword as one more opportunity to make a positive difference in the lives of women everywhere.

In speaking to thousands of women over the years, I have often said, "Let your mess inform your message." In writing this book, each of these women has revealed the mess that gave rise to her epiphanies, breakthroughs, and successes. Each woman's chapter is close to her heart, written in her authentic voice. Each writer's style is individual yet conversational, as if she is sitting across the table from you over a cup of coffee or tea. And each woman shares powerfully because her life lessons were hard earned. All these collaborators have something valuable to say. Because of the refinement process they shared while writing, all of them say it well.

It delights me that the writers' ages span six decades, from their mid-twenties to their mid-seventies. They represent a wide range of feminine experience. Yet despite their differences, they are alike in one important respect—like me, they are passionate about empowering women.

During their online collaboration, these writers discovered that their similarities mattered more than their individual differences. While their backgrounds and voices were diverse and they lived on different continents, they came together to write and stayed together in friendship and support . . . through illness, death, financial hardship, severe injury, and pandemic quarantine. Together, they laughed and grieved and celebrated. In sharing their writing with one other, each woman found she could recognize an aspect of herself in another woman's story—just as you will be able to identify with something revealed in every woman's chapter.

This collection is emotional, engaging, and empowering. I invite you to experience it personally. Then I encourage you to share these life-changing conversations with others, too.

Empowering Women With Words was written to empower *you*.

SANDRA YANCEY is the founder and CEO of eWomenNetwork, a multi-million-dollar enterprise connecting over 500,000 women through chapters across North America, Canada, the UK, and Australia. The eWomenNetwork Foundation she created has awarded cash grants to 115 nonprofit organizations and scholarships to 167 emerging female leaders of tomorrow.

An award-winning entrepreneur, Sandra is recognized by the International Alliance for Women as one of the world's 100 Top Difference Makers and by CNN as an American Hero. She is featured in *Chicken Soup for the Entrepreneur's Soul* and is a #1 bestselling author of five books. Sandra is also featured in and producer of The GLOW Project, named by the Orlando Film Festival as "one of the most inspiring movies ever created for women."

Find out more: eWomenNetwork.com

MY PAGE AND MY STORY

RHONDA PEOPLES

Each day I'm living my best life, ever. Today, I live in my ideal house; I have my ideal husband and my ideal children. I enjoy creating and expanding my life with other human beings. I love my mother, father, and siblings more today than ever before. My relationships are better than I could have dreamed. I'm fully self-expressed and live my life authentically, every day. Each day I create my best life, ever.

But it wasn't always like that. Before I discovered what it is to be a fully actualized human living in a world of possibilities, I lived the default life most people plug into every day. I believed the stories I told myself and I unknowingly wore the filters and shackles that came with those stories. Freeing myself was a process.

Let me show you how I did it by starting with some what ifs . . .

What if, when you first meet someone, you could freeze time for a moment? Then, what if you could look at a page that flipped down over their face? What if that page could show you how they came to be who they are today?

A person's My Page would reveal the events of their life along with what those events meant to them. It would show their suffering, joy, love, and pain. You'd be reading the story they created about the events of their life.

Then you'd understand why they say what they say and why they act a certain way. You might be able to see things through their unique pair of life-glasses. And you'd have access to forgiveness and compassion for them, along with every human being on earth, when you consider that we all have an invisible My Page.

We all have stories we've created around events that happened in our lives. An event doesn't have to be labeled something big or bad or wrong or unjust—it was just an event. We created a story around the event and gave meaning, something more than, or something other than, what actually happened. Usually this is where our misperceptions or feelings get involved with what happened.

From the time I was a child, I began telling myself stories around events that happened in my life, stories I hung onto most of my life. These stories acted like wearing an invisible pair of glasses that colored everything I saw. They also determined what I did and (mostly) didn't do throughout my life. These stories were my head trash.

They were what had me stand in the background, hiding from people. They had me telling myself that people were judging me, that something was wrong with me, and that I wasn't good enough to talk with people. When my stories told me I didn't have anything important to say, and even if I said it, people wouldn't listen to me anyway, I believed that, too.

I didn't know it then, but there was something more waiting for me to discover. There was another way of seeing things. Another way of thinking and believing. But before I could make that discovery, I had to reveal my *stories* for what they were. This meant taking another look at what had happened in my life and what I'd made it mean.

I was the oldest of six children; five of us were girls and the youngest was a boy. The first three of us were raised with both mother and father in what I considered a dysfunctional home. The second group of three were raised by my mother alone, who seemed to see herself as having been victimized by her divorce.

My mom and dad were pretty young when they started having children. Mom was twenty-one and Dad was about nineteen. I remember their parties, drinking, fast cars, late nights, and brutal fights—both verbal and physical.

I lived in two houses as a child. The first one was the Cul-de-sac House, where I shared a room with my two younger sisters. We had bunk beds, and that's where Mom would come to hide from Dad when he came home drunk.

I remember one night in particular. It was summertime, probably two in the morning after the bars had closed. Dad came home, drunk, and I could hear Mom and Dad yelling in their bedroom. Then Mom came running into our room and grabbed us kids, pulling us into the lower bunk with her as if to shield herself from Dad. Meanwhile, he stumbled around the kitchen, loudly ripping open drawers as he looked for a knife. While he tore up the kitchen he was screaming, "I'm gonna kill myself!"

I was desperately scared for my mother. Since they'd been fighting, I was afraid Dad was going to use a knife on my mother before he killed himself. I was only six years old, and I felt such terror knowing I couldn't protect my mother, myself, or my siblings. Mom was huddled behind us on the bottom bunk as if we could protect her. I knew that if Dad came in with a knife, having us as a barrier wouldn't stop him.

At six years old, this was the first of many stories I would create. I made up at that moment that I wouldn't be weak like her. I'd be strong. I'd become strong enough to take on a man. I didn't need anyone, especially a man. I lived the next fifty years of my life proving I was strong enough, and I did it alone, because I didn't need anyone else.

While I was growing up, I struggled in school. I mostly hated math class. My teacher always pulled my ears when I answered incorrectly. My mom would go to the school and stand up for me when I was younger. She'd let the math teacher have it, saying, "You've no right to touch my daughter!" Those were the times I knew my mother loved me.

I've seen pictures taken of my parents in that first house; they were smiling and seemed happy. I don't remember the happy part. That house represented terror for me—punishment, discipline, crying, fighting, and fear. That house was darkness to me.

I made up my second big story when I was around twelve years old and ran for student council secretary. I was excited and made a zillion posters. As part of the campaign, I had to give a speech in front of the entire school. I remember standing in the cafeteria/auditorium up on stage with nine or ten kids, each waiting our turn to speak.

This was the same stage that was used for the school plays, the same place where we all came to eat lunch every day. The auditorium was completely familiar, but everything seemed different from the stage. The tables, now folded up along with their attached benches, had been moved alongside the wall. The whole school was there—all the students were sitting on the floor with their legs crossed, looking up at me.

I remember walking to the podium across the stage's wooden floor. The sound of my feet on the hardwood echoed throughout the auditorium. I had my notecards with me. I set them on the podium and looked out at the entire school. They were all watching me, waiting for what I was about to say.

Then I woke up in the nurse's office.

I couldn't understand why I was there, lying on a cot. What had happened? I started to sit up.

The nurse said, "Stay down so you don't pass out again."

"WHAT?" I was mortified. "I fainted in front of everyone in the entire school?" I dreaded facing everyone again.

The ridicule started the next day, the beginning of my horror stories around my school years. Everyone was talking about me and staring at me, pointing me out as The Girl Who Fainted. I heard the whispers behind my back. I felt everyone judging me. After my spectacular fainting spell, I felt judged by the other kids for everything . . . for everything I did, for the clothes I wore, and for the way I looked.

I was already very tall (my adult height is 6'1") and back then girls' and women's clothing were pretty standard. But my long legs weren't standard. Throughout my school years, I was called names like Digby (the biggest dog in the world), Jolly Green Giant, and Honda Rhonda.

Experiencing this ridicule and judgement, I began to tell myself stories about what I imagined was happening in these events. I didn't realize that I was placing shackles on myself, limiting who I could be as a human being. I would wear these shackles for most of my life.

After fainting, the story I told myself was that I couldn't speak in front of large groups. I lived my life never questioning this story that I had created. When forced to do public speaking, I'd blank out during the experience because I was so terrified. Ironically, throughout my life, I've always been in positions where it was necessary to speak to groups of people. But because of what I told myself, I felt powerless when having to do so.

I learned to work around my tendency to blank out by memorizing everything I needed to say; as long as I stuck to my prepared script, I could force myself to speak. But if anyone asked me a question that interrupted my prepared speech, or if I had to address something out of order, I was lost. Each time I blanked out or felt lost reinforced my belief that I couldn't speak in front of groups. I was just another person, one of many, who couldn't do public speaking. I had "proof."

My belief in my story and my collection of proof held me back in many ways. In high school, I really wanted to go to debate class, but couldn't because I knew I'd have to stand up in front of the class. I wanted to try theater but didn't because I knew I'd have to stand up in front of the class and an audience. I wanted to dance, but I'd never dance in front of people because that seemed too close to standing up and speaking in front of them. Mostly, I hid all the time.

If I couldn't hide, I devised strategies to cope. When I knew I had to be in a group of people, I always had an exit strategy for how I was going to get away from the group without them seeing me. In meetings, one of my strategies would be to wait until others were talking on the other side of the room before I'd get up to go to the bathroom without being noticed. I'd sometimes sit in agony for hours, needing the bathroom desperately, while I waited for a distraction because I never wanted to call attention to myself. My need to hide, not call attention to myself, and being small plagued me for many years, well into adulthood.

After feeling shamed and judged at school, I told myself I was a nobody, no one liked me, and I was different because my family wasn't like other families. (We were probably like many other families at the time, but it didn't occur to me that way.) I was ashamed of my family. The people I went to school with all seemed to come from loving families. I lived in an abusive family where the kids were beaten and yelled at daily. These were the *stories* that were true to me; this was the imprisoned hell that I lived in constantly as I grew up.

As an adult, I'd forgotten how I had taken on these stories, that I had attached certain meanings to the experiences I was having, and those stories became the shackles I placed upon myself. I lived life as it was all true. Until a couple of years ago, I couldn't walk through a mall without hearing people laughing and being sure they were laughing at me. I'd even look over what I was wearing, wondering if I'd worn something odd, or I'd check my hair because maybe it was out of place. Automatically, I knew without a doubt it was me they were laughing at.

This, and so many of the dysfunctions in our family, were like sickly, bitter seeds planted in my garden of life. Yet they grew. And they sent out tendrils that twisted around my adult thoughts and emotions.

By the time I was thirteen, we were in the Brown House, our second house. That was where The Drinker began exposing himself to me. He'd call me into the bathroom to have a conversation while he was in the bathtub. Sometimes I'd wake up in my bed with his hands inside my shirt. When that happened, I acted as though I was still asleep. The Drinker did these things.

My dad was still my dad; I knew my dad loved me and I loved him. But I learned to separate my dad from the stranger he became when he was drinking. At first, I was afraid to tell my mother about what was happening because I imagined she'd say it was my fault. I also worried that telling her would cause a huge blowup with my dad, or it would be discussed in front of the whole family. It took all I had to tell my mother.

Mom was working nights, so I called her at work and told her over the phone. As surprising as it seems now, I don't remember hearing any reaction from her then. Nothing happened after that phone call, either—there was no blame, or blow up, or family confrontation. From my mother, there was no running to me and hugging me, asking what she could do for me, no consoling me, no tears for Rhonda. She didn't bring up the subject again.

Dad was still in the house. He still drank. Fortunately, his exposing himself and physically touching me stopped.

Another story I told myself was that nothing happened to The Drinker because what I had to say about it wasn't important enough to deserve any action. I didn't have anything important to say, and even if I did, no one would listen—I had proof. I lived my life believing that story to be true until a few years ago. Now I realize my mother had her own My Page that would also get in her way of doing things.

There were moments when I thought she loved me. (That's another story; in fact, my mother has loved me since my birth.)

She'd talk to me when we were in the car together—I was her confidante—and she'd unload everything on me. I thought that meant she loved me, because she was talking to me instead of yelling, and in my mind, talking was closer to loving than yelling.

I watched my mom always being involved with things outside our home. I admired her participation in organizations, her support of our church, her strength of conviction, and the way she'd organize things to perfection. Yet, at times I thought, *This is a coverup for who she really is.* Because at home she'd have a beating fest with her own children.

It seemed like everything we kids did was wrong. Not good enough. I never understood it. We all had chores and things we took care of at the house. We were good kids, so what was wrong? Yet another story got created.

Despite Dad's behavior when he drank, I loved hanging with him when he was sober. He taught me so much. Even today I keep a yard up just the way he taught me, change my oil on a regular basis, and always keep a clean car. My dad was a man on the move; I'm a woman on the move. He got up early in the morning for work and came home late at night; for most of my life, so did I.

I think I was in high school before I realized what he did for a living: sales. He didn't graduate high school and was an awful speller, but otherwise he was good at all he did. He always had company cars and wore nice clothes to work. He was important. On the weekends, he played softball and raced cars when I was young.

Dad was always working on the cars at home, and I was right there with him, handing him the tools he'd ask for. I did whatever I could to not have to go inside with Mom. Dad was also the handyman of the house, always tinkering. That's something I got from him and passed onto my daughter: being able to work on anything and not have to depend on a man to do it for me.

As I got older, Mom and Dad were my softball coaches. I loved softball; I could throw a softball as hard and as far as Dad. It was an advantage to be tall in sports; I'd never feel too tall there, where I was a powerhouse, and everyone knew it. That was my happy place, and my parents helped me be there.

I loved going to my grandma and grandpa's house. They lived a couple of hours from us, and we would visit often. At their house, we watched *Hee Haw* on TV with Grandpa, and Grandma gave us our baths outside in the metal tubs she used for "washin'".

Grandma only went to town occasionally, but when she did, she'd handle all her business then. Grandpa would be in the local tavern while we followed Grandma around. I remember going into the bank with her; everyone dressed so nicely, and it was always very quiet there.

"Don't speak," Grandma would tell me and my sisters, shaking her finger in our faces. "These are important people!" You can guess how that reinforced the story I'd made up, that it was always other people who were important, not me.

When I was a teen, I was looking to get out, so when I graduated from high school I moved to Arizona with my cousins. I left my family with a rush, freedom ringing in my ears. I never looked back. As soon as I left home, the wild came out. I didn't care about the judgment of my older cousins; whatever opportunity came my way, I was doing it! My life was sunbathing, floating down the Salt River, working for wealthy people who needed someone to clean their houses and watch their kids, and partying.

I stayed in Arizona for a few years, living with my cousins and loving the freedom of my life. Then I moved back to Indiana for about five years or so. That's when my life changed drastically. I had met a man that I loved—we lived together, I became pregnant, and my daughter was born.

I made up my mind that she wouldn't live the life I had. She'd have the confidence that I didn't, and she'd be settled in who she was and proud of it. Never would she experience the events I did. I'd make sure of that! I'd protect her. Once I realized her father wouldn't be true to his word to her, that he would make promises that would be broken, we left. She was two when her Arizona life began. She became the light of my life. I would raise my daughter as a single parent for ten years.

Arizona was the beginning of my car business life, and that's a story for another chapter, which is at the end of this book.

Years passed when I experienced uncertainty about things in my life. I was unsure of myself, though I was making more money than I'd ever made before. I felt unsettled, though I was building a home. I was still acting like I didn't need anyone, though I was beginning a wonderful relationship with the man who would become my current husband. Looking at my life from the outside, what I had was exactly what most people would wish for. But even though I had all of that, I wasn't satisfied.

Toward the end of my career in the car business, I joined a direct sales company. They'd engaged a coaching company to help people identify what stopped them or stood in the way of their success. They'd learned that when things got tough, humans would act a certain way or revert to stories that would have them quit. The sales company wanted us to have access to tools to deal with this and show us how to get out of our own way, so they arranged for a group of us to attend a course. It was in this program that I learned about being vulnerable and I was finally able to see myself without the filter of my stories.

The people in my sales group knew of me but didn't know who I really was. I'd never wanted to share anything about myself, so they only knew how I appeared to them. I remember looking around the room during the course and making an instant assessment of my own: I was outclassed. These people obviously came from money. They lived in upscale neighborhoods, drove high-end cars, and wore Rolex watches. They'd been educated at top schools.

Then it came time to hear their assessment of me. They said they thought of me as a tall, beautiful blonde who was smart, attractive, and bourgeois. They thought I acted as if I was too good for them.

Ha! They think I'm smart, beautiful, and upper-middle class? I thought to myself, amazed. *They think I act as though I'm too good for them? That's crazy!*

Their perception of me and my self-perception were miles apart. I knew I was tall, but I'd never considered myself to be smart or beautiful. Bourgeois wasn't in my vocabulary. (I didn't even know how to spell it.) I felt worthless and was so set on proving myself that I was shocked to hear that I came across as too good for everyone else. Since I hadn't shared who I was with the people in my life, they based their opinions of me on what they thought they saw, and they'd created their own stories around me.

Hearing others' perceptions of me was my first step toward self-realization; this began the series of amazing revelations that altered my own perceptions and changed my world. Up until then I was always looking for somebody to emulate.

I'd always been looking outside of myself for how I was supposed to live my life. I'd kept my fears and insecurities to myself, put on a false front, and did my best to be strong and prove myself. It wasn't until I started communicating that I realized how I was just like everyone else—we were all hiding, we just did it differently.

In that program, there were many exercises we all did together, but there was one that stood out for me. It started my true awakening and gave me my first real sense of myself in this world. For this exercise, we sat in a semi-dark room with music playing. The course leader talked about our mothers and fathers and said things to them on our behalf, as if we were children again.

"All I ever wanted was for you to love me, Mommy!"

"Why can't I make you proud of me, Daddy?"

I became aware of the sadness in the room. This scripted conversation with our mothers and fathers continued, becoming more intense and emotional. There were howls of unacceptance, screaming, and begging for attention among the attendees. This wailing was coming from the same people who wore thousand-dollar suits, expensive cufflinks, and Louis Vuitton shoes with matching purses—the same people who usually spoke with a language proficiency that raised them above anyone else in whatever room they occupied.

Suddenly I realized that these people had grown up wanting and needing things from their parents just like I did. When all of us were kids, they'd experienced the same fears, thoughts, anxieties, and wishes for their parents' approval as I had. Our backgrounds were wildly different, yet we were just the same.

That weekend I found out that being vulnerable wasn't a weakness. Being vulnerable gave me strength and allowed others to be vulnerable with me. This understanding put me on a whole different level with people.

Please understand that it took several courses and more time for me to unleash that vulnerability. It took the strength, experience, and patience of a team of people that was committed to me letting go of the armor I wore daily. Once I broke through that armor and began removing it, my authentic expression began to flow. I started using a different language within myself and in speaking to others. It wasn't easy, sometimes it was even painful, but removing this armor allowed me to speak from my heart freely, and I'd do it all over again if I needed to.

I began to realize that others in my life were dealing with the same issues and circumstances. They would say or do things in our interactions—not necessarily because of me, but because of their own head trash. I discovered the many ways people hide themselves from others. Some people hide in money, some in arrogance, and some by lashing out at others. We all do it differently.

I thought about the life my mother must have lived as a child. I knew that after her own parents divorced, she'd had to live with her father and four brothers because her mother couldn't afford to keep her. I knew a little bit about the things she had to deal with as she grew up and the events that she'd created a *story* around.

I had no idea what my father had to deal with as a young boy. I didn't know how he grew up, what events in his life informed his own stories, or what he'd made them mean. I didn't know what made him run away from his life and turn to alcohol.

I do know my parents did the best they could, or they would have done it differently.

I've learned that, as we grow up and our dreams get bigger, it's usually ourselves and our stories that stand in the way of our progress. We get in our own way. Our stories clutter our space.

Being bravely vulnerable jumpstarts our forward movement. By sharing our feelings and our stories, talking about things that happened when we were kids, and revealing what we made them mean helps clean up and clear out that cluttered space. This allows room for growth.

Maybe you've heard this before: if you clean up your closets and your drawers, and if you clean out that messy garage, you make room for more good things to come into your life. This applies to clearing head trash clutter, too. Completing your stories from the past creates space that allows for a new beginning to emerge.

Today I'm focused on that with my whole family. I've found that when vulnerability is present, people feel safe, and things unlock. Shackles begin to drop off.

My mom called me one day and said that she was working on an annulment. She and my father had divorced many years ago, but as Catholics, divorce wasn't acceptable. Dad was dealing with cancer, and Mom wanted to grant him an annulment (using the grounds of their forced marriage due to her pre-marital pregnancy) because she wanted him to have safe passage when he died.

I was blown away at what my mother was saying. She'd always been very violent when it came to speaking about my father. Although they behaved civilly during family functions, in private Mom could spew venom about Dad.

As I listened to Mom tell me what she was doing for him, I felt this urgent rush to call my father and forgive him. I wasn't sure that he fully knew about what The Drinker had done to me; Dad often had no memory of things he'd done when he was drunk. Regardless, I knew his subconscious knew, and I didn't want him dying with that on his conscience.

I'd done a lot of work on forgiving him, separating the facts of what happened from the stories and emotion I'd created around them. I was ready to let him know. I'd started allowing my Source of everything in the universe, God, to direct my life a few years prior to that. So, I knew this was something I needed to do. It was time.

When I called Dad, I shared my experience of The Drinker. At first, he was silent. Then he started crying. He said he didn't remember any of it. He expressed deep remorse. He couldn't believe I was still willing to talk with him. I told him I wanted him to know that I'd forgiven him, and I needed him to hear it from my own mouth. Because I'd taken away all the meaning of what had happened when I was a kid, it no longer had a hold on me.

I *moved* my dad that day. I allowed him to see past whatever boundaries he had in communicating; I let him see more than he ever thought could be possible in communication. I forgave him, and he accepted my forgiveness. Now, today, I watch Dad reach beyond what he knows to be safe as he learns this thing called real communication.

You see, once I realized that all human beings are caught up in stories and saw how the world occurred differently to others based on their own experiences, I loved everyone. I knew it was possible they were living inside the same hell I'd been in. I also knew they might have been living inside the additional hell they created for themselves with the stories they thought were true about who they were . . . just like me. How could I judge them? How could I use my perceptions of them to judge them for what I thought they were doing or who they were being? This is true for my parents as well.

Don't get me wrong—what my dad did as The Drinker was real and it was wrong. Imagine the hell he must have been living in to have committed such an act! Knowing there was some reason, some story of his own that had him do it, lit up a new path for me. It led me to understanding and to opening my heart for forgiveness.

I discovered we're all walking around in this world doing one of two things: either we're seeing love and opportunities in life, or we're stuck seeing the world through the view that we had created with our stories. This view was created by events that we made mean something, usually as we were growing up. Stuck in this view, we mainly see the wrongs of the world and we stay connected to our victimhood in life.

I made the choice to see differently. I made the choice to see love and life's opportunities. I made the choice to say, "It's time to start living life, not surviving it."

Today, I have a life I love. I'm married to the man of my dreams. I've raised four wonderful children who are out in the world creating opportunities for themselves. I sit on the Board of Directors of three different women's organizations, after having created three women's organizations of my own. I own and operate my own training and coaching business. I co-founded the Empowering Women Alliance. I'm a VP of Sales for a hemp company. I'm a National Keynote Speaker, inspiring women to find the power inside them and to find out the truth about the world they live in. I'm also a writer and author.

I'm on the court of life, every day, taking on my limitations so that I can experience the breakthroughs that come with staying with it. I also have a coach of my own who keeps me on the court of life and helps me stretch past the boundaries of however I'm currently living.

The work I did released my voice. I can speak again, authentically. I'm sharing my story because there are thousands of women who've experienced versions of it. They're holding onto the meaning of the stories they created around what happened, which has taken away or diminished their internal power, and which has muted their authentic voices.

I share my story to give you permission to reclaim your power and voice, too. You can give yourself permission to know the facts of what happened in your life, to reveal and release the meanings you've attached to events, and to forgive any person who committed any act against you. (Imagine what your perpetrator's My Page must look like, and what hell they must live in, every day.)

The work I do around what it is to be a human being in this world has allowed me to also share my experience with more and more people. But the power of communication that I focus on, that I'm committed to daily in all relationships, has encouraged so many others to share their My Pages and stories with me.

My mother started sharing her stories with me, allowing me to really be with her in a way I'd never experienced before. Her sharing has given me access to the ability to hear her not as my mother, but as a human being who has a My Page of her own. This allows me to have compassion for her and for what she must deal with daily.

Stopping to look at my head trash, giving up whatever judgements I harbor, and truly listening to the human being in front of me provides intentional freedom. In pursuit of this freedom, I'll continue to peel the onion of my life so that my experience of this world is the magical experience God wants me to have.

My wish for you is that you take this opportunity to discover your own My Page. I hope you'll realize that your life is being shackled or driven by the stories you've created in the past and unknowingly still hold onto today. My suggestion is to get a coach to work through this with you.

A coach can help you find out what you don't know and also help you discover the invisible pair of glasses you've been looking through. It's human nature to stay in the comfort zone of life and not play a game you don't know how to win. A coach can help you learn how to get on the court of life and work through whatever needs to be worked through.

You're worth it. The world needs you to be vulnerable. Your vulnerability is the source of your strength and your power. We all need to be vulnerable because our shared vulnerability is how we connect. Vulnerability reveals our shackles, being unshackled brings out our power within, and that power has us stand as the women and leaders we are. The world needs our vulnerability and our strength.

RHONDA PEOPLES has been called an authentic light in the world. Her extraordinary leadership style leads people to new discoveries in their lives. While Rhonda is encouraging and supportive, she also has been known to "push people over the cliff" with love.

Thirty years' experience in the sales industry made Rhonda passionate about teaching others the underappreciated beauty of authenticity in sales. She also is an empowering coach, dynamic public speaker, and Codebreaker Technologies trainer. In her coaching business, she leads women to discover and own their greatness, to recognize and break through their personal glass ceilings, and to create and claim six to seven-figure incomes.

Rhonda founded several women's support groups and is a member of NAWBO, the National Association of Women Business Owners. She serves on the Board of Directors for Eagles Wings of Grace and coaches Team Management and Leadership Programs for Landmark Worldwide.

Contact Rhonda for speaking engagements, coaching, or training:

>LinkedIn: Rhonda Peoples
>Email: rhonda@rhondapeoples.com

Find out more about Codebreaker Technologies B.A.N.K.® sales methodology, scientifically validated to accurately predict buying behavior in real time:

>crackmycode.com/trueauthenticself

THE POWER OF PURPOSE

DEB ANDERSON

If you look at the tapestry of my friendship with Susan Johnson, the surface picture of our lives makes it seem as if we don't have a lot in common. (See Susan's related chapter, "The Power of Possibility.") Susan's been married, had children, earned a master's degree, and maintained a respectable corporate career before becoming an entrepreneur and coach. In contrast, I never married, never had kids, never completed a degree, and amassed an eclectic résumé of careers, training, and entrepreneurial experience before becoming a coach. Yet when you look behind our surface tapestry, underneath where the messy threads of our lives entwine, then our stitches, tangles, and knots begin to look a great deal alike.

Early in our friendship, our conversations went deep—we talked as if we'd known each other a lifetime instead of only weeks. We shared that life had not been working out the way either of us had planned or expected, and circumstances or trusted people had dealt us some painful blows. We'd both felt loss; we'd both been lost. Despite having years of education and training at our disposal, we'd struggled to figure out why we'd often been stuck or frustrated, spinning our wheels. We wondered why there were so many times when we couldn't gain any traction. Or, if we were moving forward, why we weren't getting anywhere truly satisfying. We talked about this a lot, asking ourselves the age-old questions:

"Who am I? Why am I here? What's the meaning of my life?"

We felt unfulfilled. Some vital part of our enjoyment and expression of life had been going unrecognized and undefined. We could almost point to the empty space where we thought the missing piece belonged. When we each found our missing piece and compared notes, we knew we had to share what we'd discovered with others, too.

I was a born storyteller. I loved hearing and reading other people's stories, and I started telling my own at a young age. Some were whoppers! For instance, one day my Kindergarten teacher taught us how to make kaleidoscopes out of cardboard tubes, paperclips, and bits of crinkled paper. I was enchanted by the project, wanting to tell everyone I knew about it. Walking home from school, I started practicing what I'd say. I ended up embellishing the day's events past recognition.

The simple, real-life kaleidoscope experience evolved to include my teacher inviting a Hollywood movie crew for Show-and-Tell. In my fantastical tale, her director boyfriend brought a huge crane-mounted camera that filmed all of us kids from above while a famous choreographer taught us to make kaleidoscopic patterns on the playground below . . . and we might be on TV!

That was the first time I remember being thrilled by storytelling. That was also the first time Mom gently scolded me for telling a story that wasn't true. She privately enjoyed my creative exaggeration, but verbally she stressed the importance of separating fact and fiction.

While my imaginative narratives sprouted and bloomed that year, Mom weeded my fanciful inventions and nipped any confabulations in the bud. She cautioned me about making things up; fiction was fine if I was careful not to pass it off as the truth, or worse, begin believing it myself.

As I grew older, I began to understand her motivation and warnings. My father often revised history to boost his ego or further his personal agenda. Dad retold events to save himself embarrassment, twisted facts to serve his own ends, and then insisted Mom and I were both crazy for remembering things differently. He backed up his version of events with emotional bullying, physical intimidation, and psychological manipulation.

Over time, as more of my innocent childhood fabrications met Mom's patient admonitions, I gathered that made-up stories were okay if told around Girl Scout campfires or written for school assignments, but not at any other time. Yet even with homework, there was something magical about capturing my thoughts and imaginings on paper. My enjoyment of writing felt larger than life, and I preferred writing stories to any other activity or playtime. Nothing was more satisfying than knowing I'd painted a picture with words that someone else could see, too.

Satisfaction in elementary school was hard to come by—most of my teachers didn't know what to do with me. Though I was well behaved, I always finished my work too quickly for the time allotted in the classroom. To keep me busy, I was usually pressed into service as a teaching assistant. But one second-grade teacher allowed me time to write instead. That year, at Parent & Teacher Night, she gave my mother a hand-bound collection of my stories.

"Debbie should write a book!" My teacher insisted.

"Maybe she will," my mother replied. "When she grows up."

"No," the teacher said. "She should write it now."

When I was in my forties and still trying to "find myself," Mom asked me why I'd never pursued writing as a career. Apparently, it had always been evident to her that it was what I should do. She told me she'd been sure of it ever since that Parent & Teacher Night. I shook my head in amazement, hearing this for the first time.

"Wow, Mom," I said. "Why didn't you ever tell me that, then?"

"I thought you always knew," she said.

I thought about this over the years, wondering how it could have seemed so obvious to everyone in my childhood, but I was so oblivious to it in adulthood. As I'd grown up, Mom and I had somehow missed talking about the possibility of me writing for a living. This realization came as a surprise because we'd certainly talked about everything else.

During my youth, talks with my mother always helped me understand people's largely negative reactions to my intelligence and verbal precociousness. These talks had begun when I started reading at the age of two. The casual lessons had included "Don't be a chatterbox" and "Don't be a showoff" (because teachers and kids won't like you), along with variations of "Don't be a smarty-pants or a know-it-all" and "Don't be a teacher's pet."

Mom also ran interference with librarians who tried to restrict me to age-appropriate books, and she defended me successfully when a fifth-grade teacher disputed a beyond-my-age story I'd written, accusing me of plagiarism.

"My daughter didn't copy this," Mom had protested. "Haven't you ever listened to her talk? She *always* sounds like she's middle-aged and just swallowed a dictionary."

But afterward, Mom suggested that when I was writing, maybe I should rein in my overblown imagination and tone down the ten-dollar words.

"Try to write like somebody your own age," she said.

In my sixth-grade year, I received the gift of a newly minted team of teachers who encouraged creativity, self-expression, and extra-credit projects, including writing. These young women saw I was an avid reader, so they shared their favorite authors and suggested books beyond the limited selection of our school library.

They didn't find anything wrong with an eleven-year-old girl contentedly dwelling in the bleak and wintry realm of Tolstoy along with the flowering fantasia of Tolkien's Middle Earth. With their encouragement, I consumed hundreds of extracurricular books, devouring classic literature and gobbling popular novels with equal gusto. I began to enjoy writing again when I realized I wouldn't be reprimanded for my choice of vocabulary, style, or subject.

I was still a kid the next school year, just starting junior high, the first time I remember someone asking me, "What do you want to be when you grow up?"

I said, "I want to be a writer. I want to write books that make people happy to read."

Then the well-meaning adult explained all the reasons why that wasn't a good idea. In addition to vicious book critics, fierce competition, and poor odds for success, one reason made a huge impact:

"Writers don't get paid very much. It'll be impossible to make a living at it, even if you're any good. If you're smart, you'll choose something more practical."

I still recall the sickly, breathless feeling that came with being hit by those loaded words; I felt as if I'd been punched in the stomach and had the wind knocked out of me. *"But there are so many stories I want to write!"* I wailed silently. At the time, while I was reeling, I'd processed the adult's statements subconsciously. It wasn't until many years later that I was able to examine and evaluate their five-way impact.

First, I'd cringed at the idea of facing vicious critics, especially since I already endured enough mean-spirited criticism from my father. If the competition for publishing was that fierce, I doubted I had what it would take to be a professional writer. I knew my writing wasn't as good as Dickens, Hemingway, or Fitzgerald. Disheartened by the comparison, and long conditioned to measuring myself by adult yardsticks, I never thought to cut myself slack for being only twelve years old.

Second, I'd begun to realize that many of my father's rants and rages were triggered by money issues. The sporadic lack of money created a great deal of upset, tension, and stress in our household. I didn't know enough about the world to protest that adult's assessment of a writer's income or prospects. In fact, I gave a great deal of weight to the cautionary advice, not wanting to be poor and stressed when I grew up.

Third, I wanted to be smart, yet my father frequently told me how stupid I was. "You talk like you're smart," he'd say, "but you're really stupid. If you were smart, you'd . . ." Then he'd complete the sentence with something I should have noticed, been able to do perfectly, or done differently, all according to his exacting adult standards. If he wasn't calling me stupid, he was telling me I was conceited (or selfish, or lazy). I walked a fine line between wanting to be seen as smart and talented, and wanting to hide my intelligence or be humble about my abilities. (I also tried my best to be unselfish and hard-working.) As a result, the adult's admonishment to be smart hit particularly close to home.

Fourth, I'd learned to keep myself quiet and even-tempered. I wasn't allowed to be defiant or show my emotions around Dad, who bristled with pent-up rage. So, I suppressed my fear, anger, disgust, upset, or impatience, especially during his lectures. I'd also learned (the hard way) not to *ever* share my thoughts, ideas, or opinions with him since he tended to interpret any hint of disagreement as defiance, and he often used information as ammunition. To keep safe, I kept quiet, and I'd gotten a lot of practice narrowing down my behavior, bottling up my emotions, and limiting my self-expression. I never thought to voice my upset or argue with the adult's assessment of a writing career.

Fifth, I was subtly influenced by my mother's understated example of practicality winning over talent or desire. In her youth, Mom was a talented artist who'd been offered an art scholarship to attend university. However, she'd also grown up during the years of the Great Depression and World War II when work was a simple matter of survival for most people, not a matter of preference. Mom had reasoned that she could always find more reliable, steady work as a nurse than as an artist. In setting aside her desire for art, and in being an exemplary nurse, she also became an advocate for practicality. I identified strongly with my mother, and I had come to agree with her.

I'd been verbally precocious and mature for my age, but at twelve my life experience was limited, and my logic was still childlike; I readily believed the adult who cautioned me about becoming a writer. Some of that advice touched upon my fears and insecurities, and the rest appealed to my unspoken needs and concerns.

So, I gave up the idea of writing. I squelched my dismay and ruthlessly guarded my practicality. I even felt shame for ever having entertained the stupid, childish notion of being a writer. After that, thinking about writing made me uncomfortable, so I avoided it. In fact, I managed to completely forget about writing for long periods of time.

I didn't realize I'd made an actual decision back then since I hadn't fully articulated those thoughts at the time. Looking back, I can pinpoint that well-meaning advice about being smart and practical as being a catalyst in my own personal formula for quashing myself. The advising adult wasn't responsible for my long-lasting decision, but that conversation marked the time when I gave up my first ambition. For almost forty years afterward, I gave up creative writing altogether.

I'd just turned fourteen when my high school entrance counselor asked me what I wanted to be when I grew up. I told him I wanted to be an architect. He seemed surprised that a young female would be interested in going into what was, at that time, a male-dominated profession. Apparently, my counselor wasn't aware we were amid the Women's Liberation Movement, because he immediately tried to discourage me.

"Oh, you'll have to do a lot of really hard math to be an architect," he said.

"That's okay," I said. "I'm good at math."

He immediately changed tack. "Why would a nice girl like you want to do something like that? You'd have to work at dirty building sites, and construction workers are a rough lot."

"That's okay," I repeated.

"Then why?"

I explained that my family moved frequently, and we often visited housing developments under construction. I'd become interested in perusing and re-imagining the sites' blueprints. I enjoyed visualizing 3D renderings of architectural plans, loved drawing elevations and improving upon designs, and could entertain myself for hours creating my own floorplans.

I told my counselor, "I want to build houses for people to live in comfortably."

I remember the expression of relief on his face when he heard this.

"Oh," he said. "You'll need to be sensible about this. If you become an architect, you'll have to build a lot of different things like office buildings, warehouses, prisons, and gas stations. I suppose, every once in a while, you'd be able to build a house, but not very often."

Although I'd recognized the counselor's misogyny when implying girls weren't good at math, it didn't dawn on me that he might be lying about—or at least misrepresenting—my potential work as an architect. I had no interest in designing the buildings he'd listed, and I had no idea of how to become an architect who exclusively built houses. Accepting his sensible counsel, I gave up that ambition, too.

I managed to hang onto the next choice of what I wanted to be for a little longer.

I'd become intrigued by the human mind and wanted to learn everything about what made people tick. Thoughts, emotions, and behaviors absolutely fascinated me. I'd always wondered why people experiencing the same situation often had wildly different perceptions and reactions. Why did some people wither while others thrived? And what made some irrationally angry, perpetually morose, or indiscriminately happy?

I'd been reading my mother's medical and psychology textbooks, and Mom, a Registered Nurse (RN), always answered my questions about things I'd read or observed. We spent countless hours talking about people's conscious and subconscious motivations. I'd also put a lot of time and thought into figuring out ways to cope with family life.

Our home always looked picture-perfect to outsiders, yet the threat of danger smoldered behind closed doors. I was constantly devising strategies for surviving my father, smoothing his easily ruffled ego, and shielding my little brother. I also wanted to understand Mom's intermittent depression and her indecisiveness about leaving Dad.

So, as a fifteen-year-old Junior in high school, I declared I was going to be a doctor, a psychiatrist. Then I did everything I could think of to achieve my goal. I deliberately tuned out my father when he'd say: "You're not half as smart as you think you are." When he told me there was no money for college, I got a job so I wouldn't be dependent on him for anything more than keeping a roof over my head until I graduated high school. I avoided my guidance counselor entirely, applying for academic and leadership scholarships on my own. And instead of wasting time at parties and dances, I played it smart by concentrating on getting perfect grades and racking up advanced placement credits so I could enter college as a sophomore.

At sixteen, I sorted scholarship offers and focused on universities with pre-med courses. Sifting through people's comments and advice (well-meaning or otherwise), I disregarded any that might cast doubt on my career choice or my ability to secure a place in med school. I was sure that this time, with this goal, I was well-prepared to follow through.

However, in my junior year at university, a mandatory session with my academic advisor changed everything. After she asked me why I wanted to pursue work in my chosen field, she proceeded to shatter what she referred to as my "illusions."

"Psychiatrists work with people who are mentally ill and emotionally sick," she told me. "This idea you have about 'helping people become their best selves' is naïve and unrealistic. When you join a psychiatric practice or facility, you won't get to pick and choose your patients. You'll have to work with the psychotics and neurotics and all the other crazies. It's not pleasant work, but it can be rewarding in its own way, and that's what you'd be signing on for. So, if that's what you really want to do for the next thirty years, then go to med school."

I didn't.

Disillusioned, I also became discouraged. If it wasn't practical to use my creative writing ability, and if it wasn't feasible or realistic to pursue my interests in design or psychology, then I didn't have any idea of what else I wanted to do for a living. I felt as stupid as my father always said I was because I couldn't figure out what to do with myself and my future.

After pinning so much hope on higher education, I began to feel that everything I'd done to get there had been for nothing. I stopped taking pre-med courses and started losing interest in other classes and activities. I chafed at professors' seemingly arbitrary requirements and restrictions. Soon I came to doubt my reasons for striving for good grades or carrying a heavy course load. I lost my motivation for studying subjects that bored me and became apathetic about preparing for a future that wasn't enticing. Even pursuing a course of study for the sake of being practical lost its allure.

Despite the effort I'd put into getting my scholarships, I began to think that sticking around to complete a college degree in some random subject was pointless. I'd given up on everything that lit me up, and by the end of my junior year, I felt really, really tired. At the ripe old age of eighteen, I burned out.

In retrospect, it's not difficult to see my pattern of disillusionment, setting aside dreams, and abandoning ambitions. I'm embarrassed to admit how easily dissuaded I'd been. It didn't occur to me to challenge the statements or assertions of those who'd dissuaded me; I didn't fight for something I could so clearly see myself doing. I didn't request or demand assistance from the university advisor who'd dismantled my life plan without offering any consolation, ideas, or options in its place. I'd allowed myself to be hobbled, both by my mother's gentle admonitions (intended to keep me safe) and by my father's harsh criticisms (meant to keep me small). And I'd tamped down or forsaken my favored forms of self-expression until I couldn't express myself at all when it mattered most.

At that time, I had no way of knowing that the as-yet-unknown field of Positive Psychology would eventually become a reality. I'd relinquished my nebulous vision of it. By giving up when I did, I unwittingly missed out on contributing to the genesis and development of a whole new and potentially rewarding discipline. Hindsight, as they say, is twenty-twenty.

It would be easy to make excuses for myself by saying, "I was young and inexperienced," or "I deferred to authority figures or to those whom—I assumed—knew more than I did." For a long while, I blamed my domineering father for undermining my confidence and inhibiting my ability to express myself authentically. But eventually, I came to realize that something else was ultimately responsible for thwarting my ambitions; it would take me another three decades of searching to find this missing piece.

After I left university, life went on. My parents finally divorced when I was nineteen and I broke off my relationship with my father. In my early thirties, I spent months in therapy to come to terms with Dad's abuse and my family's dysfunction. In my late thirties, with the help of some valuable coaching, I was able to forgive my father, reconnect with all my emotions, and become more self-expressed. My mother continued to work as a nurse and astonished me by showing up as a fun-loving, multi-dimensional and vibrant human being. My younger brother grew up to become a successful, kind, well-adjusted man with a healthy, stable home-life and a beautiful, loving family.

Meanwhile, I spent decades pursuing and abandoning multiple careers. Nothing was a perfect fit. I found subjects I enjoyed researching and studying on my own, but nothing was ultimately fulfilling. After a while, all my efforts, struggles, accolades, changes, learning curves, successes, and failures began to blur together and feel the same. Everything in my life seemed a blah shade of gray.

I felt restless in my own skin.

I wondered how to cure the restlessness. I wondered how to stop uselessly spinning my wheels. I wondered how to start getting somewhere worthwhile and where that worthwhile place might be. I wondered until the wondering finally turned into discomfort, followed by desperation, then determination.

I participated in a variety of seminars and training programs, and I had a series of breakthroughs. When my progress stalled, I enlisted the help of a coach. Whenever I got scared, sidetracked, or stuck, she was there to reassure, realign, or rock my world to get me moving forward again. At one point, after I'd been coasting a little too long and believed I was being smart by staying small and playing it safe, my coach said something that shocked me. One sentence jarred me loose of my underlying fear and stripped me of my complacency.

"I've got a good epitaph for your headstone someday … 'Here lies Deb Anderson: she died with her potential intact.'"

"How could you say something like that?" I was aghast. "That really hurt!"

Yet the moment she said it, I knew two things for sure. First, sometimes the truth hurts. And second, I didn't want what she said to be true.

My coach's half-joking epitaph jolted me into full awareness. It wasn't enough to keep doing what I'd been doing; I could no longer settle for simply making a living, or just putting one foot in front of another, day by day. I'd already spent too much of my life marking time. I'd wasted years not doing the things I most enjoyed and not pursuing the things most important to me. It horrified me to think of getting to the end of my life with nothing meaningful to show for it.

These harsh realizations gave me the push I needed to go beyond the edges of who I'd known or guessed myself to be. My comfort zone hadn't really been all that comfortable, but it was familiar. It took a bit of courage to venture beyond its confines.

Once I did, I found out what I'd been missing wasn't information, book learning, or life experience. It certainly wasn't proving I was smart, not to myself or anyone else. And it wasn't innate stubbornness or an acquired style of grit-your-teeth determination, either. Instead, I was missing a hidden inner wisdom that was eventually revealed through prayerful meditation.

In my communication with God, I began to receive answers to my questions, including some I hadn't known to ask. Although these answers came to me from a variety of sources, I attributed them all to God, the ultimate Source. My connection to God provided more than insight and inspiration; it also allowed me to reconnect to my authentic self and core values. Those essential clues equipped my search for what had been eluding me.

I persisted in my inquiry until I found the missing piece . . . my life purpose.

I discovered that my purpose is simple, yet has the potential for great depth, breadth, and growth. To my surprise and pleasure, I realized that my expression of this purpose was intended to be fluid and expansive. Although the foundation of my purpose was determined by God, I also had a say in the matter! I could co-create the different forms my purpose would take in the world. In addition, I could choose how I would show up while fulfilling my purpose.

Next, I needed to make a choice: I could ignore my purpose, or I could align myself with it. The moment I chose alignment, I recovered and re-energized my true self. Alignment with God and my purpose aligned me with the universe, which in turn aligned the universe to assist me in fulfilling my purpose. This dual alignment gave me access to the power necessary to follow through on the myriad of possibilities my purpose continually makes available to me. It also gave me the courage and fortitude to not let anything, or anyone, dissuade me from fulfilling it.

I revisited and analyzed everything I'd tried and done over the years. There was a common theme—service to others—in each career path I'd chosen for myself in the past. I wanted to help people be happy, comfortable, and able to live their best lives. I noticed which aspects of each job, career, and activity had lit me up; these flickers of light guided me toward a plan for designing a new life—a clearer path going forward. Frequently checking in with God, I was able to co-create and articulate the expression of my life's purpose in the world, which enabled me to create and explore new possibilities in my life.

Then I began documenting and streamlining the steps of my journey. I wanted to share this process so others would be able to discover and implement their own life purposes. I included all the well-marked paths and short-cuts, so others could do it in a *much* shorter time (with significantly less angst and fewer detours).

I came to see that my journey hadn't been a series of side trails, wrong turns, and dead ends as I'd once believed. Every high and low offered vantage points I hadn't recognized at the time, as well as signposts I hadn't known how to read. It was a relief to find that, although my life had been unconventional, it hadn't been meaningless. I'd just lacked the perspective to understand what it meant until I was able to view it through the lens of my purpose. Then I could finally make sense of the kaleidoscopic mélange of my eclectic life.

Now I'm thrilled every day, in so many ways, to be sharing my journey and purpose with others. I've reclaimed my joy as a storyteller, and I've learned I'm also a "storycatcher" . . . I gather others' instructive, inspirational, and empowering stories and I foster their personal storytelling. I'm writing again—novels, fiction stories, and non-fiction accounts—all written with the intention of making a positive difference. I'm designing again, but rather than drawing blueprints for houses, I'm designing and building structures for transformation and success. And I've happily exchanged the quashed dream of a psychiatry practice for the flourishing reality of a coaching method that guides others toward leading their best and most fulfilling lives.

I know who I am now, and who I'm meant to be. I'm even okay not knowing what I may find ahead on my zigzagging path into the future. Because now I'm confident that wherever my path leads, along the way I'll be fulfilling my purpose.

Everyone has a unique and powerful life purpose. Everyone.
But not everyone knows what their life purpose is.
Most of us recognize and can name several purposes we've had or continue to have in our lifetimes; they're obvious and easy to identify. A simple example is a parent's purpose to love, nurture, and raise a child. A student's purpose is to learn, and a teacher's purpose is to educate. In general, a businessperson's purpose is to create wealth by making products or providing services. But the kind of purposes I'm talking about, life purposes, run deeper and broader than the obvious. They're as varied as the people to whom they belong.

Life purposes are vital and life-affirming.
Sometimes life purposes recommend or drive a person's work, career, or volunteer efforts. Sometimes they're more applicable to relationships, social connections, or causes. They may be earthy or philosophical, they could be privately pursued or collectively shared, or they might be global or esoteric. Purposes come in every size, shape, and flavor. Some are quiet and subtle, while others are loud and splashy. No matter what form they take, all life purposes are—by their very nature—profoundly powerful and uplifting.

To be empowered and uplifted by a life purpose, each of us must first recognize that we have one. Often, we don't contemplate the purpose of our existence until we encounter pain, difficulty, or loss. Sometimes we ask the big questions because we see or hear something that really gets to us . . . something that touches, moves, or inspires us. Or sometimes we encounter something that profoundly shifts our perspective or alters our path going forward. Whatever impetus provides that initial questioning, it can give us a place to start.

Maybe you, too, have searched your heart, mind, and soul in these circumstances. Maybe you've asked yourself those same, age-old questions I did: "Who am I? Why am I here? What's the meaning of my life?" Listening for my own answers, I learned several things worth sharing with you:

- You can see and determine who you are at your core. Who you really are, what you truly value, is at the heart of the matter.
- You can discover and declare what your life means. What you're here for is important. Whether you believe it or not, you have a God-given purpose, yet you also have a voice and a choice about how it's expressed in life.
- You can find fulfillment and positively affect others. When you are fully and truly yourself—when you're fulfilling the promise of who you're truly meant to be—your personal fulfillment will also profoundly influence and positively affect others.

If your life purpose has been eluding you, then you might be feeling a sense of dissatisfaction. Maybe you've been running as fast as you can to stay in the same place. Maybe you're not sure where you want to go, let alone how to get there. Perhaps the enjoyment you've previously had in your job, career, or relationship is not as keen as it once was, or you're wondering whether it was ever there at all. Maybe you have the feeling that something is missing in your life, but you can't quite figure out what it is.

You might be having trouble making choices or decisions. Maybe you're going through a period of questioning or adjustment as a student, recent graduate, empty-nester, divorcée, widow, or retiree. You could be dealing with a change or loss, personally or professionally, or a series of changes or losses. You might have been repeating the same complaints for much too long, unable to muster the energy or focus needed to generate a solution. Or maybe, when you look in the mirror, you're having trouble recognizing or liking the person you've become.

If any of these situations are uncomfortably familiar to you, then it may be time to discover (or recover) your life purpose.

Your purpose is at the heart of your driving force—it's the answer to your underlying "why." When you're in alignment with it, you're happy to get up in the morning, you persevere in the face of insurmountable odds, and you feel the most alive.

Aligning with the source of your purpose supercharges everything you think, say, and do in relation to fulfilling your purpose. When you find your purpose and tap into the source of its power, your life becomes profoundly meaningful.

It all starts with love, light, and joy:

- What do you love? What lights you up? What brings you joy?
- What could you talk to someone about for hours and still feel like there's more to say? What activity could you blissfully participate in for days on end?
- What really touches, moves, or inspires you?
- What are you completely passionate about? (If the word "passion" is too strong, then replace it with another word like "fascination," "interest," or "curiosity.") What fascinates or interests you? What are you curious about?
- What have others said you're good at or complimented you for that you truly enjoy being or doing?
- What are you contentedly engaged in when you lose track of time? What holds your attention so thoroughly that you seem to lose yourself? What exciting way of being has you so enraptured or focused that you forget to eat or sleep?
- What causes you to experience wonder or awe?
- What calls to you or pulls you? What refills your well or recharges your batteries? What way of thinking, feeling, doing, or being fuels you or empowers you? What feeds your soul?
- What lights you up and makes you feel truly alive?

When you begin asking yourself these questions, you'll come to realize that you already have the means of overcoming any invisible barrier that might be standing between you and your answers. (When you begin asking God for guidance, answers may come even more easily.) Your life purpose may be temporarily obscured from view, but when you seek it, you'll begin to recognize clues, signs, and markers leading you to uncover it.

You were born with the inherent ability to live your life fully. If circumstances, situations, people, and events (or your stories about them) have interfered during your life's journey, then know this: you have the right and ability to move forward unencumbered. You have the God-given right to be your true self. You have the capacity to determine your ideal destination and the authority to request a guide when entering uncharted territory. You have the built-in capability of finding the original path you lost, discovering a completely new pathway, or trailblazing an alternate route.

You can choose to live your life full-out at any point. You can choose to live full-out starting *right now*.

Start by acknowledging who you truly are and exercising your right to unfettered self-expression. Boldly own every fabulous, flawed, and quirky aspect of your unique, true self. Seek what lights you up. Communicate with God. Access your source of insight, inspiration, and supercharged power. Discover your purpose; create your possibilities. Then harness your personal power of purpose and dare to be the joyful, naturally glowing, fully realized person you were always meant to be.

DEB ANDERSON collected careers, licenses, and certifications much like a vacationer gathering souvenirs of her travels. Her shortest job lasted only thirteen minutes in a phone sales boiler room, and her longest career was twenty-six years owning and operating a marketing and promotions event business.

Deb's formal and autodidactic education, compulsive reading habit, and decades of experience in checkered careers led her to become a Certified Life Coach. After ten years' training in transformational coaching, she created Purpose & Possibility Coaching and co-created its online courses.

Deb also co-founded America's largest quantum physics study group dedicated to exploring the blurred edges between science and spirituality; renowned participants have included quantum physicists, scientists, theologians, and international speakers such as Dr. Joe Dispenza, Dr. Bruce Lipton, and Dr. Candace Pert. Additionally, Deb is a co-founder of the Empowering Women Alliance. Her first fiction book, *The Smallest Gift: A Story of Christmas*, will be released in 2023-24.

Find out more about Purpose & Possibility Coaching and online courses:

    PurposeandPossibilityCoaching.com

THE POWER OF POSSIBILITY

SUSAN JOHNSON

The day I met Deb Anderson, we started talking about the things closest to our hearts right away. (See Deb's related chapter, "The Power of Purpose.") We became instant friends, bonding from the moment we shared our vulnerabilities and resilience. We shared our personal stories and then expanded our conversations to include other women and their stories. So many women's life tapestries share common threads! We've always been interested in tugging on those threads to find out where they lead, marveling at the many ways they connect all of us to one another.

One of the first connections we noticed was how both of us had experienced a lifelong struggle to find purpose. Our specifics were different, but the underlying theme of our questions had been very similar:

"Why am I not satisfied? What's missing from my life?"

Answering these questions provided a great deal of meaning and significance in our lives. As our friendship grew, we delved deeper into this conversation. We learned it wasn't enough to simply find and articulate our life purpose.

Creating purpose-inspired *possibilities* causes the key pieces of life's big puzzle to snap into place and energize you. Some of these possibilities are future-oriented: new paths to explore, innovative endeavors to undertake, and exciting projects to develop. Other possibilities are more present-oriented: fresh outlooks to adopt, original thinking to encourage, and empowering "ways of being" to step into.

We were already grateful for the transformative power of purpose; soon we came to appreciate, and be awed by, the tremendous power of possibility.

Skipping along the Hawaiian shoreline was my favorite thing to do when I was six years old. I twirled and kicked up sand while wearing my favorite outfit, an outrageous pair of bright pink culottes with screaming yellow trim. I sang songs over and over until I drove my parents crazy. Inside the house, I played endless tunes on the piano, picking out the notes by ear. When it rained, I was always outside, tipping back my head to enjoy the raindrops falling upon my face and churning the earth beneath my bare feet into mud. Then I'd take a leaf from our palm tree in the yard and go mud sliding down hills in our neighborhood with my best friend. We'd laugh and slide and play, completely delighted in making a glorious, muddy mess.

You could say that I danced to my own tune, but that would be cliché. It would be more accurate to say I was a vibrant explosion of color in the world, overflowing with song and creativity. I was a lover of people, animals, and everything beautiful in the wonderful world around me.

Then I went to school.

There, a discovery slapped me in the face like a bully—I was different. I'd been born with a droopy eyelid, due to having been born prematurely. Gawking, stares, and whispers greeted me in class. I felt alone and disillusioned—if you can be disillusioned at so young an age. School had been the possibility of another colorful adventure until I found out what it felt like to be avoided and sometimes taunted.

To protect myself, I began to put up my shield against others. Little by little, I put away my life-colors like crayons in their box, orderly and contained. I became more muted and tried to blend in like a chameleon. Slowly, I conformed to social norms, just another societal clone.

When I was fourteen, I ventured out from behind my shield to begin ice skating. My skate blades sliced through the mist rising from the ice, marking my path as I skated toward the possibility of being myself again. I began to let others see the real me, and I became a part of a group of skaters who accepted me as I was. The little flower curled tight inside me blossomed, blooming vibrantly once more as I swirled and skated through the mist. Soon, I chose bright and beautiful dresses, and I went to competitions. I felt beautiful and unstoppable. All was well in my world.

"I found a doctor who can fix you," my mother said in my junior year of high school. She said this knowing I'd felt broken by all the negative comments over the years. After seeing me bloom in the ice-skating world, she may have thought this would be another positive step.

My younger sister was a model, and Mom had told me modeling would never be a possibility for me. Even though I'd known she was right, her words had stung. My older sister was beautiful, smart, and popular, and my younger sister was beautiful, smart, and a model. I wasn't sure where that left me on the scale, though I knew I'd never have the possibilities and opportunities my sisters had. I'd even given up on the idea of just being normal because I'd already had two unsuccessful surgeries at this point.

As I contemplated Mom's words, "fix you," I wondered, *What would that look like?* Then I began to be excited about the possibility of looking like everybody else. *Surely the taunting would stop, at least,* I thought. I had an ice-skating group of true friends and knew that being "fixed" wouldn't change our experience together. However, thinking about how others in school would react to a new me made me smile. *Maybe the other kids won't say I look like a freak anymore,* I thought. *And maybe I won't see them staring or hear those under-the-breath murmurs anymore, either.* So, I agreed to another surgery.

The doctor did fix me. My eyelid was re-built to be much more normal looking. But my inner vision and trust in people couldn't be so easily put back together. I still had my shield of protection up against the world, and I only let it down around my group of ice-skating friends and my best friend at school. I never fully brought myself out into the world, never wanted any scrutiny that could bring bullying and judgment. Ice skating was a brief respite from those self-imposed shields; it was a special world that allowed me to glimpse the possibility of fully being me.

High school brought new challenges and growth opportunities in an unexpected way when our house burned down, leaving nothing but ashes, tears, and depression. I'd been working at my first job at a burger joint when my boss got a call that my house was on fire. I came home to find a burned-out shell.

Inside, all that remained of a once beautiful home was charred debris. I was relieved my younger sister and her friend had gotten out safely and were at our neighbor's; my older sister had already moved out on her own. My mother, a realtor, couldn't be located by the authorities until much later because she'd been working away from her office. When I arrived, the firemen had already put out the fire and were cleaning up.

In horror, I thought of my puppy, Niama. She was a dear sweet girl, named after a character in a book I'd loved. I'd been busy house-training her. Slipping through the firemen in the front yard, I went around back, desperately hoping Niama would be waiting for me in the backyard. Instead, I found other firemen shoveling her body out of the house and onto the back porch. I cupped my mouth with both hands, as if that would hold the pain and agony at bay. I began to weep. The firemen looked up at me in surprise, covered Niama with a cloth, and escorted me back to the front yard.

My mother finally arrived after most of the cars and emergency vehicles had departed. She looked at the house and was in a state of shock. She put my younger sister in her car, and then turned to me.

"Karen and I are going to stay at my friend's house," she said. "Where are you going to stay?"

At that moment I felt completely abandoned and alone. I wasn't sure who'd take me in. I had no other clothes to wear. Mom got in her car and drove away with my sister. I wanted to scream at her.

"I'm only sixteen!" I cried silently. "I want to be with you. Don't leave me here on the sidewalk alone!"

I wanted so badly to be with my mother and sister after this tragedy, but instead I had to ask friends' parents to let me stay over. My best friends' families had no trouble letting me stay at their houses. They even let me borrow clothes so I wouldn't have to wear my ash-stained burger uniform to school. Eventually, my mom secured a rat-infested rental house down the street from our burned house and let me move in with her and my sister.

When I'd been eight years old, praying alongside my grandmother, I'd asked God to come into my heart. I went to church with whoever would take me in the neighborhood, since my mom was usually too busy to go. I went to churches of many different denominations, and I learned to appreciate the special beauty of each one.

As I'd grown older, I'd gotten a car of my own. I'd also gotten busy with my friends, skating, and high school. I'd stopped going to church.

Yet, during the time of the fire, God came through for me and my family. He brought people together around us in the community. A church several miles away brought us new Bibles, and church members came to sit and talk with us. We were given new clothes, kitchen wares, and other necessities.

I was deeply moved. I also realized something profound: when God was all I had, He was all I really needed. He took care of me when my mom was unable to. He gave me what I needed when I needed it most. I began to understand that God was the source of strength when I needed to be strong, and He was the source of comfort when I needed comforting.

Even realizing this, after the fire, I fell into sadness, grief, and depression over my loss. But my depth of despair took me into the depth of God's love. He inspired me.

This inspiration came in the form of a healing poem; writing this poem in high school helped me express my sorrow. True to His nature, He turned my tragedy into something positive. My poem, entitled *The Fire*, won the National Federation of State Poetry Societies award that year. What had started out as a devastating event turned into the possibility of a deeper relationship with God with a new church family. God even turned devastation into national recognition.

By experiencing this series of events, God also introduced me to the concept of creating possibility from nothing.

I persevered through the remainder of high school. I was able to rise to the challenges that accompanied me due to holding onto my reconnection with God. As a result, I began to glimpse possibilities based on my new inner vision of me.

I ended my high school years being semi-popular, having both regular school friends and my ice-skating friends. In fact, I'd started dating a boy from my ice-skating group who took me to my high school prom. Then he went to college out of state, and I went to college with my skating friends. There I met my future husband.

Because ice skating had helped me blossom, it made sense for me to go from amateur skater to professional. I went on to become an ice-skating coach as I continued my university studies. When I graduated, I married and stopped coaching for a time while my husband and I learned to ice dance together.

After our two boys came along, I settled into being a mom. I satisfied my need for being colorfully creative by throwing great parties for the kids' birthdays and Easter. Being a mom was the best. I loved everything about it, even when motherhood became difficult, and the possibilities of creative self-expression became fewer. I served at church as well, singing in the praise team and teaching Sunday school. Colorful possibilities began to drop even further down my list of priorities once my youngest son began having serious health issues.

Joshua had been a premature baby, weighing only three pounds and four ounces. When he was able to come home from the hospital, his doctors arranged for a nurse to come in as well. We were told we needed to isolate him and not let him be exposed to anything, especially RSV (Respiratory Syncytial Virus) or any other viruses and bacteria.

We literally kept him in a safe space, a clean room, just like in the hospital. In the beginning we'd have to scrub up to hold him, wearing masks and gloves just like a nurse or doctor. To help him survive, we had to keep him away from the world for a year. We were told that he'd catch up physically and soon outgrow his need for such extensive vigilance and care. But he didn't outgrow the need for extreme caution. He kept getting sick.

In elementary school, it became obvious that a cold, which would inconvenience another child, would make Josh twice as sick and take him three times longer to recover. He suffered one severe illness after another. He had asthma. He had sleep apnea. As soon as he recovered from one illness and returned to school, he came home sick with another, and we didn't know why. No one knew what was wrong with him. Our constant worry and his frequent illnesses were exhausting and frightening.

Throughout all of this, I put myself and my own needs aside. I could sense my true, authentic self being muted again and my personal possibilities being limited, but my number one priority was being a mom and helping my children be healthy and happy. I didn't realize what I was doing to myself at the time; and while I certainly didn't begrudge devoting myself to my husband, kids, and job when called for, my day-to-day challenges and routines were masking the fact that I was slowly losing myself.

Without realizing it, I'd also put God on the back burner of my life once again. When I stopped reaching out to God, I started losing access to another vital, vibrant aspect of being myself. Without my connection to God, I lost access to my source of co-creating possibilities. I was blind to losing myself, bit by bit. In fact, I was so oblivious to my deep personal colors fading beneath my beige-on-beige surface story, that for a while I thought I'd "made it."

I remember the day my carefully crafted beige façade began to crack. I'd been working at my desk in my private office, and I leaned back in my executive chair for a little break. I'd been in the Human Resources (HR) field for over a decade at this point, and was the Technical Recruiter, Human Resources Manager, and Marketing & Sales gal for an amazing startup.

I looked around me, glancing at the stylish décor, the framed degrees and awards, and the homey family photos artfully arranged. Beyond my office door, I could see rooms that had been previously empty, now filled with people I'd helped to bring on board. I felt a sense of accomplishment. At that moment I realized that I had a great paying job, a wonderful husband, two kids, two dogs, and a terrific house. I was living what seemed to be the epitome of the American dream . . . and it wasn't enough.

Then I understood. It was all a shell—nice to look at, but hollow inside. God wasn't there; neither was I.

Despite all the good things I had going for me, my love for my children, and all the things I'd stuffed into my life, I felt empty. I felt alone, and I wasn't happy. And on top of it all, I felt guilty about not being happy.

I also felt guilty about letting my relationship with God fade. I'd put all my efforts into trying to keep the kids well, to find a diagnosis for Josh, and to do my job. Without realizing it, I'd melted back into the beige mold of what others wanted and expected. Somewhere along the way, I'd not only lost my connection to God, but I'd also lost my connection to the possibilities of my colorful self—I'd lost the real me.

I think that in addition to putting God aside, one of the reasons I wasn't happy was that I sensed there was something else I was meant to be doing, some greater God-given purpose that I needed to fulfill. I wasn't fulfilling it in my current position. Unfortunately, I didn't have a clue what that something might be, and not knowing what was missing was frustrating.

I thought, *There must be something wrong with me!* I felt that I should be content, grateful that both of my children were surviving. I should be happy with my job—in many ways it was the best job I'd ever had. I loved the company I worked for, all my coworkers, and the opportunities I had there. And yet, I felt hollow. I couldn't even begin to guess what else might be possible.

How can I know what else is possible if I don't know what else there is?

There was another reason I felt lost. My marriage wasn't going well. My husband and I had been growing apart, not really communicating, and not taking time to be together as a couple. We'd been trudging through the days and making it through each challenge that came our way, but we weren't doing it as a united front. Our marriage had been reduced to putting out fires while caring for the kids, and we hadn't been stoking the fire we needed to be happy together. We dealt with what was immediately in front of us and lost any memory or notion that another way of being together was possible.

In caring for Josh, and in fighting for his health, I'd felt alone. In reality, I wasn't, but it certainly felt like a very one-sided effort. My husband went to work, made money for us, and was a great co-provider, yet emotionally he wasn't there. He rarely accompanied me or filled in for me at Josh's medical appointments. I carried the heavy burden of being the medical sleuth, caregiver, wife, mother, and chief homemaker as well as being a workforce professional, and I'd begun to wear down. Yet I couldn't imagine any other possible way of keeping Josh alive and getting him healthy.

It didn't help that I felt my husband never understood or appreciated me enough. I'd given up so much of myself to make sure Josh survived and our sons had a good life. (Which, to be fair, I'd willingly do all over again.) However, somehow, I'd also missed out on getting appreciation and understanding for all I did and who I was.

We also had a lot of monetary problems. We'd reached the point where we ended up in bankruptcy. While my husband and I were working to recover financially, neither of us were investing anything into our marriage. And as you know, when you don't invest in something wholly, eventually it will begin to erode and fall apart.

Meanwhile, I homeschooled Josh to protect him from normal childhood illnesses, but he continued to get terribly sick. My mother-in-law found out that she had immune issues. All of us began to wonder if that was what Josh had, too. I found a specialist who was able to diagnose him with a very rare disease called X-linked Agammaglobulinemia, requiring infusions of artificial antibodies once a month. All in all, it took me fifteen years of persistence, research, and trial and error to help the medical doctors discover the nature of Josh's illness and be able to help him. That long haul made both my husband and me battle weary.

For a long time, my husband and I had been trying so hard to get through life and survive. When our finances imploded, it didn't come as a surprise. When our marriage exploded, it was like watching a train racing toward a section of track that hadn't been maintained. I knew the wreck was going to happen, I could see what was coming, but I couldn't stop it.

My husband had been gone mentally and emotionally long before he left me physically for another woman. He told me one day that he loved me but was not *in love* with me. Soon after that, he moved out of our family's house.

Many people don't realize that divorce is like experiencing a death. My husband of twenty-eight years was gone, and I missed him, even though I'd been unhappy about so many issues in our marriage. I'd always believed we'd fight our way through our problems and eventually get back on track. But without honest communication and perseverance, there was no hope. He rejected the idea of couples counseling to salvage our marriage, and he started a new life without me.

Our divorce devastated me in every way. My inner girl who used to sing and dance along the shores of Hawaii had been completely silenced. I no longer saw any sense in dreaming or dancing, much less creating new possibilities. I'd lost my reasons, my "why" for persevering. It was a struggle just to get out of bed. But I made myself get up, and stay up, for my kids' sake.

They were reeling from the loss as well, and even though they were young adults, they still needed a grounded, caring mother. My older son almost dropped out of college while trying to deal with the upset, and my youngest had to deal with his feelings about his father as well as the challenges of his compromised health. I was dealing with waves of grief that continued to wash over me, threatening to drown me at any moment.

I had to force myself to respond to life again, move forward, and look for new possibilities. I became determined that my husband's departure from our marriage wouldn't blow up what was left of our family. I began to find and build family activities—things the boys and I could do together—so we could continue to bond and not fracture. We took singing lessons together. I created a play and had them sing and act in it to raise money for a youth group downtown. I began to feel again.

I also began to feel God again. I turned to Him, reminding myself of everything He'd already done for me; I began to trust everything He would do in the days ahead. I remembered that He'd called me to love and serve Him, and I wondered what might be possible by answering His call.

I began to see that God was the source of the comfort, strength, and support I needed to be able to heal. Slowly but surely, I also understood that God was the source of power I needed to continue to be a caring and strong woman and mother. Eventually I came to the same realization that I'd had after the fire: God was the ultimate Source of everything I needed in my life.

My boys grew up. Amazingly, Josh managed his own health needs and went away to university, finishing a five-year degree program in four years. He also met his wife there. My older son, Kyle, did exceptionally well, too. He graduated from university with honors, has thrived in his career, and is currently engaged to be married.

With both of my boys grown and launched, I found myself wondering what was next for me. *What do I want to accomplish on my own? What's my next chapter in life? What might be possible?* I went to multiple seminars to find out what I needed to know about myself. Exploring new ways of seeing and thinking helped me learn a lot more about how I'd been designed as a human being, how I'd become who I was, and—even more importantly—who I wanted to be in the future.

After several years of looking inward, working on myself, and learning how to be the colorful real me again, I decided to take everything I'd learned and ask the big question: *What is possible?*

I'd learned that possibility didn't come from the past. It might be informed by past ways of thinking or being, but it's not dictated by them. A new possibility isn't meant to fix anything, either. True possibility is meant to be inspired, seemingly out of nothing, because it's co-created with God to be fresh and compelling.

What is possible? I asked in prayer and thoughtful meditation. The answer I got was to turn my focus outward to help others. I chose to be certified as a life and health coach, and to add career coaching to my skill set. That was when things really began to click for me.

I'd been a licensed counselor for ten years, in Human Resources for fifteen, and an ice-skating instructor on the side for five. Now, I was journeying into new territory on my own, but I was also meeting fellow sojourners along this path.

I kept asking, *What is possible?*

I found ways to utilize that creative spark inside and started painting splashes of color from my internal pallet onto the world around me. I was tapping into my "aliveness," that superpower inside me that had been wanting out. Once I tapped in, my ideas began to flow and the people I needed began to show up in my life to surround and support me. I couldn't wait any longer to discover new possibilities and put my ideas into action.

One of the ideas I've put into action has been to co-create Purpose & Possibility courses. I also used the insight I'd gained during my research, the perseverance and resolve I'd developed during my battle to restore my son's health, and the healing work I'd done after the divorce to start a new venture. I designed my company Invigorated! to guide those with health and life issues back to vibrant living.

Years ago, I'd mistakenly thought I'd made it. Now I know there's no end called "making it" . . . it's all about making the journey with God, enjoying the journey, and learning from the journey. How I show up and share my passion for the journey is what makes me who I am. When I step out of my limited thinking and do something new despite my fear, I continue to grow; when I invent fresh possibilities and add something positive to people's lives along the way, then I'm truly succeeding.

Possibility is one of your birthrights.
When we're children, everything is possible, and the impossible is just something good that hasn't happened yet. As we grow up, exterior forces apply pressure to shape and sculpt us as well as limit our possibilities. Parents, siblings, spouses, extended family, teachers, friends, peers, society, and circumstances all have a hand in our sculpting. Our own experiences, thoughts, emotions, and expectations play a role, too, so that the shaping takes place within and without.

Michelangelo, the famous sculptor and artist, once said, "The sculpture is already complete within the marble block, before I start my work. It is already there, I just have to chisel away the superfluous material."

Imagine that the shaping of your life is like the shaping of a sculpture. If all the forces that shape you have been benevolent, talented, and wise, then as you grow, the material chiseled away is the stuff that isn't necessary to you becoming the best and finest version of yourself. The finished work eventually is revealed to be an adult who is well-balanced, self-expressed, happy, productive, and fulfilled.

However, if any of your sculpting and shaping forces have not been of Michelangelo's caliber and benign intent, then you may not believe you're the best and finest version of yourself. You may feel the absence of choices or opportunities, or you may have a vague sense that something more might be possible. Plus, you may not have an idea of what that "something more" is.

We're not inanimate sculptures, of course. We're living, breathing, loving human beings with an impressive ability to adapt and an expansive ability to transform ourselves. We're capable of reshaping our bodies, minds, and futures. Also, unlike sculptures, we can move, act, and make progress in our lives. Just as each of us is born with an infinite number of possibilities, we each have a hand in designing our own destiny.

Unfortunately, we can forget that more is possible, becoming resigned to doing what's required, expected, or demanded.

Many of us try to fit ourselves into a neat and tidy box. Once we've settled in, we close the lid and then wonder why we aren't happy or thriving in that dim place where our colors are muted. We listen to the multitude of voices in our lives, both internal and external, telling us why we should do this, or we shouldn't do that, and we go along with their compelling arguments for staying inside the box.

The longer we stay inside, the harder it becomes to hang onto our dreams or generate new possibilities. Soon we begin to believe that our glimpses of possible futures aren't really possible at all. Many of us start to feel trapped, forgetting that we're the ones who climbed into this pseudo-safe space in the first place. Sometimes we're surprised to notice that our personal lights are sputtering in the dark, and our box walls are closing in around us.

All of us who've experienced being in a box have things in common: we don't spend enough time honoring what lights us up; we don't nurture our life spark; and we don't consistently shine through our uniqueness. We tell ourselves that doing what lights us up isn't practical, responsible, valuable, or safe, or . . . well, you can pick your own self-limiting words here.

But whatever adjective you pick also holds down the lid on your box. Staying inside the box not only stops you from doing what lights you up, it keeps you from finding and fulfilling your purpose and creating new possibilities, which in turn keeps you from living life fully and completely.

You're meant to expand, light up fully, and shine.

When you choose to be true to what lights you up, when you pursue whatever makes you feel radiantly alive, and when you utilize all your colors and all of who you're meant to be, then your life is filled with joy and meaning. It's never too late to throw off the lid and climb out of your box. It is possible—at any point—to discover your life purpose, create new possibilities, and then live in a bright and colorful new future.

Getting real

Creating new possibilities is simple . . . but it isn't easy.

It requires you to get real about who you are, and who you aren't. It necessitates taking a good look at where you are in your life, what you have around you, and who you're being. It demands that you get real about the game you're playing and ask yourself whether you truly like whatever it is that you're winning. This means you must own up to your part in occupying whatever box you might be in. It also means choosing to take a good look at your life without self-recriminations, judgment, or blame—that you accept who, what, and where you are simply as "what's true in this moment."

Clearing the way

The reality of "what's true" is just a place to start, and the next part is also simple, but it's not easy, either. It requires something of you, too.

Clearing away clutter makes space for something new to show up.

This means identifying and cleaning up your messes—literally and figuratively—or at least putting a plan in place to finish cleaning them up. It means discarding the clutter in your life—physically, mentally, and emotionally—and giving up whatever isn't serving you. It doesn't mean you have to burn down or rid yourself of your old life, but it does require you to acknowledge "what's true" about your life as it has been and as it is now.

After you've acknowledged what's true, you can choose what you want to set aside. You can choose to discard whatever isn't working for you and get it out of your way—temporarily or permanently. Then you can choose, just for a while, to set aside whatever works well for you. You can set it aside while you clear the way and make space for inviting and creating something new.

Inviting something new

Inviting something new to show up is both simple and easy.

It's also fun because you've already done the hard work needed to get you to this point. Standing in your newly cleared, empty space, you can create something that didn't exist before or invite something new to show up.

Here's how:

1. Imagine your newly empty space as a clean slate extending as far as you can see in every direction. This space isn't cluttered by your past, filled up by your present, or populated by a future that mirrors your past and present. When you've cleaned up your past and emptied the busyness and clutter out of your present, then your future is a completely clean slate.
2. Ask for guidance. While you're standing in this clear, empty space, before you invite something new to come into it, you can ask for God's guidance, whom I believe to be the ultimate Source of love, light, energy, and possibility. Standing in your clear, empty space, close your eyes and ask: *What is possible?*
3. Look and listen for your answers. Use all your extra senses—your mind's eye, heart, gut, and inner wisdom. Listen for God's whisper and look for a shining glimpse of an exciting new future. It will feel vibrant and compelling, causing your inner spark to brighten. This vibrancy will encourage you to say "yes" to a possibility.

You'll be invited to step into a new future that didn't exist before. Each time you co-create and say yes to a new possibility, you'll open yourself to more possibilities that light you up. When you're lit up this way, you'll continue to generate even more light and even more possibilities.

So, now that you know what's possible, stop playing it safe. Come out of your box. Be you! Dance in your own uniquely personal version of bright pink culottes with screaming yellow trim. Get lit, show your true colors, and share your special gifts. Above all, dare to dream and then dare to act when you create new, thrilling, and inspiring possibilities.

The world is waiting for the wonderful possibility of YOU.

SUSAN JOHNSON earned a BA in Psychology and a master's degree in Counseling. She has aided people in accessing, claiming, and growing their personal power for more than twenty-four years. Early in her career, she counseled sexually abused children and their mothers. Then she was invited to recruit for Intel, which opened the door to becoming a recruiter for several other companies. Although she enjoyed working in this field for many years, she also craved connecting with others more personally and profoundly.

Susan returned to her passion for working directly with individuals and groups as a Certified Life and Health Coach. She founded Invigorated! to assist people to achieve vibrant living naturally. Her holistic approach includes preventing and reversing disease by developing a completely healthy body and mindset. She is a founding member of the Empowering Women Alliance and has co-created Purpose & Possibility online courses.

Susan helped organize the Free to Laugh comedy event which raised funds for Sold No More, a non-profit fighting sex trafficking. Active in her Texas community and church, she travels frequently to Arizona to share her infectious laughter and quirky sense of humor with family and friends.

Find out more about Invigorated!:

>YourInvigoratedLife.com

Find out more about Purpose & Possibility Coaching and online courses:

>PurposeandPossibility.com

AN ODE TO ORDINARY WOMEN

SUE HARRIS-WILLIE

Let's imagine two women preparing to enter a marathon race.

One of them, Jill, has been a distance runner all her life and has a physique designed for running. Jill's an outstanding runner. She has the stamina and training to match a Boston Marathon winner. Based upon her best times for the distance, and what she knows of the times of the other runners, Jill believes that, barring some catastrophe, she could run her best time and be the first woman to cross the finish line in this race. That is her goal.

Our second runner, Anne, has no idea where she'll finish relative to the other runners. She's been training for over a year to run in this marathon. Though she doesn't have the lithe torso and long, lean legs of a natural runner, she's finished strong in each race she's participated in during her year of training. Her goal is to finish the twenty-six point two miles with her best personal time. Anne is an ordinary marathon runner.

Anne and Jill are both looking for a win in this race. They've both trained rigorously in anticipation of this opportunity. They're both committed, dedicated, and passionate about running. Each of them is keen to test her enthusiasm, grit, and endurance against the course. Each is as fit, strong, and healthy as she has ever been.

Now imagine that we're among the spectators on the day of the race. Both Jill and Anne are running strong. Their training has paid off. From the start we see Jill among the front runners. Anne is hidden by the bulk of runners in the middle of the pack. Each of our runners is running steadily at her best pace. Jill remains with the thirty or forty front-runners. The distance between Jill and Anne gets wider with every footfall. They are both in, and not in, the same race.

Now let's join the crowd near the finish line. Each spectator is waiting in anticipation for their runner to break the ribbon or cross the line. The first woman in the field of runners is in sight . . . and then crosses through to the finish. Hoorah! It's Jill! A crowd gathers around her. She's plied with Gatorade, water, a towel, and offered thousands of exclamations of congratulations.

While rejoicing for Jill's success, we don't fix our attention upon the crush of people crowding around to meet, greet, photograph, question, and congratulate her. Instead, we turn back to watch the other runners as we wait and continue rooting for Anne.

We spot her. And we note that while maintaining her best-time pace, she's running alongside those in the final third of the runners. Determination and fatigue are etched across her face as she runs her race, surrounded by hundreds of others. It's obvious to all onlookers and her companion runners that she's not going to win the marathon by achieving the fastest time for completion. Yet she runs on to the finish.

When Anne crosses the finish line with her best finishing time, after more than half of the other marathon runners have completed the course, she'll be recognized by many onlookers as a contender who also ran. And she'll know herself to be a winner.

A winner. How can that be? Because Anne is an ordinary woman who knows the value of her own win.

Anne and Jill both value the accomplishment, effort, dedication, and determination it took for Jill to win first place in the women's division of the marathon. However, let's suppose that both women also prize the equal efforts of *all* the runners. Then they can both celebrate the success Anne achieved as well . . . as an ordinary runner.

The ordinary woman doesn't allow the achievement and ranking of other runners to be the measure that defines her personal win. She's able to acknowledge, and celebrate, what others have achieved without diminishing or even comparing it to her own accomplishment. She set a goal to run and finish. She ran. She finished. She holds that to be a win. This is an example of the exercise of freedom and power in the mind and heart of an ordinary woman who embraces being ordinary.

I'm here to shine a little light on the ordinary woman within us and the ordinary women around us. I'm writing to the women who say, "I'm not a . . ." or "I'm just a . . ." without realizing there's a beauty and power to behold and acknowledge in a woman's being who and what she is in a small, medium, or large sphere of influence. There's a world of wisdom, wonder, and worth in the lives of ordinary women.

I'm an ordinary woman. I say that often. I say it with comfort, esteem, and joy. Often when other women hear me say I'm an ordinary woman they wish to disabuse me of the notion, or at least insist that I not say that about myself. But I resist their insistence. For I know that we ordinary women are a force to be reckoned with, and a presence to be celebrated.

I haven't always thought this way. There was a time when I believed that if a person wasn't at the top of the proverbial heap, she wasn't living at the peak of her potential. Fortunately, life, circumstance, and reflection have taught me to think differently and to question whether I want to be at the top, bottom, or anywhere at all on a heap. I now know that a person can be giving her all and living her best possible in-this-moment life and still show up last in comparison with others. Such comparisons are odious, erroneous, and blinding.

Having been knocked down hard by life a few times, I desperately wanted to garner feelings of importance, status, and self-value. I thought the way to achieve those ends was to find a way to be outstanding. But, trying to be, do, or have more than the other people around me was detrimental to the relationships I wanted to build and maintain with them. There had to be another way. When I began to see that the power of life and seeds of joy weren't only in the big and grand things in life, but also in the small and ordinary, I came to understand that the ordinary in life is valuable, beautiful, powerful, and essential.

I'd thought what was needed for me to garner esteem was to be like the maidens in fairy tales. I figured I needed to be either extraordinarily gifted or deservedly deficient in some way for good fortune to smile upon me. But when I was able to see that the Life-Giving Spirit that pervades all is also the God of the ordinary, I was able to take hold of a sliver of hope.

There's power available to the ordinary woman who's awake to the source of her very being—the power of life, growth, possibility, influence, and change. Such wakened women have access to the power of recreation, rejuvenation, and hope.

There are millions of ordinary women making a dynamic difference in the world and in the lives of others. Many of these women haven't stopped to recognize in themselves and one another their beauty, power, and worth. Because of the significant difference they—and we—make, each one of these millions of women is worthy of acknowledgement.

These ordinary souls, the majority of women in the world, are the foundation and scaffolding of much of what we behold, rely upon, and love. These women are primary elements in the everyday successes of work, life, and relationships. Yet, our presence, contributions, and influence are treasures we rarely reflect upon.

Webster's Dictionary defines "ordinary" as "customary, usual, regular, normal, familiar, unexceptional and common." We ordinary women need to redefine and embrace those descriptive words; we need to take exception to anyone hearing in those words anything less than what is phenomenal about us. What is customary and usual is our reliability. What is regular and normal is our trustworthiness. What is familiar is our faithfulness. And what is common is our number. For we ordinary women are everywhere.

Every aspect of nature is held and sustained by the power that is potent within the ordinary woman. It's the source of creation and creativity, health and hope, life and renewal, strength, and satisfaction. There's nowhere in life that this power is not.

From before we were conceived, the potent power that vitalizes us was at work drawing sperm and egg together. Like Mother Earth, ordinary women nurture life's seeds in the soil of the everyday and cultivate a crop of expression that is steady, stable, and yet often surprising. We inspire, invest, and co-create life in ourselves and in others. We may appear commonplace, but in our own rhythms we are each as unique as every day's sunrise and as changing as each night's moon.

Our creativity, independence, and strength are rooted in a growing reliance upon this power as expressed via our intuition and inner wisdom. We practice listening for the still small voice of Spirit within us, and we respond to its leading. Subsequently, we experience an increasing sense of wholeness. These are our guidelines for health, harmony, and happiness.

While busy with the tasks, commitments, and relationships of our daily lives, we have a myriad of chances to see and to acknowledge the dynamic, and precious ordinary women around us. We often miss these opportunities to acknowledge ourselves and others because our view of things is distorted.

I've been wearing glasses for all my adult life. They're necessary for me to see clearly. Without my glasses, my range of vision is very limited and my view and understanding of the world around me is distorted.

When I was a sophomore in high school and my need for glasses was first discovered, I rejected the idea of wearing them. This was primarily because I had no idea what I was unable to see. I had no notion that there was more to be seen than what was familiar to me, so I didn't experience an absence of anything. Fortunately, there were loving, wiser people around who insisted that I get glasses despite my objection.

When I put on my first pair and walked outside, I was surprised, amazed, astounded, overwhelmed, and delighted. The world was so different! The clear and clean impact of all that had been unfocused before was so sharp it was almost kaleidoscopic. I was entranced by what I beheld in every direction I looked. At the same time, I was shocked and felt momentarily sad at the discovery that I'd been missing what everyone else had been seeing.

I kept lifting up my glasses and looking out from under them, then putting them back down again in order to reconcile the world I'd been missing. With twenty-two hundred vision, I'd had no idea that people could distinguish individual leaves on a tree from a distance. I hadn't known it was possible to recognize and hail a friend from more than a couple of arm's lengths away. I didn't realize that to a person with twenty-twenty vision, things some distance away had crisp, clean edges to them. With my glasses on, I could distinguish the distant mountains and I could see the texture of my breakfast cereal while eating it. The world was transformed for me as a result of my new (external) lenses.

Our inability to see ordinary women properly is caused by a similar impairment to our vision. In this case, it's due to viewing through a distorted, out-of-focus lens through which we view them and ourselves. Most of us acquired this invisible lens at a very young age, and we've been viewing the world through its distortion for so long that we don't even know it's there.

The distortion is caused by the comparisons we make as we look at our lives and the lives of others. We're socialized to measure our success, status, ability, and even our value in comparison to the success, status, ability, and value attributed to others. Then, over time, we internalize this way of looking at and evaluating ourselves and our lives so often that we're unconscious of doing it. We weigh ourselves on a scale that we view through myopic eyes as we encounter other people's lives and stories.

When we have this distorted point of view, we not only see others through our biases, but we also add or remove weight from our pan-scales of judgment based upon whether we perceive the other person as happier-than, slimmer-than, poorer-than, better-than, healthier-than, higher-than, older-than, richer-than, more-than, etc. Then, having weighed ourselves in comparison, we make judgments about how we fare, what we look like, and how we matter based upon our calculation of how we measured up—or down—to them. Sadly, we often go on to determine the value of our contributions and our very worth by these same measures.

We don't have to be subject to this way of being in the world.

There's another way to look at our lives and the lives of our sisters on the planet. We can learn to see and prize in the ordinary woman a magnificence that we have habitually overlooked. We are free to choose another way of seeing her and ourselves. We can learn to disassociate from other-centered assessments and judgements. We can learn to listen to the voice within us that calls us to live, enjoy, and value our own unique lives . . . for the sheer joy of it.

Being able to view, embrace, and celebrate ourselves and other women as ordinary may be, for many of us, an experience akin to getting upgraded glasses. It may result in a stunning and welcome change of view. With our vision and experience of ourselves shifted from odious comparisons to honoring embraces, we can begin to see beauty where we overlooked it before. We can see in a new way the things that delight us about ourselves (and others), bring them into focus, and then express gratitude for them. We can delight in our own lives, free from the weight of comparison.

To be an ordinary woman does not mean being a woman who eschews excellence, dynamism, contribution, invention, creativity, or the beauty of discovery. Honoring the ordinary does not mean living a mundane life. The ordinary life is rife with possibility, power, and unlimited potential. There are resources for life-changing adventure on every plane, in each relationship, and in every dream honored by the one who holds it.

When celebrating herself as an ordinary woman, each woman is strengthened in bringing forth her gifts to the world. By delighting in her own ordinary existence, an ordinary woman can more easily grasp the freedom to choose her own path and execute her own independent choice.

An ordinary woman who is awake to her freedom can choose to respond to the call of the muse within herself rather than march to the cadence of a drum beat outside of herself.

Within each of us resides the Source of life and the Light that illuminates every soul. This Essence, our Wisdom, is also the seed of our becoming, the source of our self-expression, and the foundation of our "yes" to life's invitation. In this life Source, we've been given a choice and a response-ability to nurture the seed, honor the source, and confidently speak and even shout our yes aloud. We're called to be our own first cheerleaders. We can be thwarted by circumstances, set back by loss or illness, or have our hearts bruised by death and discouragement. Yet, we rise again because we are part of the wholeness of life—and we know it. When we know and nurture that connection, we're free to embrace a way of knowing our value. We can assess how we are and how we're doing in a way that doesn't involve comparison with others. In fact, it frees us to explore a new vista of relationship—cooperation.

Some may ask, "What about outstanding women?" There are, have been, and undoubtedly will be women in the world who stand out. Shouldn't they be acknowledged? Indeed, yes. It's a gift to have both outstanding and ordinary women in the world. What's often missed is that sometimes they're one and the same.

What's outstanding and what's ordinary is a matter of choice, comparison, and preference. We know that outstanding is not necessarily better, just different than ordinary. But different how? Think of these examples:

Let's say we have twenty-six letters in our collection. Twenty-five of the letters are lower case. One of them is an upper-case letter. If we place them all together on a table, we note that one is outstanding from the others. It's different. It's unique. But it's not better.

Let's consider a collection of twelve twenty-four-carat gold pins. Each pin is uniquely crafted, gem-encrusted, and priceless. Which one (or more) of them is outstanding? They are, each and every one, worthy of being worn with pleasure and pride. And yet, because not one of them is noteworthily different from the others, each pin in the collection would be, according to Mr. Webster's definition, ordinary. And at the same time, each pin could be considered outstanding in some way in relation to the others. Perhaps one has more filigree, another a particularly striking setting of rubies, and yet another a wonderful turquoise stone inset in it. Each of these could, in our judgment, be outstanding depending upon our definition of what constitutes standing out.

So, which is it? Are we ordinary or are we outstanding? I say, "Yes!"

The majority of outstanding women have been and are lauded for the way their lives have touched others and made an impactful and/or life-enhancing difference in the world. Though things have changed in recent times, many of the ordinary sisters who came before us and who we now herald as outstanding were not recognized or praised for the ideas, achievements, and contributions they made during their lifetimes. There are thousands of women whom we could call to mind as having been or being outstanding among the women of the ages.

Many women we know as outstanding today were (or are) ordinary women who had a dream, vision, calling, or desire and chose to follow it. It's the fame and acclaim awarded to them now that marks them as outstanding to us. These women were originals: Anne Hutchinson, preacher; Rosa Parks, activist; Florence Nightingale, nurse; Madeleine L'Engle, author. They weren't following someone else's path or principles. The choices and attitudes which distinguish them are actions and behaviors that were a part of their ordinary life.

Sojourner Truth is a sterling example of an ordinary woman who we now see as outstanding because of what she did in the ordinary course of her life. Sojourner was a tall, strong, and very dark-skinned emancipated slave who, though she was illiterate, was very wise. On one notable and historic occasion, she became a spokeswoman for women's rights, even as she was a spokeswoman for the rights of enslaved Black people to be set free as human beings.

During the Women's Rights Convention of 1851 in Akron, Ohio, Frances Gage, a leader in the movement, invited Truth to speak. Not all in attendance supported that invitation, fearing that Truth's stand for freedom for slaves and abolition would bias listeners against her and the cause of women's rights. Truth's speech, entitled *Ain't I a Woman?* was galvanizing. Her ideas about equality resonate today as we continue the effort to bring disenfranchised groups and individuals to humanity's table on an equal, honoring footing.

So, let's not compare ourselves with our sisters. Let's not judge ourselves by their status, acclaim, or accomplishments. Instead, let's look to them for solidarity, inspiration, and fellowship.

As Hellen Keller once stated, "There is no king who has not had a slave among his ancestors, and no slave who has not had a king among his."

I'm grateful for the doors opened and ceilings shattered by the women among us who stand out. We shudder to think where we would be without women who stand out and without the contributions they've made. Yet, I'm here to say that while being a front, middle, or end of the race runner, an ordinary woman can also be estimable, beautiful, and difference-making in life's race. An ordinary woman can be inspired, and she can be an inspiration to others. Here's an example from my own life.

One day a few months ago, I shared with a woman friend the title and some insight about a book I was reading. She was so inspired by what I said about the book, (*Well Read Black Girl* by Gloria Edim) that she checked it out from the library and read it. The book, and my comments about it, ignited her compassion and imagination.

As a result of that small interaction, she's established a book resource that gets books into the hands of underprivileged and disadvantaged Black, Brown, and Native children. These books contain stories and images of grown-ups and kids like themselves between the covers. Now, many of these kids haven't had access to books in their homes, and many haven't had a book of their own. Getting books to these kids is amazing all on its own. But even better, these books reflect aspects of these kids' ethnicity, race, culture, and language.

I know this because my friend met with me recently to tell me how my few earnest words made a difference in her life and that of many children. This is an example of an ordinary woman making a difference. I shared enthusiasm, an opinion, and information. My friend took those and generated an idea and a small institution that is now making a difference in hundreds of young lives.

Many times, we don't see the ways in which our lives, efforts, and stories touch and influence the lives of others. Our lives are never just about us.

I have a friend who spends four days a week with her two elementary-aged granddaughters. Her son is a single father and my friend lifts some of the parental weight by spending quality time with her granddaughters. She makes the girls breakfast, reads to them, plays various games with them, helps with homework, reading, meals, and baths. She sits with and cuddles them for hours over the course of the day. Amid these and other ordinary tasks, she tells them how they are loved and chosen, special, beautiful, smart, strong, and clever.

These girls have a mother who is physically part of their lives, but emotionally and socially absent. By their mother's own account, her girls are "a lot of trouble to deal with." The girls know that their mom feels this way about them, and it undercuts their confidence. What their grandmother brings to their lives is foundational for them as they build their image of themselves as chosen, loved, and wanted. Her presence and care are fertile soil in which they can plant, nurture, and grow positive self-regard.

This dear friend, along with many grandmothers (and mothers) like her, is an ordinary woman running in the middle of the pack. The profound influence of her love and nurturing of these girls can never be accurately measured. Yet, we who have lived through and looked back upon our own childhoods know that the value of her ordinary presence, though inestimable, is truly priceless.

My friend is running the grandmother race. She won't win any trophies or awards. She may never know just what a difference her contribution to her granddaughters' lives will make. She is an ordinary woman living life and sharing love. And that's phenomenal.

This often-quoted poem by Lucille Clifton expresses what I believe is true for every ordinary woman:

listen,
you a wonder.
you a city of a woman.
you got a geography
of your own.

listen,
somebody need a map
to understand you.
somebody need directions
to move around you.

listen,
woman,
you not a noplace
anonymous
girl;

mister with his hands on you
he got his hands on
some
damn
body!

(Lucille Clifton, "what the mirror said")

    Indeed, my ordinary one, you're worthy of notice and attention. You have many shades and you're engaging. Similar some may be, but your terrain of mind, interests, soul, skills, spirit, and talents are singular—yours alone. You're familiar, but not wholly known. You have a spiritual, social, physical, mental place in this world and your presence adds beauty, power, and interest to those places. Though there may be many like you, we call you by *your* name. You're exquisite, memorable, influential, and inventive living your ordinary life. We wonder what will come of the lives you touch, the dreams you influence, the ways you shift the world.

    For the ordinary woman, achievement and winning are centered around the mind-and-heart attitude with which each woman runs her life's race. An ordinary woman finds her primary sense of worth and fulfillment within herself. She's learned to listen to and trust the still-small (sometimes-shouting) voice within. Acting upon that trust allows her to set goals that are heart, mind, and soul-satisfying. Striving for and meeting those goals, regardless of the judgment of others, is her win. Her finest prize is her own self-regard and that of the Source that enlivens and defines her.

Should the acclaim from others come her way, she'll receive it with grace. She'll no doubt find it satisfying. But it will adorn, not define her success.

She's an ordinary woman.

SUE HARRIS-WILLIE is a self-described ordinary woman. She says she does not have a clue how to "throw on the diamonds and pearls" to highlight interesting aspects of her life. Yet her unassuming manner naturally invites others to step into the extraordinary experience of sparkling, honest, and meaningful conversations.

A life-long learner, Sue earned her master's degree in Rehabilitation Counseling. She studied sign language because she wanted to know what it would feel like to be a majority member among minorities, in this case a hearing person entering a deaf world. Her social experiment exposed the unconscious nuances inherent in any cultural paradigm.

Sue recognizes the force that moves through women who have clear intentions, are challenged and humbled, and then take risks anyway. She successfully risked a later-in-life marriage and launched her own business. Sue now uses her training to help others bring order, energy, balance, and joy to their homes and businesses as a Professional Organizer.

EMBRACING TRUTH

MING LOVEJOY

In navigating life, make truth your North Star.
Since ancient times, the North Star has been used for navigation. The earth's magnetic field and its movement in relation to our earth's molten core are constantly in flux. As a result, magnetic north can shift, rendering a magnetic compass unreliable. However, the North Star always points true north. True North is a constant.

Relying on something in constant flux as your guiding source can take you off course, whether in your travels or in life. On a journey, if your navigational system is off by even one degree, you could miss your destination by hundreds or even thousands of miles. Imagine what being off course like this could mean in life.

Knowing your starting point on a journey also impacts your experience. If you start out thinking you are a human having a spiritual experience, for example, your journey will unfold one way. But if you remember that you are a soul having a human experience, your journey will unfold differently.

The greatest truth I know is that you were created from Divine Love, within the very heart of God, the Source of Love, Life, and Light. Divine Love is your true identity and inheritance, that seed of pure potential within you. Like the North Star, Divine Love is a constant. It is truth. This truth is the ultimate navigational tool you can carry within you, like a GPS for your soul.

Sometimes truth is a seed.

When I was four years old, Auntie Lu crouched down next to me in the garden. Her voice was soft and alluring. She pointed to a flower, whispering in her British accent.

"Did you know God is in everything?"

Earthy and etheric, Auntie Lu enthralled me. Her full name was Lucille, and like the meaning of her name, she was truly filled with light. She was lovely, graceful, and wise. When she spoke, her words resonated truth. She pointed to a big rock, a bird, some trees, and to an insect that hummed in the air near us. She told me that God was in every living thing, including me, and that everything was connected. She said that God had made me, with so much love, for the very special life I was to lead. She told me that I was loved more than I could imagine.

My auntie's words were seeds she planted carefully and deliberately in me. They were sacred seeds of trust, hope, and truth. They were fertile seeds, held in the fragile husks of her words, potent with the promise of nourishment and provision. They were seeds of my potential, containing both heaven and earth within them. Auntie Lu's essence, which embodied truth to me, and her voice, fluid and life-giving, helped sow those seeds into my being. And, like seeds must do, her light-filled words would disappear into the dark and dimly lit earth of my subconscious.

Sometimes truth is lost in judgment.

My parents weren't "believers." Yet, I witnessed in their lives a tension between spiritual skepticism and what I call "irresistible grace." When pain pushed, the Divine pulled. My mother consistently resisted this draw. My father, who held great curiosity and reverence for the mysteries of life, kept his spiritual doors and windows open, not just to the possibility, but to the likelihood of a magnificent and beneficent Divine. My parents seemed to be two sides of the same coin, one who saw her spiritual cup as half empty and one who saw his as half full.

My father was Burmese, and my mother was of Scottish descent. They tried for ten years to conceive. Unable to bear children of their own, they finally decided to adopt. My sisters and I were gifts.

In naming us, my parents indulged their preferences for the unique. I was named "Mingulay," after a Scottish island in the Outer Hebrides. This name delighted my father for its Asian tone, and he always told me that Mingulay sounded much like the Burmese words meaning "my little daughter." They called me Ming from birth.

One of the great blessings of being adopted into this family was that I felt safe in our home, which felt solid and fortress-like. My father and mother were steady, sound, and stable, the certain center of my universe. We had a comfortable, even affluent life. I knew I was loved and especially privileged.

Yet, I felt disconnected. Being adopted nagged at the core of my identity, and my judgment of the label haunted me. Adopted. The word made me feel awkward, embarrassed, and alien. Somehow, it defined me; it meant that I was lost, abandoned, and unidentifiable. It was grafted to my identity, as I was grafted to my adoptive family. I didn't understand then that "adopted" actually meant I was "chosen," which is the true meaning of the word.

Sometimes we must search for the truth.

One of my favorite storybooks as a child was *Are You My Mother?* Like the baby bird in the story, I felt forlorn and reckless in pursuit of discovering where I belonged. While I was amused and comforted by the simple ending of the children's story, I didn't understand how profound it could be in making sense of my own spiritual journey.

Much like the baby bird, the story I made up about me was built on partial and faulty information. I had no way of knowing I was creating a story from my own judgments that would cause me to suffer by my own hand. Being adopted left me with an unrelenting sense of separation, which was the first crucible and container for my early personal transformational journey.

Sometimes we have to dig for the truth.

Several years ago, I wrote a poem that speaks of this painful, enlightening, and fulfilling process. In my poem, "Dig," I wrote:

> Archaeologist of my emotions,
> Here, in the landscape of myself,
> I dig.
> Mountains of memories,
> Artifacts of dashed desires,

Protruding from the ground,
My feelings' lost and found,
Map of my underneath.
. . . Fragments of feelings,
Confused by our experience,
Buried and lost,
Confound us.
From these forgotten pieces
And imperfect impressions,
We write the histories we believe,
And build civilizations inside ourselves,
Which we populate for centuries,
Or, so it seems . . .

Sometimes truth appears to be just out of reach.

My childhood was one of loneliness. I was desperate for friends and wanted a connection with others that I couldn't seem to get or keep. This unquenchable longing, along with my perceptions of rejection and an inability to feel connected, drove me to hate myself. Miserable and anxious, I came to reject my worthiness, which led to self-loathing and later, to self-harm.

From the time I was tiny, the extrovert in me turned outward in an insatiable quest for attention, affection, and approval. I became an ardent charmer, animated performer, and ruthless competitor. Driven by an intense appetite for the love and acceptance I desperately wanted, I was fierce, persistent, and downright aggressive in my tactics and behavior. My dear parents overlooked the forcefulness, even the brutality, others witnessed in me, which earned me the nickname, "Ming the Merciless" from our babysitter.

My father nicknamed me "Champ" for my physical ability and performance. I became my father's little hotshot performer and felt like a superstar when his big smile, applause, and kudos proclaimed my merits and worth. Winning championships as an equestrienne momentarily filled the insatiable hunger of my emptiness. Achievement and adulation became nourishment to me.

On the other hand, loneliness and longing still lurked, hindering my equilibrium. Soon my fixation on performance and perfection overran my balance. My excessive fastidiousness became a burden to me as well as an obstacle to fellowship with others.

My envy, jealousy, and shame limited the depth and sustainability of my friendships. My assessments and judgments of my classmates were harsh and intimidating. Eventually I was filled with anxiety and stress I couldn't subdue. The harder I tried to remain in control, the more anxiety and stress controlled me. I developed extreme and addictive behaviors, including eating disorders.

No matter how hard I tried to outrun the emptiness inside me, to fill it with praise and recognition from my parents, teachers, and coaches, the sinkhole of my self-worth continued to devour everything in sight. It was insatiable. It seemed as if the more I fed this sinkhole, the bigger it got.

Sometimes truth is a crucible.

At sixteen, I began to starve my body. I used all the survival tools I had at my disposal: competition, drive, achievement, and discipline. My body was something I thought I could completely control. And I could be really good at it. Soon I began to binge, consuming huge volumes of forbidden foods (all foods were forbidden), and then to purge. I vomited in an effort to deny consequences and erase the weakness I had displayed in my out-of-control food splurges.

The anorexia/bulimia demon would plague me, without ceasing, for the next twelve years. It accompanied me as a seventeen-year-old through the United States Equestrian Team's Screening Trials and training for the 1980 Olympics, where I gorged and vomited throughout weeks of training camp. It dogged me through high school and college. It ruined my health, destroyed my fertility, blighted my relationships, and bankrupted my bond with myself. It followed me like a living nightmare, a savage adversary inside me, doing its utmost to take me out.

The desolation of faithlessness is like a magnet for the Divine. But it was my brokenness, misperceptions, and feelings of unworthiness that confused me so I couldn't recognize and receive Divine Love. Fortunately, the melancholy of self-annihilation created a God-sized hole in me, waiting to be filled.

Sometimes truth comes in a download.

I earned a coveted place at a top university, and my time at Princeton was also an incredible period of spiritual exploration. I prayed daily. I begged God to deliver me from my self-induced prison of agony and misery. I remember praying nightly as I walked through campus from the library to my dorm.

One night I looked up at the starry sky and asked Jesus to please help me, to take this burden from me and set me free. Often, I felt like I was whispering my desperate pleas into the void. And sometimes I felt like I was yelling my reckless request into a sky filled with God. Either way, part of me wanted to rail against Jesus for not instantly answering my prayers. But another part of me knew I wasn't a victim; I was doing this to myself.

That night, Jesus instilled His wisdom into me like a download. He showed me that I could be free from my disease, and that freedom was a reward for honesty and humility. He showed me that my pride stood in the way of my healing and that I needed to be vulnerable and admit I had a problem. Even with this realization, I wasn't ready to admit His truth and receive His gift.

This download was much like the seed that Auntie Lu had planted in me. It would take years for me to receive its truth in my heart and to nurture that truth in the dark and fertile ground of my troubled yet seeking subconscious. I was unwilling to admit I had a problem. Meanwhile, in bondage to my addiction, I recognized the part of me that longed to feel connected to God's Divine Love and promise of freedom.

Sometimes truth is obscured or hidden.

Twelve years of addiction, evasiveness, and secrecy took a big toll on my body by eliminating my menstrual cycle for years and throwing my hormones and digestion into complete disarray. I was weary. Still, I would be intractable and obstinate in my self-abuse.

At twenty-eight, I had seen several of my classmates marry and begin families. Their world seemed heartbreakingly out of reach to me. Yet I longed for love, and the desire to be married and to bear children was budding in me.

The truth I had buried began to push through, surfacing into the light. I knew I needed to make a change; I longed to start over. I realized that my self-abuse was destructive and unsustainable and that I had a lot of healing to do.

Sometimes truth is delivered in love.

One day, I met a nice young man. He was down to earth, clean cut, gentle-mannered, spiritually oriented, and exceptionally kind. We fell in love. I wanted to share my life with him and have his children. We decided to marry.

Almost immediately, I experienced a "honeymoon" healing from my eating disorders. Sadly, it wouldn't last, though it gave me a reprieve and much insight.

I felt liberated. I had done nothing to "deserve" this deliverance, yet it was mine.

It was a blissful time. I was in love and felt loved. I perceived my own value in a new way. My body began to heal. I was yielding to a power much greater than myself, a power that literally could transform me physically, emotionally, and spiritually.

Filled with thankfulness, I began to explore various modes of healing, including working with a psychotherapist and an acupuncturist to address many issues. I had no idea what would be revealed to me this way. Truth would be added to my perspective, changing my life dramatically.

Sometimes truth comes in a vision.

One day, my acupuncturist loaded me with needles. As I relaxed with my eyes closed on the treatment table, deep peace settled on me like a heavy blanket. Then images began to emerge. I had a vision in which I experienced two simultaneous perspectives: being inside a vision while also observing the scene. The unfolding imagery didn't resemble my immediate surroundings. Overwhelming emotions consumed me as volumes of tears welled up in my eyes and streamed down the sides of my face. I soon realized I was having a memory from before my own birth.

In the vision I floated above a bed in a room with pale green walls. The scene below was black-and-white tinged with muted green. I saw a woman with medium length dark hair whose face was blank; I couldn't make it out. She was reclining on a bed with a green cloth over her abdomen and legs. She seemed disengaged.

I realized she was in a hospital room. The air was cool, almost cold. A doctor and a nurse were in the room with her, both preoccupied, while the dark-haired woman reclined in bed. Everyone seemed disconnected from one another.

Then I felt a wave of energy. Immediately, I was aware I was observing my mother just before she would give birth to me. I had the sense that I, in what must have been the soul of my preborn self, was floating above the scene, observing.

My feelings were overpowering. I was alarmed by my awareness and by what I saw. I was filled with dread while viewing this dismal scene. No one seemed connected and I was terrified.

Oh, no, I thought. *NO. I can't do this!* I was filled with dire dismay, denial, and refusal to acknowledge that this melancholy scenario could actually involve me and my life. I was a soul resisting participation in the scene that was about to be my birth.

Suddenly, I saw two photographs appear in the corner of my vision. These feather-edged cameos hovered above the woman's bed. Unlike the greenish monochrome of the scene, these two images were in 1960s technicolor. One pictured the man I came to know as Ezra, my dark-haired, Asian-looking father, and the other showed Janet, my ginger-haired, light-complected mother—my adoptive parents. Ezra and Janet lit up the corner of this bleak scene with vibrant color.

Who are these people? I wondered in the vision. Then I sensed my preborn self was being told or reminded that these two had longed for me and were excitedly awaiting my arrival. As soon as my soul recognized my parents-to-be, I realized everything was okay. The scene was no longer melancholy. It was okay for me to be born.

This vision, a soul-memory, was one of the most powerful experiences of my life. On the acupuncture bed, I was consumed with grief, compassion, and understanding. Heavy tears flooded my eyes and poured out in what seemed like an endless flow. My vision and the insights that accompanied it had broken through a dam. The barrier I had constructed to hold the harsh judgments and brittle misunderstandings I had accumulated over the years was breaking down. My heart was broken open. I was completely undone, and it was all okay. I was changed.

Sometimes truth moves us.

I would never be the same again after that vision. However, it would take me decades to fully integrate this new perspective, the truth about my birth, and how loved I truly was.

My sweet man and I left Silicon Valley to pursue a shared dream of growing our own food and living peacefully and sustainably in rural northern California. Nestled in the foothills of the Trinity Alps Wilderness, we settled in a tiny community. It would provide fertile ground for healing. There, I would come home, be home, and learn to create a home.

Sometimes we find truth in community.

A loving community of warm and vital, goddess-celebrating women welcomed me like mothers and midwives. In these women I witnessed true community and interdependence. They showed me what it looked like to be willing to do deep personal work, to surrender completely, to honor life in every stage, and to grieve loss. They showed me how to embrace life and death in its messiness, with the compassion it called for and the grace it promised. They invited me into their circle, showing me benevolence and care. They taught me how to speak truth in love.

Within this playful and serious community, this "tribe" of earth-honoring, ritual-loving, truth-drumming women, I was steeped in the fertility of the earth and its beautiful cycles. I learned the principles of balance and how to steadfastly follow a healing path.

I wanted to start a family. Until then, dreams of pregnancy had seemed distant; I believed I wasn't fertile. The awareness that I wanted children began to reveal some of my inner obstacles. The more I sought the truth, the more my identity would unfold before me, revealing the lies and judgments holding me in bondage. As I began to welcome the truth of Divine Love and follow its direction, I noticed insights, shifts, and gifts flowed more easily to me.

Sometimes we find truth when we have the courage to seek it.

As I began to search for the truth, I realized I didn't even know who I was. Who was I?

My parents had told me a little bit about my origins: the name of my birth mother (Donelda), the hospital where I had been born, and the names of the doctor and attorney who had facilitated my adoption and placement. I aligned with an organization called Adoptees Liberty Movement Association (ALMA) and dug into my search.

My ALMA mentors warned that adoptees tended to romanticize the story of our birth mothers or parents. Romanticizing is human nature. However, the circumstances of my birth might accompany a hidden story. Bringing this story to light could disrupt lives and marriages, cause sibling conflicts, and even renew pain for my birth parent(s), their spouses, and siblings.

I decided to go for it anyway. At this point, I had to know the truth. It felt like my life, my fertility, and my future depended on it. Finding this truth seemed to be the breakthrough I needed to move on with my life as an adult, a spouse, and hopefully, a mother.

Within several months, I found several siblings who had also been given up for adoption. I discovered that my birth mother had been married eight times and she lived in Toronto. I reached out to her in a phone call.

"Are you Donelda?"

"Yes?" She answered in a gentle, lovely voice.

"The Donelda who gave birth to a baby girl in Chicago in 1960? A baby you gave up for adoption?"

"Yes?" Her voice softened even more and quivered. "Who are you?"

I told her who I was. I said I had searched for her and was so happy to find her. We both wept—in deep relief, forgiveness, and a sense of redemption. We each were reclaiming someone we had lost.

My mentor had warned me about the potential reality of an adoptee's birth parents, their circumstances, and their lives. During my search I had been told that the truth about them could be far from the idealized notions I held. Despite the warnings, I was swept up, imagining.

As I flew to visit my birth mother in Toronto to spend a week together, I projected a sentimental fantasy onto her. I envisioned the beautiful woman with the lilting voice I had heard over the phone. I imagined the kindly person who would be my mother, and I invented lovely scenes of our dynamic reunion. It didn't take me long to come to my senses when I arrived.

Sometimes we find truth where we least expect it.

I stepped off the plane and saw Donelda. I had to laugh at myself, saying silently, "Ming, what the hell did you expect?!"

The tall woman who greeted me shifted her raised hand to adjust her oversized brown wig. She wore a hodgepodge collection of layered clothing over a bright pink dress, topped with a ragged, cobalt blue coat and embellished by a multi-colored scarf that was obviously frayed and stained. At one point, her scuffed, black, high-heeled pumps might have been stylish.

My beautifully imagined birth mother was essentially a bag lady.

I went with Donelda to her home in a public housing tenement. Her one-room apartment was stuffed to the gills with her hoardings, an archive of dumpster treasures. I could see at a glance it was a monument to all she had lost.

Everywhere I looked, I saw things for babies. Her collection included baby clothing and blankets, an old buggy, broken strollers, and a fractured cradle. The half-dozen broken baby dolls she had retrieved from the trash were missing arms and legs.

A once-white wicker bassinet was the centerpiece of the room, complete with broken fronds sticking out here and there. This was where she put her doll babies to bed every night. Donelda also had a rocking chair where she cradled and rocked the dolls before their bedtime.

"I am 'Mama Donna,'" she said. "Like the Madonna, who gave up her son, I gave up mine, and I know how God feels." She was straight-faced and completely serious.

I was surprised, amused, and cynical. Before arriving, I had learned that Donelda had been diagnosed with a histrionic personality disorder, which explained a lot. Yet, this was the mother who had given birth to me. While she entertained me with her provocative behavior, attention-seeking, emotional shallowness, and exaggerated emotional displays, the pathos of her life washed over me. It saturated me.

Visiting with her was a mind-bender, but my eyes and heart were wide open. I wanted to glean all the between-the-lines stuff, the meaning of everything. I was claiming it all. I wanted the stark, raving truth, and Donelda delivered.

Sometimes truth consoles us.

As I gazed across my mother's shabby apartment, with its many symbols of a devastated life, I looked back at all the years I had subjected myself to feeling unworthy and despicable. I tallied all the times I had laid waste to the gifts I had been given. And I observed the pathos of her life with a surprising amount of gratitude and love. The tragedy of Donelda's life offered me a poignant window from which to view the generous gifts of mercy in my own life.

I felt these gifts. I was witnessing the truth—about my mother and about me. As awkward and wretched as it seemed, these truths consoled me. I realized that our suffering, while it may seem in vain, exists for a purpose: to wake us up to the holiness and sacred intimacy we have with the Divine who made us, and to understand this principle in our relationships and life.

I was flooded with understanding and compassion for this woman who was so pathetic … and so dear. My heart was opening to her, and to myself. I was overwhelmed with a feeling of a love that was whole and fulfilling. It was abundantly merciful and forgiving. It was peaceful. It was accessible and available to me, and I realized it was a Divine gift.

Sometimes truth lights paths to understanding.

As I sought to understand why we suffer, I would come to see that God uses that part of us that is living and eternal. He uses our emotions, like His blood symbolized in the wine of communion, to feel. Our feelings are the flags or signals that command our attention, so we don't miss the mark, the sign, or the wonder. That wonder is the truth that we are loved, without condition, by the One who created us.

Healing my emotions through this immersive experience with Mama Donna would help me reframe a lifetime of negative judgments. It changed my perspective, forever. It took all that I had falsely deemed to be true and redeemed it. It transformed my relationship with myself.

That night, my mother and I engaged in an awkward and tender ritual. I climbed carefully onto her lap as she sat in the rocking chair where she rocked the broken baby dolls she had rescued. She held me in her arms and rocked me, stroking my short hair. She spoke to me in coos and loving words.

It was the mother-daughter bonding sacrament which had never taken place when I was a child.

We were doing it now, at sixty-four and thirty years old. Our ceremonial role play seemed to give each of us comfort. We gave ourselves permission, without judgment, each satisfying a deep need and longing. Then I climbed into my rickety cot. She tucked me in, and I fell asleep.

Sometimes truth surprises us.

The next morning, we went sightseeing. As we walked down the city street, Donelda started boldly and beautifully singing "Lara's Theme" from the movie *Dr. Zhivago*. Perhaps it was her personality disorder on full display. My modesty about spontaneously singing in public wore off quickly and soon I was charmed by her complete lack of self-consciousness. The freedom I felt was transformative.

> "Somewhere my love, there will be songs to sing
> Although the snow covers the hope of Spring
> Somewhere a hill blossoms in green and gold
> And there are dreams, all that your heart can hold
> Someday we'll meet again my love
> Someday whenever the Spring breaks through
> You'll come to me, out of the long ago
> Warm as the wind, soft as the kiss of snow . . ."

In the subway, I used a restroom. After wiping myself, something made me look at the toilet tissue in my hand. It was stained with an abundance of bright red blood.

I stared at it.

For the previous fourteen years, at five foot six and barely a hundred pounds, my menstrual cycle had been almost non-existent. My excessive self-control and obsessions had held my fertility captive for half of my life. Now I was about to experience a shift.

I stared at the blood on the tissue I held and heard words in my head.

Who gave you this?

That beautiful blood-stained paper meant that my cycle and fertility had returned. As I looked at the blood on the paper, I mouthed the answer quietly to myself.

My mother. My mother gave me this.

I felt a rush of gratitude and love. I was grateful for her gift of life to me and for the realization that I was a woman, too, with the blessing of my own fertility. The life-giving part of me was being restored, there, in a Toronto subway station bathroom, on a glorious and crisp spring day when I sang songs of longing and reunion with the dear woman who had given birth to me. I was flooded with forgiveness for myself for all the years of self-punishment. I was comforted by the love message my heart could finally receive and understand, written in bright red.

I was a woman, born from a mother and connected to a lineage of women, to a history of women and families. My menstrual blood was part of my identity. It was an inheritance. It was permission. It was a source of power and creativity. It was my mother's legacy and it meant I was connected to her. I was joined with my history and within me was access to the future.

I wept there in that basement bathroom in the subway in Toronto. I wept as I celebrated my returning blood and the endowment it was. What a reunion! "Out of the long ago," Mama Donna and I came to one another. My drama-loving, Zhivago-singing, sweet bag lady of a mother, and this entire experience, was returning myself to me.

My monthly blood and the sacred rhythm of my fertility cycles became something I cherished and studied. It fascinated me. At last, I understood its connection to my past, to myself, and the baby for whom my heart longed.

Truth really is stranger than fiction. And my time with Mama Donna taught me to trust the truth and examine the fictions I create.

Sometimes truth fulfills us.

Later that fall, I got pregnant. I was ecstatic. From the day I found out I was pregnant and knew that a tiny embryo was growing inside of me, my cherished baby, I stopped purging. The destructive compulsion vanished.

I fell in love with my body's creative capacity. I loved its changing shape and the power it possessed to grow a new life. I became engrossed in learning about the empowerment of birth in its emotional, physical, and spiritual aspects.

My pregnancy was a time of great celebration, truly blissful in every way. I even loved morning sickness because I understood it meant that this baby was really digging in. I ate whatever I wanted, and I yielded to and trusted my body's natural desires and wisdom.

Among my community of earthy, wise women, I experienced a euphoric time of expansion. I continued learning and deepening my intuition. Not only was it a time of falling in love with my body, but it was also a time of falling in love with the one who would be my daughter.

Sometimes truth transforms us.

I drew on the power and confidence of the millennia of women who had gone before me. Birth, a monumental step forward, began to reshape my view of myself. My body had accomplished the ultimate creative act, to bring a human being to life. Now, I absolutely loved my body; I celebrated it. My body, which I had punished and starved, had forgiven me, yielding an abundance of life and nourishment.

The birth of my daughter transformed me into a mother. It gave me a new sense of identity, a knowing of myself in a deeper way. As I held and beheld my daughter, I was overcome. She was a miracle, awe-inspiring and perfect, and a blessing. She was the culmination of a journey of personal healing, the love between myself and my husband, and the bridge connecting us to the past and to our future.

Her life essence also connected me to God in every living thing. My little newborn showed me Auntie Lu's truth, that God was in me, and everything was connected. I wanted my daughter to know that God made her, too, with so much love, for the very special life she was to lead. I wanted her to know that she was loved more than she could imagine.

Sometimes truth redefines us.

I reveled in my newfound identity as a woman whose self-loathing was transforming into self-love. My healing path would provide further growth. This growth allowed me to face and resolve judgments I had about both of my mothers. My adoptive mother had never been able to conceive a child.

My biological mother had never been able to keep one. I realized that in my own struggle for identity, I had feared being like them.

In my search for the truth of my identity, I had encountered the painful prison of my judgments. I would continue to discover that those judgments could serve my personal growth and emotional freedom when I used them as mirrors. These mirrors showed my errors in perspective and revealed the fear, pain, and unforgiveness I held against myself. I came to better understand my connection to the mystical love that creates and unites all life.

I learned that facing the truths of my life allowed me to find freedom and forgiveness, which have borne fruit beyond my imaginings. Facing truth has brought me abiding peace, deep understanding, and strong faith. It has improved my relationships, brought me meaningful work, empowered my confidence, and revealed the purpose of my life.

I have learned through all the crucibles in my life. Each one was rich with truth. And though each truth held pain, accepting the pain in truth ultimately demonstrated what Auntie Lu had taught me.

In embracing truth, I have learned several gemlike facets I want to share:

1. Truth reveals itself in prayer; you can use it as a navigational tool to guide you.
2. Your desire for truth may transform you as you come to understand your own pain and the pain of others.
3. When you shine the light of truth on any aspect of your life, the dark lies you have deceived yourself into believing are revealed.

I also have learned that truth can wake you up. It can energize you like an espresso for your soul. It can sting like being splashed in the face by an icy mountain spring. Or it can revitalize you like a warm cup of nourishing soup. As you adapt to truth's purpose, you can learn to love how it recharges and refreshes you. Its wakeups, even the stinging ones, are healthy for you.

Truth helped me realize that I am loved more than I can imagine, mercy and forgiveness are my birthright, and I am made for a life of grace, peace, boldness, abundance, and fulfillment.

I invite you to know and embrace your truth, as I have done:

- Discover that truth is the place where your heart merges with the heart of the Divine, whose light and love lives within you.
- Make truth the vehicle for your transformation.
- Seek the seeds of truth that dwell inside your pain. Their fruit is your personal gift of wisdom.
- Be brave in seeking to know yourself, truly.
- Root out judgments, falsehoods, and the stories you have constructed and believed. Surrender those stories to the light of truth when they no longer serve you.
- Be an archaeologist of your own emotions. Dig in the landscape of yourself to unearth the legend of your feelings.
- Rely on truth to light your path and discern your most reliable footholds.

You were born to inherit deep satisfaction and peace, and truth is the key to your inheritance. Truth, the most trustworthy compass for your life's journey, can also serve as your vehicle to bring you freedom and empowerment. When you make Truth your North Star, you can rely on it to always guide you home.

MING LOVEJOY is CEO and Founder of *Ming Lovejoy Coaching*. She is passionate about supporting women business owners to achieve tangible results that grow their businesses and create lifestyles that they love.

Ming is a Princeton graduate, student of bio-energetics, and a leader in the network marketing industry growing a team of over 6,000 people. She is also a founding member of the Empowering Women Alliance. Her unique combination of work and life experience ensures that her clients create lasting professional and personal transformations to live more deeply and joyfully aligned with who—and *why*—they are.

Ming has mentored thousands of coaches and healers to integrate aligned growth strategies with personal well-being. Money, relationship, and health transformations that might be hard become easy with her guidance.

Find out more about Ming Lovejoy:

> minglovejoy.com

Download The Five Golden Pillars of Transformation Workbook:

> minglovejoycoaching.com

SELF-RESPECT

BECKY NOEL

The dictionary defines self-respect as "holding yourself in esteem and believing that you are good and worthy of being treated well." This makes self-respect sound simple and direct, yet I've found it's anything but. I know what it means to have self-respect because I earned it. But I think there are a lot of women who haven't had the same experience, and they may not know what they're missing.

Self-respect doesn't seem to get a lot of attention in conversation. Even when people stop to think about it, they tend to shrug and say, "Well, either you have it, or you don't." But there's more to it than that, so I started asking myself and other women some questions about self-respect.

- What does self-respect look like?
- Is self-respect something you just have, or don't?
- If you don't have self-respect, how do you get it?
- If you want more self-respect, how can you develop it?
- What if somebody tries to diminish or take away your self-respect?

I think these questions are worth having a conversation about.

I've almost always held jobs in a man's world. Working with men was both easier and harder. Easier because I generally knew where I stood with them more so than with women. Harder because I had to work harder to prove myself. But I discovered that when I gained men's respect, they supported and backed me all the way. Unfortunately, I found that many women preferred to tear me down. They were the kind of women who liked to undermine other women rather than empower and support them. Of course, I've since learned there are many women who don't do this, but in my previous experience, empowering women were in the minority.

Early in my work life, I was up for a promotion into management in the grocery business. This was definitely a man's world back then; women were cashiers, not managers. My promotion meant I'd be only the fifth female manager in the whole country. Numerous women I worked with told me, "Good luck," and said they wished me well. After I got the promotion, I learned that those same women were telling people behind my back that I'd slept my way to the top. Instead of being happy for me, and instead of being supportive of another woman getting ahead, they'd chosen to undermine me and spread lies.

I've never understood why some women feel the need to ridicule and tear down others. Why do you suppose they do that? One of the answers I've heard is, "Maybe they're jealous." That may be true. But I think maybe they disrespect others because they have so little respect for themselves. Which makes me wonder . . . what causes that lack of respect?

I was very fortunate. I grew up with loving parents who didn't verbally or physically abuse me. They taught me to be independent and strong. They respected me, which helped me develop self-respect and inner strength. I was taught that I could do anything if I tried hard enough, worked hard enough, and didn't give up. They set good examples. In my family, no matter what, you finished what you started. And, if at first you didn't succeed, you tried again.

But what if you didn't have loving, confidence-building parents? What if no one told you that you were good enough—that you could do anything you put your mind to? Where do you get self-respect then?

I've learned that when respect and self-respect are demonstrated, a girl has a much better chance of respecting herself as she grows up. Knowing what respect and self-respect look like is a real advantage. Girls who don't get that, who have families that behave in a way that's abusive or disrespectful, are put at a disadvantage. They tend to grow up thinking that's just the way things are, or that they're stuck with it.

When I was a community service officer with the police department, it became very clear to me that we learn our behavior, both good and bad. That's why domestic violence and child abuse can continue generation to generation, because kids learn it from their parents and because people continue to be psychologically and emotionally affected by it.

If kids watch their mom behave in ways that show she has no self-respect, or if they watch her allow her self-respect to be chipped away by tolerating their dad's lack of respect or bad behavior, then kids assume that this is the way life works. If they watch their mom get belittled by their dad all the time, and they see that she just takes it, then that leaves an impression. Or, if everything she says is run over, downplayed, or ignored, then they see that their dad doesn't take her seriously and that their mom doesn't take herself seriously, either. (It works the other way, too—men can also be put down.)

When those things happen, then the girls in the family often grow up to behave like their mom because that was the behavior demonstrated for them—they don't know anything different. For the same reason, the boys in the family often grow up to behave like their dad. It's the same for all kinds of domestic violence. When kids watch their mom and dad constantly fighting or their mom being beaten, then they often grow up to repeat the behavior they learned. In abusive situations, it's no surprise when boys learn to beat their girlfriends and wives, or when girls learn to take it from their boyfriends and husbands. That's what's familiar, and as far as they've been taught, that's what's acceptable. That's learned behavior.

Fortunately, men and women can learn to be respectful and to have self-respect. At any point, it's possible to break the cycle. It's possible for a man to say, "No, I'm not going to lash out," and for a woman to say, "No, I'm not going to take it." Usually that happens through intercession, or after a shocking wake up call. It can also happen when people realize another way of behaving is possible, or when a different behavior is demonstrated by someone who's a positive influence.

I understand this first-hand, not only as a former officer, but as someone who's been there herself. I know what it takes to say, "No," or "No more." I know what it is to make the decision to stop putting up with bad behavior, and I know what it costs to value self-respect more than the idea of staying married.

That's why I divorced my husband. I put up with his alcoholism for fourteen years and told myself it was okay because in most ways he was a wonderful man. He was well respected in his career. He was loving and caring, and he wasn't physically or verbally abusive. But sometimes I still felt like a victim in my own home. I shared a house with my husband, but I felt like I was on my own with no one to talk to. There were too many times I had to eat dinner and watch a movie by myself because he'd passed out after drinking.

Then one night, on Christmas Eve, something happened I'll never forget. He'd fallen asleep after a heavy night of drinking and was snoring loudly, like 500 freight trains. So, I woke him up to get him to stop. Instead of just rolling over, he got up, came around to my side of the bed, and stood over me. Then he raised his fist.

I was shocked. But I'd always said I wouldn't stand for a guy abusing me, and I wasn't going to let him get away with trying to hit me or intimidate me. I tapped my chin with my finger and said, "Take your best shot, because if you hit me, I'll fucking kill you." That's exactly what I said. And he knew I was serious. I could see the look on his face, and it was like he was thinking, *Oh shit*. He put his hand down, and then he slept in his chair the rest of the night.

I was awake all night. I knew my marriage was over and I'd have to leave.

Looking back, you might think I'd been stupid for not realizing right away he had a drinking problem. It's not like I could claim I didn't know he drank, because I saw him drink the first time I met him. But back then, I think I was just naïve. I excused his drinking in the beginning because he'd recently gotten divorced, and his ex-wife had disappeared with the kids. I thought he was just drowning his sorrows. I figured he'd stop drinking once he was with me and we got the kids back because then he'd be happy.

Back then I didn't know much about alcoholism or how people rationalize being with an alcoholic, how they make excuses, and how they minimize the impact of alcoholic behavior. I unknowingly did all of that. And I made the same mistake so many women make about marrying a man with a problem . . . I thought I could fix it.

I'd listened to stories like Johnny Cash's when he'd talk about his wife, June. This famous country music singer-songwriter would always say things like, If it hadn't been for this woman, June Carter Cash, I'd be dead now.

She saved me. He'd go on about how I loved her so much and I wanted to do right by her, and she stayed by my side and was always there to help me stay away from drugs and drink. So, in my mind, I thought I could do that for my husband, too. I kept thinking if he loved me, he'd quit. In the beginning, I thought I was making it work, but like I said, I just didn't know that much about alcoholism.

We'd gotten married and settled in together, along with his two kids, and I became a wife and an instant mother. I loved him and I loved those kids. Everything should have been fine then, right? My husband went to work every day where he did a great job, made good money, and was very respected. But after six o'clock, as soon as he got home, he wanted a drink. So, I was there at six o'clock to remind him not to drink too much, to suggest that maybe he didn't need that extra drink, and for the most part I made that work for us. We made it through like that for more than eight years, just like Johnny Cash and June.

Then I got promoted to Night Manager at the grocery store. I started going to work at five o'clock; my husband got off at six. That's when our marriage started to die. Every night he was home by himself. I wasn't there to curb his drinking. And it didn't take long for his drinking to get out of control. Oh, for a long time he was a functioning alcoholic. He still went to work every day, but he drank every night. I'd call to check on him, but half the time he didn't answer the phone because he was passed out drunk. He'd sober up by morning, go to work, and then come home and drink. This went on for years until it finally started affecting his work.

I think that made him finally admit he had a drinking problem. He told his boss and his district supervisor, and he checked himself into rehab. I was thinking, *Oh my God . . . we're over the hump! We're going to make it!* I still wanted to believe in him. He was supposed to be in rehab for four or five weeks, but he didn't even stay a week before he checked himself out.

He came home saying, "They told me I was doing so good I could come home."

Well, I was naïve back then, but I wasn't stupid. "Really," I said. I questioned him while thinking, *This can't be true.* The problem was, I wanted it to be true. So, I went along with it, for a while.

Then, typical alcoholic that he was, and typical naïve spouse that I was, we fell into a new pattern. Over three or four days, he'd gradually start drinking more until I'd blow up and say, "This isn't working!" I'd threaten to leave, so he'd stop drinking and be good for a while. And then he'd start to slide again. I finally realized he just couldn't do it. He couldn't give it up. And even if I could be there every hour of every day for him, I couldn't stop him from drinking.

The morning after he almost hit me, he wrapped his arms around me, apologizing. I stiffened up in his arms. I couldn't pretend things were okay. I had to face up to the reality of alcoholism in our relationship. I didn't want to lose respect for myself by acting as if what had happened didn't matter. I realized he couldn't, or wouldn't, change. I knew my marriage was over, and I was brokenhearted.

I was also worried. I'd just changed jobs the month before. I'd left the grocery business to go to the police academy, which was something I'd always wanted to do, even though it meant taking a $12,000 per year cut in pay. It suddenly became very real to me that ending my marriage also meant I'd need to move out . . . and when I moved out, I'd be going from a two-income household to just one. . . and my income would be much less than I'd been earning before.

I had these panicky thoughts like, *Oh, my God. I'm forty and I'm changing careers. I'm leaving my marriage of almost fifteen years. I don't know where I'm going to live.* But then I reminded myself that I'd said I'd never let any man abuse me, and I'd been raised to keep my word. Maybe I should have wised up to the whole alcoholism trap earlier, but I hadn't understood or wanted to believe it for a long time. Now that I did understand and knew the truth, my life, my sense of ethics, and my self-respect were on the line. So, I made the best choice I could: I left him.

I think what helped me was having grown up in a family with parents who set boundaries. They taught me to respect those boundaries, which helped me to respect myself. My parents had also wanted to know what I thought about things, and they listened when I talked. We talked about everything, and we spent time together as a family, like at dinnertime. We kids were allowed to speak our minds without being afraid, we were allowed to have an opinion, and we were treated fairly and individually. My parents were respectful of one another and of us kids, and we kids respected our parents and their authority as adults.

Spending time together as a family was important then, and it's important now. Unfortunately, nowadays so many people are on their phones or they're watching television, not really spending time with one another. I know that a lot of people didn't have the same background as I did while growing up, or don't have those advantages now. As a result, many don't have good experiences to draw from or good examples of respectful behavior to follow.

Even though I'd had good examples, I still got caught in a long-term situation that took its toll on me. After my divorce, it took me a year or two to get back to being me, the real Becky. I hadn't realized how much of myself I'd let go or given away while being married to an alcoholic.

Now that I'm older and more experienced, I can see the warning signs more easily. But I couldn't see them then. Just like I can now spot a functioning drunk in a few seconds, I can also spot the red flags when someone's missing self-respect, or when relationships are in trouble. I'm also experienced enough to know self-respect is something that grows when you cultivate it.

It's never too late to build self-respect.

First, you have to want it. Then you can start developing it. It can be built up gradually, like building muscle. Just like weight training, you can start out weak and end up strong by lifting small, light weights and then bigger, heavier ones until you're finally able to bench press your own body weight.

You can always get started by asking for help.

That's what I did. I reached out to my sister. She was a good sounding board, and she helped me stick to my guns once I'd decided to leave my husband. My step-kids were grown by then and my husband and I hadn't had kids together, so that wasn't a concern. But I had a lot of other things to consider, and I had my sister to talk to.

Ultimately, it was up to me. I knew I needed to move out, regardless of how hard it would be. I went out apartment hunting and rented a place three weeks later. I chose to move out while my husband was at work, though I'd already told him I was leaving.

I know from experience that just finding someone to talk to, someone you can trust, can make a huge difference. Getting out of a scary or abusive situation is the number-one priority, and getting support is a close second. If you don't have a trusted family member or friend to take you in or be there for you, somebody will always be available to help, even if it's someone at a women's shelter.

A lot of people don't know that most police departments offer referrals and access to resources. Many of them have a community service officer like me. You don't have to be afraid of calling the police, and you don't have to call 911, which is for emergencies; you can get their phone number online and then call your local police department directly for information and assistance. You won't have to give them details or press charges to get help with rape crisis counseling or domestic violence and abuse resources. You can also get referrals to safe houses, shelters, addiction and rehab programs, mental health services, community food banks and services, and housing and financial assistance.

There are people at each of these places or services who are experienced in whatever your situation might be, and they know what to do and how to help you. There are even organizations that can give you some money to help get on your feet; they can help you find a job, and get you educated in that job, if that's what you need.

You just have to be able to say: "I need help. I can't do this by myself." Believe me, I know that's the hardest thing for some of us to admit. But you don't need to be ashamed of needing help. Admitting it isn't weakness; it's a healthy sign of self-respect because you're looking out for yourself. And you don't need to be afraid of sailing into new, unchartered waters. If you come to a realization like I did, if you're facing difficult choices, if you're upset because you think your marriage is over, or if you're saying you're not going to do this anymore (whatever "this" is) and you need help to make changes, then there are caring people and professionals out there to help you.

And if your circumstances aren't dire, but you need to grow your self-respect, there are people who can help with that, too. Another strong woman can be a positive role model or a mentor. You can look around to see who demonstrates self-respecting behavior—you can learn from her. You can talk with someone you admire, such as a co-worker or a good friend. It can really help if they're someone you can open up to. If your earlier background was—or if your current situation is— abusive or severely dysfunctional, you can always talk to a therapist, counselor, or pastor who's been trained to help you identify your learned behaviors and then develop healthier ones. No matter who we are now or where we came from, we all need someone to be there for us if we're going through rough patches.

Another way you can begin building or strengthening your self-respect is by keeping your word.

When you say you're going to do something, do it. Start small. Make small promises you can keep. If you make a promise to yourself, honor it the same way as a promise made to someone else. Then, as you begin to trust yourself, and others begin to trust you to keep your word, make bigger promises, and keep them too. The more practice you get keeping your word, the better you'll feel about yourself. You'll develop your "muscle" for respecting yourself, and others' respect for you will grow, too.

In the same way, you can build self-respect by sticking with something and following through on it, even when it's hard or unpleasant. This could be anything: maybe taking on a project at work, school, or home, committing to an exercise program, or cleaning out your desk or a room in your house. Seeing something through can make you feel proud of yourself.

If you're a mom, then I think following through is even more important. Your kids learn from your example. It doesn't matter whether you're a stay-at-home mom or a going-out-to-work mother, your follow through counts. The more you stick with things and follow through, the better example you'll set, and the more self-respect you'll feel.

Choosing to do something well can also give you self-respect.

It doesn't matter what you choose. You know the saying, "If it's worth doing, it's worth doing well" It's true. You can take pride in doing any job well. Whether you're a volunteer, a minimum wage employee, or the president of a Fortune 500 company, you can choose to do your task or job to the best of your ability. If you do that, it doesn't matter what you do—convenience store clerk or CEO—because whatever it is you can be proud of the way you do it. You can be proud of doing your best and doing an honest day's work. Having a good work ethic is a great way to build your self-respect. Which brings me to the subject of ethics in general.

Self-respect and ethics go hand in hand.
One of the things people have always said about me is that I'm ethical. Right and wrong isn't just an idea for me, it's a way of life. I mean, I wouldn't take a paperclip that didn't belong to me, and I couldn't keep quiet if I knew someone was doing something unethical. I used to drive everybody crazy at work because I would speak up and stick to my guns about something that I thought was right, or important.

But I know how important it is for a woman to stick up for something she knows is right. I also know how important it is to say, "No." There are lots of reasons to say no and lots of ways to say it. Sometimes no is a matter of preference, and sometimes it's a matter of self-respect. Another muscle to strengthen is your ability to say no when it counts, and then stick to it.

I've never had a problem saying no to things I knew were bad or wrong; I've always been able to stand up for myself and others and been willing to back up a no with action if necessary. But it's taken me most of my life to learn that it's okay to say no to things I'd normally enjoy doing but shouldn't take on because I'd be spreading myself too thin. Now that I'm retired, I've had to give myself permission to say no to volunteering too much.

Self-respect has a lot to do with your values.
When you know what you value and what your values are, you have a choice whether to honor your values or not. The more you honor and uphold them, the more you can respect yourself for choosing what's important to you over what seems to be important to someone else. If you let someone run over your values, then you're letting them run over you—you're letting them devalue you. If you stand up for your values, you're also standing up for yourself. That's why it's so important to figure out what your core values are, or what you want them to be, and then hold true to them.

When you know your core values and somebody impinges on them in some way, you have a choice to make. As I see it, you have three choices. First, you can stand up for yourself and risk a confrontation. Second, you can take yourself out of the situation because you want to be safe and keep your core intact. Or third, you can give up . . . you can basically say to the other person that what they want in that moment is more important than who you are at your core, and just let them have their way. The first two choices allow you to build or maintain your self-respect; the third choice diminishes your self-respect. I believe that most women facing these situations have trouble making a good choice because they don't even know what their core values are, let alone feel that their values are truly valuable and important.

That's another way I was lucky about how I grew up; I had a family that showed me what good values looked like. My family's strong values got me off to a good start in life, and as I got older, I added my own.

When I went to high school, the popular drugs were marijuana, LSD, and heroin. Several of my friends smoked weed and a few dabbled in LSD. I wasn't interested in doing drugs. Whenever we'd go to concerts together, I could expect that joints or tabs of acid would get passed around, and there would always be people pressuring me to just try a hit. I wasn't judgmental about their choice to do drugs back then, but I'd get irritated at constantly having people tell me, "Becky, come on, just loosen up and have some of this!" I was always very firm about saying, "No."

After a while, I told them, "Look, I don't care what y'all do, that's fine. We can still be friends. But do not pressure me. Don't ever ask me again because I'm not doing it. You say it's fun, and that's fine for you, but I can have fun without that stuff. So, let's just leave it this way . . . I'll respect your choices, and you respect mine." And they did.

I hear a lot about how peer pressure is so much worse nowadays. In some ways, that might be true because now there's social media to worry about. But I believe the basics are still the same now as they were in my day; peers apply pressure, and kids have a choice to give into the pressure, or not. Kids of any age (or in any era) can be taught the skills they need to stand up to peer pressure the same way they can be taught self-esteem and self-respect.

Not long ago, a friend's eighteen-year-old daughter went to Europe with a group of college students for a six-week educational trip. Once there, most of the kids' "education" consisted of sex, parties, and drinking. When the students weren't sleeping with each other, they were bringing strangers back to their rooms for sex. My friend's daughter had gone on the trip to sightsee and learn about European history and culture, not to party. Pressured every day to have sex and get drunk, she stood firm, even when she was ridiculed by friends and strangers alike, even when she had to lock herself in the bathroom to get away from the partiers! Every day, for six weeks, she upheld her values instead of knuckling under to theirs. That's self-respect.

The flip side of self-respect is having respect for other people's choices as well as your own.

Respect means not pressuring them or bullying them. Respect means accepting them for who they are and for who they're not. And I think that those of us who have self-respect are more likely to respect others.

I've seen many women fall short of self-respect or getting respect from others because they're not clear in their minds about what they want and what they don't want. They don't have a clear sense of who they are and what they deserve. They've never spelled it out to themselves, let alone others.

A woman with self-respect will say, "This is my life. These are my goals. These are my values. This is who I am. This is who I intend to be in the world." And if somebody comes into her life and tries to diminish her, push her, or change her, she's sure enough about who she is to say, "No," "back off," "this is who I am," or "this is what I want." She'll let that person know straight out what she will or will not stand for. Or she'll simply choose to not spend time with that person.

Sandra Yancey, a businesswoman well-known for empowering other women, says something about this that's absolutely true: "You have to know what you stand for, or you'll fall for anything."

And I say, "Know what you stand for, so you won't be a pushover."

I believe it's important for women to take a stand for themselves and also show one another how to do it. To support each other and stand up for one another. To build each other up, not tear each other down. To give one another encouragement. Providing any of these things can go so far in helping someone gain self-respect. Finding other women who demonstrate these qualities can show you how to grow your self-respect. Women who provide encouragement can help you boost your self-respect.

As women, we all need to practice building each other up. We need to do this instead of tearing each other down, stabbing each other in the back, or being catty. We need to cultivate our self-respect and show respect to others. We need to be telling each other, "You've got this; you can do it!" and "Go forth and conquer!"

So please start practicing now. Start today. Tell another woman, "You are worthy. You matter. You are loved. You can do anything!"

And then, repeat after me . . .

"I am worthy."

"I matter."

"What I value matters."

"I am loved."

"I can do anything. I CAN."

Yes, you can.

BECKY NOEL knew as a young girl watching Perry Mason on TV that she wanted to be a criminal attorney. She earned a BS in Criminal Justice in Texas, then was sidetracked from attending law school by family and work commitments. Eventually, she segued from criminal law into law enforcement in Arizona, attended the police academy, and became a Community Service Officer.

Becky was named city-wide Employee of the Year and served the Tucson Police Department with award-winning distinction for twenty years. As the National Instructor of the Crime-Free Multi-Housing Program, she taught at other law enforcement agencies across the United States. She was also an exceptional Personal Safety Instructor and speaker for organizations and businesses.

Throughout her career and following retirement, Becky served several nonprofit organizations as Board Member or Director, including Executive Director of an international nonprofit. For ten years, Becky satisfied her love of horses by volunteering at Therapeutic Riding of Tucson (T.R.O.T.).

Find out more about community services available in your area:

> Many police departments have a Community Service Officer like Becky, and all have access to a variety of referrals and resources. Instead of calling the emergency number, you can call your local police department <u>directly</u> for other information and community support services.

FREEDOM COMES AT THE PACE OF GRACE

CHRISTY LEE

Scroll. Click. Scroll. Stare. Ponder.
What could I do to look like that?
Wow, she is the definition of Super Mom!
She is so creative and talented—I wish I could do that.

I feel the lies of comparison creeping into my thoughts. I desperately seek peace while society screams its own agenda at me. *Work hard.* There is no time for rest. *Work harder.* There are too many people and tasks to take time for myself. *You are falling behind.* I will only achieve success by striving. *Always be one step ahead.* Say yes to all opportunities. *Network. Clean. Study. Cook. Strive.* I'm so tired, and still don't feel I've done enough.

Does this sound like a narrative written about the ebbs and flows of your life? If your answer is yes, I want you to know you're not alone. I've been there and am still tempted daily. Society has instilled in us the picture of what a perfect woman should be—a picture we want to believe is within our reach.

At home, we're expected to be the best moms, wives, and caregivers. In the workplace, gender discrimination tells us we must work twice as hard to be respected. Through the media, we're plagued with reminders of society's value of outward beauty. Within our culture, we may also carry unrealistic expectations: a perfect woman regularly works out, makes healthy home-cooked meals, lives sustainably, volunteers, and meditates. All these standards are dictated as one-size-fits-all, not taking into account our individuality—our differences, likes and dislikes, or our varied stories.

My story is one of highs and lows—one minute racing to finish first, the next finding victory in simply finishing. All while learning to mute society's voice and listening to God's voice instead. I invite you into my story to share what I have learned. I want to empower you to find peace in who you are and your unique success, regardless of expectations the world tries to set for you.

From the age of three, I participated in countless activities. I joined clubs like 4-H, played five or six sports, and danced. My schedule was constant hustle and bustle, but I loved it. I was a social butterfly who never wanted to miss out. At times, I even held my pee for hours to make sure I didn't miss a moment. I had FOMO (Fear of Missing Out) before the term was even invented. To me, life was about building memories and relationships around activities.

While I truly did love these activities, I can't say that was my only motivation for deciding to say yes. Part of it was a desire to be successful—I was building my resume early. Not to show off or please anyone, but rather to outshine my flaws and cover up my insecurities, including a deep shameful feeling of irresponsibility that came with my distracted forgetfulness.

Busyness had taken over my life. It ruled my activities and my thoughts. Like a lot of women, I had a thousand thoughts swirling around in my head and found it hard to focus on just one. This meant I didn't give much thought to things like turning off the oven, holding onto my wallet, or completing simple and straightforward tasks. Because I was juggling my busy lifestyle with other priorities, I had the option of viewing these forgetful incidents with an eye toward granting myself grace. Instead, I gave way to feelings of shame and inadequacy.

In high school, I went on a class trip to Costa Rica. While I was there, I bought a butterfly knife as a gift for someone back home. However, I was completely unaware these knives are illegal in forty-eight states. While buzzing around and packing my bags to go home, I thought I had placed the knife in my checked bag. Instead, it found its way into my carry-on. It went unnoticed by Costa Rican security before I boarded, but after we landed, US security found the knife.

I was taken aside. Airport security deemed the oversight to be an innocent mistake and said they would let me go. *Whew!* I thought. *What a relief.* However, thirty minutes later, my teacher said New Jersey police wanted to talk to us before we could board the next flight home. My stomach dropped. I was separated from my teacher and taken to a back room. A stranger approached me saying, "Whatever the officers ask you, don't say a thing. Remember your rights." My heart rate spiked as my body began to shake. A group of five or six officers entered the room and asked my name. Unsure if I was even allowed to speak, I sobbed instead.

The officers continued to interrogate me as I barely breathed out answers. Mostly saying "I'm so sorry" a lot. I also heard the words "jail time". It took all I had not to fixate on those words and the horrors I could soon be encountering. My body was wet with sweat; my face was covered in tears.

After what seemed like an eternity, I was set free. The terror I had been feeling started to fade, quickly replaced by shame and guilt. I felt terrible about my simple mistake. On the flight home from New Jersey, my thoughts continued to spiral around what could have happened to me, my teacher, my classmates, and my parents if I had been taken to jail.

When we landed, I was excited to see my family after a couple of weeks away and the traumatizing last few hours. I walked towards the airport waiting area where my parents stood and saw the looks on their faces. They knew what had happened. At that moment, I just needed a hug. Instead, my dad turned me around to look at a posted sign.

"No knives, guns, or weapons allowed."

Looking back, I know he was worried about me. I realize he didn't know how to express the love and fear he felt. But at the time, his response elicited deep regret and anger in me. Those feelings lasted several weeks before I forgave my father. I thought I had forgiven myself, too.

While this event still stands out in my list of experiences with distracted forgetfulness, other incidents piled up over the years. I truly tried to focus more on details to prevent forgetting or losing anything, but I'm still known today as a chronic loser of objects. While this phrase is used in a loving, joking manner these days, there is a small part of my soul-wound that still stings when I hear it. Part of me still wants to disprove this label.

I can't put my finger on why I felt such great shame for these forgetful acts; I wasn't deliberately shamed by others. My dad reminded me how beautiful I was every morning, my mom affirmed my potential, and others in our community praised me, too. But I didn't trust a single word because as much as I didn't want to disappoint anyone, these incidents kept happening.

When I disappointed someone, not only did I get the look—you know the one that puts a knot in your stomach that takes hours or days to go away—but I also felt a wall rise up. For me, this wall of distrust created separation between the person I loved and me. I despised the wall because all I truly wanted was trust and deep connection with people. Yet I seemingly ruined those trusting connections with a single instance or repeated acts of "irresponsibility." I felt immature and lesser than, as if I had a deep character flaw.

In an attempt to invalidate my label, I tried to prove I could be responsible. However, my efforts just resulted in participating in even more activities and striving for more accolades and affirmations. The more I strived, the more my mind raced . . . and the faster it raced, the more I forgot or lost things . . . and the more distracted and forgetful I was, the more I disappointed people. I knew what I was doing wasn't working, but still, the cycle seemed impossible to stop.

While one narrative in my story about growing up focused on shame for my irresponsibility, another narrative spoke to the definition of success I thought I had to live up to. With my mother as a prominent figure in our town, my older sister as an exceptional student athlete, and my natural drive to want to be accepted, I put pressure on myself to be the best I could, in every area of my life.

No one can deny that our culture affects the way we see the world and the decisions we make, so I'm not going to dismiss the fact that the busy American lifestyle was influencing me during this time as well. I already wanted to be the brightest student, best athlete, and most social person. I longed to be respected by older figures as well as a leader to my peers, impressive in my service, and spiritually mature. If I had also been immersed in the "comparison culture" so many of us experience today through social media, I believe my drive to always be the best would have been even worse.

As it was, I strived every day, knowing I could always be better. I was pretty good at it, too. I found plenty of temporary success, though deep down I knew my striving and outward accomplishments were never going to fulfill or fix me. They only covered up what I felt inside—deep shame and insecurity—and the underlying belief I could never do anything of significance because of my lack of dependability.

While I'm still healing some wounds and sorting through erroneous thoughts from my early years, my story isn't rife with heavy burdens. I'm deeply grateful for my childhood, and I remember being filled with so much joy growing up. My family and friends loved me despite my flaws, and I had all I needed. And for that, I recognize my privilege.

"Christy, how are you doing?" My college mentor asked me as we sat for coffee in our favorite study spot.

"I'm good! My friend is really struggling, though—" I started.

"No," she interrupted. "How are YOU? I love your passion for your friends and family. I can tell you truly care. But I'm not here to mentor them. I'm here for you."

I stopped. I thought about what she said, but I was not sure how I felt. I hadn't shared how I felt, out loud, in a long time.

While I was a social person who loved authentic relationships, I didn't do a lot of sharing myself. I didn't think it was necessary, helpful, or healthy. I thought my role in relationships was listening and helping, not sharing my burdens. I shared my feelings with the Lord in journals, but no one else knew my heart of hearts. No one knew the pressure I felt building inside of me every minute, or that I couldn't shake the disgrace that haunted me.

I had justified internalizing my feelings because I still had hope. I knew I wasn't okay, but looking at the big picture, I knew, ultimately, I would be. I had a God who loved me despite my flaws. What I didn't realize then was that keeping all of this bottled up could only work for so long; God created us with a need to communicate with one another, too.

Something clicked that day in the coffee shop, being with a friend who truly wanted to know my heart. I changed. I was shocked when I started speaking about my emotions and realized it was an experience I hadn't really had before. Sharing how I truly was at the deepest level produced a lot of tears, but also a lot of freedom. I started sharing my shame and fear of irresponsibility. I shared about my faith and how I often ran into doubts. I shared my thoughts and emotions that day, and the love my mentor shared with me allowed me to keep on sharing myself again and again.

I started a journey of true vulnerability that allowed me to find healing and forgiveness. This doesn't mean I am fully healed or never act out of a place of shame and fear, but this marked a new beginning. It opened a door to relationships with others as I began to heal. I found out how vulnerability could lead me down a path of healing the contrition I carried.

The rest of my college experience had ups and downs as I began to learn the delicate balance of work and rest. I continued to be involved in as much as I could, getting only three to six hours of sleep a night, and working to achieve perfection in everything I did. But I chose to do each of these activities because they all brought me joy in a unique way.

I studied abroad in New Zealand, where I initially started striving again, this time for having the most epic photos and adventures. Eventually, that grew old, so I intentionally eased into the Kiwi's more laid-back culture. I never wore shoes and I longboarded to class. I didn't worry as much about where I went or who knew about it. Instead, I began to enjoy simply being.

I let myself be me . . . who I really am. Being the real me got me into some sticky situations at times, but those were the real adventures I craved anyway. I loved life for its simplicity, and nature became my favorite place to dwell. When I returned to the States, I channeled this newfound freedom until I graduated.

I made a quick transition to graduate school to obtain my doctorate degree in Physical Therapy. I got married, moved to a new city, accepted a graduate assistantship, started working again as a group fitness instructor, and opened a branch of a ministry called Faith & Fitness in our new community. The barefoot, longboarding, laid-back woman had slipped away when I wasn't looking, and my all too familiar striving spirit returned.

One day I was baking cookies for some friends. I got distracted cleaning the house, running around upstairs, and talking to my husband. When I went downstairs, I smelled something burnt.

"MY COOKIESSS!" I yelled. What followed was an explosion of cussing and rage that was foreign to me. I slammed the pan of ruined cookies to the ground. My heart raced. I yelled at my husband as if it was his fault, too.

After about thirty seconds of raging, I fell to the ground amid the scattered cookies and began to cry.

"What's wrong with me?" I wailed. "Why am I so upset?" I felt heavy with shame.

As I processed this event, I discovered it had nothing to do with burnt cookies. Rather, a lifelong accumulation of striving and busyness had culminated in complete emotional exhaustion and irrational thinking. My feeling of not being good enough had exploded with my temper in a split second.

I had been coming home every day weary and burnt out; my family and husband had gotten my leftover energy and attention. I had so badly wanted to make a difference in the world. I wanted my life to matter. I wanted my minutes to all be counted as worthy and productive. I had kept racing, not realizing I had been leaving behind the most important part of my life. Although I had felt it happening, I couldn't shake the feeling I had to keep going anyway, because I couldn't back out now, right?

And did I even want to? I had huge dreams and there was no way I could achieve them if I stopped hustling. American culture yet again affirmed this—my achievements told me my sacrifices were worth it, and the momentary admiration I felt because of my hustling was like a drug that kept me seeking more. I had gone to leadership conferences, read books, and listened to podcasts all my life telling the same message: sacrifice is a part of being successful.

But I was making the wrong sacrifice.

I can't tell you the day I realized this wasn't the way I had to live. Rather, I credit many circumstances and individuals' influence that started to change not only my behavior of striving, but my belief system behind it. I didn't need to hustle; in fact, it was hustling that was holding me back from true success. Turns out, when I'm running around, I neglect what really matters. My family gave me a beautiful perspective on this. It also causes me to forget, but with people like my husband, Eric, who shows me immense grace every day, I can break that cycle. When I'm stressed, I'm less creative, unable to give a hundred percent in my work. My bosses opened my eyes to that. I also cast my relationship net so wide that I had no capacity for depth. My dear friends gave me insight to that truth.

When I'm spiraling into the sea of insecurity and all I want to do is turn away and just work harder at something else to cover it up, I'm reminded that I am loved first and fully by the God of the universe. Because His Son has already covered my faults, I can instead float in the wave of freedom. I can choose a new definition of success. This leads me to the first life lesson I learned that I want to share:

1) The definition of success is personal.

Success by the world's standards generally means getting ahead of the competition and accumulating money and accolades. It means looking like the women we see in the media, having lots of friends and influence, and never messing up. I decided it was time to create my own definition. Not what society determines to be accomplishment or what I perceive others want me to achieve, but truly my own definition:

Success is doing the best I can with what I have been given, accepting and growing from my failure, bringing light and life to the world through the grace of Jesus, and loving those around me genuinely. Success is not determined by what I do, rather by who I am, (and as a believer in Christ, by whose I am).

I also created a definition of what success is not:

Success is not owning a successful business, leading hundreds of people, being the best _____ (fill in the blank) in the room, or knowing everyone in town.

Though I take ownership of my new definition, I'm still a work in progress. Ownership is the first step.

2) Comparisons are chains that can be broken.

I can create my own definition of success, but if I don't live it, it's pointless. I find the most considerable barrier to truly living in freedom is comparison. Comparison sneaks up like a sneeze we aren't expecting, unwelcome and with so much power exploding in an instant. It may not seem when we look around at others that our tiny desire to "do what she's doing" impacts us. But over time, we start to change. Our desire to belong turns into wishing we could do more or believing we're not good enough as we are.

I have my doctorate degree in Physical Therapy. It took a lot of sacrifice, hard work, and mostly the grace of God to get there. To be honest though, most days I don't think of it as an accomplishment. Rather, I tend to look at the eighteen other certifications, degrees, or accolades I think I should have. When I choose this mindset, I'm robbed of gratitude. I'm chained to self-deprecation. I'm unable to fully run in freedom toward what I can already do because I'm wearing shades of comparison that fog my vision to see only what I should be doing.

Comparisons are chains only if we let them be. These shackles can bind us to chasing after dreams that were never really ours in the first place. If I choose to envy a woman with perfectly luscious straight hair over my crazy curly frizz ball, I'll miss the beauty of a messy bun. If I waste time and energy trying to be better than my peers, I might miss the opportunity to get to know them or enjoy the life stage I'm in.

However, without the shackles, comparison can turn into a healthy dose of motivation and learning. I can use comparison to learn from those who are doing Physical Therapy or this whole "owning a business" thing better than I am. I can be inquisitive, creating my own concepts and practices with their help.

While training for triathlons, comparison can steal my joy. I'm tempted to compare my times or distances on a social media app for endurance sports because I'm afraid of not being good enough, of being too slow, of my heart rate getting too high, or not putting in as many hours. When I give into this temptation, not only is my training not as much fun, but I also miss the whole purpose of exercising.

Conversely, when I shatter the shackles of comparison, I get to enjoy the beauty of nature and the awe of creation surrounding me while appreciating what people can do with their bodies. I'm inspired to push myself in a healthy way. I get to support and encourage others without putting myself down.

This non-comparative mindset is not one that comes to me naturally. It takes practice and dedication for the chains of comparison to finally fall. But it's worth it.

3) Nobody likes to be "should" on.

For me, being should on sounds something like this:

    a) You should never disappoint anyone.
    b) You should look super fit.
    c) You should eat healthy—organic, vegan, or carnivore.

d) You should stay up all night to get stuff done.
e) You should spend all your free time serving or volunteering and more.

We as human beings are bombarded with thoughts of how we should do this or that; however, this mentality is based on what someone else says. It's a standard that wasn't written for you or me. If I live by those standards, I'll fail every time. Worse yet, I'll feel guilty that I'm not living up to someone else's expectations of what I should be doing. If you're like me, there is nothing worse than living with guilt boiling up inside of you.

While I'm still should on externally and I'm sometimes tempted to should on myself, I now have my own pace to run and my own destination to set my sights on. Therefore, if the should-driven action doesn't take me further along my clear path, or at the pace I'm choosing to go, I can reject it with confidence.

Recently, I wrote down a six-figure goal for my business this year. I'm twenty-six years old and I started this business in the middle of a pandemic. While a goal like this may be attainable, it's not an expectation by any means. With a should-be-able attached to it, if I don't hit the goal, it places the blame on who I am. It places emphasis on striving. It also forces quick, not fully thought-out actions. So instead, I changed my goal: I'm going to build a solid foundation for my business so when it starts to grow, I'll be ready. No should, no striving, just taking my own path one step at a time.

It's time to shove the shoulds out of our way in everyday life, too.

The other day when I woke up, my mind was flooded with the to-do list I hadn't completed the day before, along with all the tasks waiting for me in the day ahead. This isn't unusual for me. However, instead of getting straight to work, I decided to take a step back.

I asked myself if these tasks were truly urgent, or if they were shoulds I needed to shove. It turns out that over half of them were attempts to feel better about myself—shoulds about the work I'm creating or the service I'm providing versus being comfortable with who I already am. Serving and working are great. But when they come out of a place of should, they don't produce the fruit I want or expect. Instead, they generate anger, fatigue, and distraction.

On this particular day, I chose to first sit and enjoy my cup of tea on the porch and then go on a run to think and pray. I discovered that the days I choose to evaluate my priorities first are the days my service and work are more efficient, productive, and life giving. I'm thankful for grasping this life lesson and getting better at determining what actually matters.

4) Humility means embracing your strengths and acknowledging your weaknesses.

Quick! Write down five of your weaknesses. Now, write down five strengths. Which was easier? Odds are your weaknesses come more easily. Why? Because we women are self-critical. We beat ourselves up for not being perfect. When we see a flaw, we do our best to cover it up, make up for it in another area of our lives, or ignore it altogether. All the while, we're trying to stay "humble" by not admitting our strengths.

Let's stop doing this.

Humility isn't ignoring our strengths; it's embracing them. For me, this looks like giving thanks to God for giving me these gifts. It's thanking all the people who have poured time and energy into helping me grow. It's identifying what my strengths are, then using them to bless people around me instead of hiding them or letting them go to waste. What does embracing your strengths look like for you?

Humility is also about acknowledging our weaknesses. While this may be uncomfortable, it's also wildly good for us. Weaknesses teach us lessons and force us to rely on each other—they make us who we are. Without them we miss out on the beauty of grace. They may mean we experience the valleys of life, but they also mean we can experience the mountaintops. Hardships and pain lead to learning life lessons that allow us to glean wisdom and resilience.

Embracing our weaknesses also provides opportunity for deep connection with others who are hurting—to help someone going through similar seasons. It humbles us to remember how broken we all are, how we need a God who cares for us, and how we need each other. It helps us carry love and appreciation for the little things in life. With failure and weakness comes loss and pain, and that is to be mourned. However, if you're sitting in fear and silence because you don't want to fail or let anyone to see your flaws, I encourage you to be vulnerable instead.

Brené Brown, a research professor at the University of Houston once said, "Vulnerability sounds like truth and feels like courage. Truth and courage aren't always comfortable, but they're never weakness." I found out that making the jump into vulnerability is like jumping off the boat; even if you sink, it's worth it because eventually you'll learn to swim—or maybe even experience the miracle of walking on water. No one wants to miss the miracle, but you will miss it if you're not willing to jump. So, jump with me, Sister. JUMP!

5) Freedom comes at the "Pace of Grace."

I first heard this phrase from Michael Todd, a pastor and speaker who talks about listening to the pace of the season. Not to strive as I had been doing, rather to stride or "walk with long decisive steps on a clear path." I also heard that, instead of automatically chasing after the next grand, sexy goal, I could step back and ask, "What do I really need?"

A couple of years ago, I started listening; I noticed what showed up in the world around me. I saw many incredible humans missing the little pleasures in life due to their racing. I observed broken relationships, marriages, even families because of increased stress. Passions were bulldozed because they became an overwhelming pressure to achieve rather than a fun endeavor to explore. However, I also noticed others who enjoyed simple delights like the sound of birdsong, or simply being. As I saw their delight, my heart received a call, and as I listened to it, I began to desire more and more of that simplicity.

I admitted to myself that many of the physical illnesses I had experienced were directly correlated to seasons in my life where I was burning the wick at both ends. I realized that over the years I had lost my sense of playfulness and my free spirit. I had become obsessed with my calendar because I didn't want to be forgetful anymore.

All the knowledge was there, but I didn't start to take it seriously until recently. I quit my part-time job, stopped volunteering, and finally spoke the word "no". At the time, all I was committed to was school and one group I attended for community. Then the pandemic hit and even those activities were stripped from my schedule. I still had to study for my National Boards exam, but the date to take the test was up in the air, too.

Time. I had time. And I wanted to use that time to truly rest, be still, and give myself grace. I wanted grace—that unmerited gift of forgiveness, favor, love, and mercy.

I had beat myself up for years. For what reason? Because I didn't measure up to my perceived standards of love, relationships, responsibility, or success. Now that I had the gift of time, I discovered it was time to stop beating myself up. And it was time, regardless of whether I deserved it or not, to give myself grace.

My husband and I moved to Tucson, Arizona two months after the pandemic hit. With these new discoveries I was leaning into, I vowed to say no to most everything until I was sure it was what I wanted to do or where I wanted to be. While the pandemic shutdowns initially aided this endeavor, I now have a much deeper reason for choosing to slow down. When someone asks me to do an activity or I'm faced with a decision to commit to a task taking time and energy, I ask myself:

1. Who will this impact?
2. What sacrifice(s) do I have to make to say yes?
3. What will I gain if I commit?
4. Why do I want to say yes?

You see, if I answer that my husband will get significantly less of my time and energy, or I'll be so stressed that none of my friends and family will enjoy being around me, then saying yes isn't worth it. If I must sacrifice what I love or what I feel called to, then I can't say yes. If my answer to "why" is because I want to overshadow an insecurity or not let someone else down, then the decision to say yes isn't a healthy one. I'm not perfect at this process yet, but that's the point of learning to live at the Pace of Grace!

These lessons I have been learning may seem like basic concepts for some, but they've been hard won revelations for me. I have to remind myself frequently to put them into practice. I ask myself daily, *Am I choosing to fight against the ever-present cultural tide of societal expectations and busyness?* The days I don't, I flow with the racing river, and sometimes the life I desire to live flows that way too. So why struggle to swim across the current? Why search for eddies and slower-moving byways? There are huge advantages to not allowing myself to get sucked into Western culture's definitions of all we should be as women.

You may find that bypassing the cultural tide also allows you to find your life-giving, creative nature, use your skills and talents to empower others, change the world around us, and live a life of peace. That is what I hope for you—that you, too, discover more joy, peace, hope, love, and freedom in your life because you choose to live at the Pace of Grace.

CHRISTY LEE has been described as "so friendly she can even make friends with walls." Her outgoing spirit and desire for connection have helped lead many professionally and in their walks of faith.

Dr. Lee earned her Doctorate in Physical Therapy at the University of Dayton in 2020 and her Bachelor of Athletic Training and Kinesiology at the University of Miami in 2017. Working eight years in the health and fitness industry, she now dedicates herself to learning and teaching ways of overcoming barriers to health and fitness beyond medication and surgery. Blending holistic healthcare into traditional practice, she empowers others to reach their full potential.

Christy is passionate about her community, pro bono clinics, and leading at her church. She helped found and is a Board Member of the non-profit organization Faith & Fitness. She loves to travel and cook with her husband, and she encourages others to join her as she runs, climbs, cycles, swims, hikes, lifts, and simply sits outside.

Find out more about It Is Well Physical Therapy, developed to empower you to become confident in your physical, mental, emotional, and spiritual self so you may pursue what you love without fear of failure:

    itiswellpt.com

BEING CRUNCHY

DEBRA MUSE WOLFF

Digesting Data

You walk through every day of your life processing information. You sort it using your senses: what you see, hear, taste, smell, and feel. Millions of bits of data are analyzed, categorized, and used immediately or stored for the future. It's how you operate, how you regulate, how you survive.

Just like your body digests the foods you consume to extract nutrients, you also ingest, absorb, and metabolize information, separating the chaff from the kernel of wheat, the waste from the worthy. An innate wisdom is at work in your digestive process, essential to your health. Likewise, properly digesting the data you consume can help you make wise decisions and enhance your well-being.

I've discovered that this process is greatly enriched by what I call the "power and practice of being crunchy." I invite you to explore these ideas, equip yourself with information, and gain access to the tools you already possess. I hope you'll read my story as a means to enhance your own life, be empowered to ask questions, and also be encouraged to seek and consult your own inner witness.

Your Inner Witness

You possess an internal knowing: the wisdom of your inner witness. The phenomenon of listening and responding to this knowing is underdeveloped in the United States. Culturally, it's believed the more knowledge you have, the more access you'll have to things like power and safety. However, it's your inner witness that brings true value and clarity to life and provides real safety and power. It helps you navigate your life with authenticity and alignment, and it's a source of confidence—a belief in yourself and your abilities—giving you freedom from doubt. You're connected to your inner witness, which is an inseparable part of you.

Knowledge vs Truth

You've heard it said: "Knowledge is power." However, what if what you know isn't the truth? If that's the case, what you know may not serve your best interests. In fact, if some things you think you know are false or untrue, then your knowledge is actually detrimental to your aims. Many times, what's considered common knowledge isn't sourced or grounded in truth; it may be counter to wellness.

Getting Wisdom

In my life journey, especially as it relates to health and well-being, I've found applied knowledge and the wisdom to use it truly powerful. To get to wisdom, you have to push past what is common and comfortable—to acquire *un*common knowledge. Inquisitiveness and being unafraid to ask for help from within brings you to a higher, healthier dimension of existence.

This practice is what's recently been termed as "crunchy," meaning green-leaning, counterculture, neo-hippie. (At my age, though, "neo" doesn't apply. I'm an original hippie.)

The slang use of crunchy infers a lifestyle of conscientious nature-lovers who buy their food in alternative markets rather than big-box grocery stores; they upend tradition if there's something better to replace the status quo. A stereotype implies crunchy people eat crunchy foods like granola, nuts, and raw foods instead of fast food. There's some truth to this.

"Being crunchy" means breaking what's brittle and fracturing what's fragile to get to the truth and goodness inside—this reveals the core of truth and values you can count on to guide you. Being crunchy requires you to consume, check in, question, evaluate, resist, and even push back against commonly held beliefs that may be outdated, unfounded, or outright false.

The yield from this is the satisfaction of taking personal responsibility for the decisions of your life. The reward is freedom and joy.

Back in the 1960s, being crunchy was personified by a man whose life was the embodiment of the ideal natural lifestyle. Euell Gibbons was a lanky, mild-mannered naturalist known for his eating habits: wild-grown foods like fruits, nuts, berries, and all things foraged. Gibbons was one of the first to challenge an America succumbing to the fast-food craze.

The news of Euell Gibbons's untimely death at sixty-four was surprising considering his lifestyle. Unfortunately, this health food guru and pioneer became jokingly remembered as having eaten rocks and twigs. His death was an unfortunate setback to the growing interest in natural and organic food. This became clear when I promoted his crunchy eating style at home. At family dinner, my brother asked, "If it's so healthy, why did Euell Gibbons die so young?" I didn't have an answer as I passed him the meat and potatoes, a meal always accompanied with cow's milk.

Cow's milk. Just saying that makes me smile. Fifty years ago, what other kind of milk was there? Today we have almond/cashew/macadamia nut milk, coconut milk, oat milk, hemp milk, rice milk, kefir, lactose-free milk, and milk from A2 cows. (Those Jersey and Guernsey brown beauties produce a more gut-friendly A2 beta-casein milk, a protein that's easier to digest.)

Because I got the value of what Gibbons espoused, I took up eating Grape Nuts, a cereal I deemed healthier than sugared cereals. I admit it felt like eating gravel, and it left my mouth raw if I hadn't waited for it to soften after adding milk. Eating it definitely took time and commitment. (It wasn't a premier choice if I got up late for school.) However, with no sugar added, I grew to savor the flavor. My palate grew accustomed to the natural sweetness that comes from chewing starch long enough to break it down in your mouth, where digestion begins. I learned the importance of chewing more, sweetening less.

I wasn't just learning a new way to eat and digest food, I was learning a new way to think about information, nourishment, and health. This growing awareness and understanding would help me shift to a more empowered custom. Ultimately, I would be able to share it with others to help them experience their own personal well-being transformation.

Being crunchy applies to getting the wisdom that comes from cracking the shell of knowledge to get to the sweetness of the life-giving truths that apply to your life. The result allows you to savor the entire experience of data digestion and enjoy the wisdom it yields. Wisdom is the best, most empowering fuel for your life.

My Path to Food Knowledge

During my adolescence in the late 1960s, my family traveled out east on Long Island to waterski in Hampton Bays, occasionally stopping for burgers, fries, and a shake at the "Golden Arches." I was enthralled with the explosion of flavor—the perfect combination of fat, salt, and meat on an ever-so-slightly sweet, fluffy bun. Little did I know, our special occasion happy meal was to become a sad way of life for so many; it's now known as the Standard American Diet, which truly is S.A.D. This way of eating leaves you craving carbohydrates and fat. It usually causes pounds to pack on in unwanted places, especially in your blood vessels in the form of plaque (cholesterol). It's full of calories, yet empty of high-energy nutrition.

Thankfully and healthily for us, eating out like this happened rarely in my childhood. There were perks to being frugal, such as home-cooked, well-sourced meals from the garden, bay, or chicken coop.

I began my wellness journey about the same time my mom returned to working evening shifts as a nurse. She left me to fend for myself in the kitchen. I'd always been privileged to have Mom at home to cook for me and my three older brothers while Dad worked "out back" as a business owner and heavy equipment engineer.

Knowing Dad's idea of a meal was Nilla Wafers and a glass of milk, Mom tasked me with the job of making dinner on the nights she worked. From market to table, I was responsible for the buying, prep work, serving, and clean-up. I wasn't a fan of the directive, but this is where I began to develop my culinary skills and interest in the relationship between food and health.

I read *The Joy of Cooking* like a primer and became a great cook. I proudly showed off my haute cuisine to family and friends. What I prepared was always the food pyramid on a plate: cooked protein/dairy, carbohydrates, veg, and fat, keenly arranged and eaten simultaneously with gusto.

At the height of my food foray, a family friend announced she was changing her life to become a vegetarian, eating a macrobiotic diet. Fifty years ago, my initial thoughts and feelings were: *Wait, what? That's senseless! That's unhealthy! Everyone knows you should eat meat. What do you mean you don't drink milk? Everyone drinks milk. You eat soybeans? Who eats soybeans? Did you say "toe food"? Brown rice? Everyone knows rice should be white. You steam your vegetables and eat them crunchy?*

At that time, I was far from humble. It didn't occur to me that something different from the balanced meal I'd been taught might actually be beneficial. My mind and spirit were closed to embracing something unknown to me.

What we don't understand we tend to ridicule, discredit, control, or annihilate; it's instinctual but not enlightened.

Since learning about the macrobiotic diet in the 1970s, I've observed the coming and going of dozens of diets:

- Atkins
- Weight Watchers
- Nutrisystem
- Alkaline and pH Miracle
- Mediterranean
- South Beach
- Eat for Your Blood Type
- Paleolithic (Paleo)
- Ketogenic (Keto)
- Scarsdale
- Zero-carb
- Drinking Man's
- Low-FODMAP
- DASH
- Raw Food

There's even a Cookie Diet (it's not what you think). Not to mention fasting: intermittent fasting, water fasting, juice fasting, and meal supplement fasting.

In the face of all the dieting and diet products available to us throughout the recent decades, one thing is glaringly obvious. Americans aren't getting healthier, they're getting sicker.

The Awakening of My Inner Witness

When I graduated nursing school, I became a registered nurse at the age of nineteen and made a pledge, much like doctors take an oath.

The doctors' oath was written by Hippocrates, a Greek physician in the fifth century BC, who's considered by many to be the father of western medicine. The Hippocratic Oath holds that the physician and his assistants in caring for their patients should not cause physical or moral harm.

Nurses make the Nightingale Pledge. This was written in 1893, named in honor of the founder of modern nursing, Florence Nightingale. Like the doctor's oath, its intention is to assure we nurses always act in the best interest of our patients.

When I started hospital work as a nurse, it didn't take long for me to realize there was something very wrong with the medical system. Forty years later, I believe it's gone from bad to worse. Despite my pledge to do no harm, I found it increasingly difficult to keep my promise in a system I surmised was broken.

America's medical technology is state-of-the-art, and Americans spend billions on healthcare, so you'd think most Americans should have stellar health. Yet the nation as a whole is more ill than ever with ever-increasing heart disease, diabetes, dementia, and cancer. Research shows increased rates of obesity and degenerative diseases (including diabetes, autoimmune, cardiovascular, neurodegenerative, and skeletal inflammation). Autoimmune conditions affect the largest number of people. The US is one of the least healthy industrialized nations in the world.

Why?

A friend of mine, with her twenty-five-year nursing career in Emergency Room medicine, shares my concern. She attests, "People come in [to the ER] sicker and sicker." The reality is, nationally, Americans have lost their grounding. Many have come to believe a lie that our bodies must succumb to degenerative disease with inevitable trips to the doctor's office and to the ER or hospital to keep death at bay.

Waking Up

The possibility of this becoming my personal reality hit me when I was in my forties. I found myself feeling exhausted all the time. I was also anxious and having difficulty staying warm. While I'd always led an active life, was physically fit, and ate well-balanced meals, it was crystal clear to me that something was wrong.

I saw my doctor and had standard blood tests drawn. My TSH (Thyroid Stimulating Hormone) lab result was abnormally high, indicating I was experiencing thyroid gland dysfunction. I'd like to say I acted immediately, but that would be a lie. Despite being a nurse, I didn't make my own health a priority. However, months later I got a direct message from God when my doctor showed up at my yard sale. She recognized me as her patient, sized me up, and emphatically told me to get to the office to be checked out. I complied.

At the office visit, she said I had Hashimoto's Thyroiditis. My body's immune system was attacking my thyroid gland (hence the suffix "itis" which means inflammation of an organ). I'd always had a slender body and no difficulty with unwanted weight or hair loss; I didn't fit the typical picture for having a hypothyroid condition. Because of my symptoms and abnormal labs, the doctor ordered an ultrasound.

Surprisingly, the sonographer found that my thyroid gland had grown internally to the posterior, unnoticed. I didn't have a goiter (anterior neck thickness at the mid-throat, which is more obvious in most women with thyroid enlargement). The findings indicated my thyroid had grown so large it extended down to my sternal notch near the attachment of the collar bones, just above the sternum. My condition had gone undetected for years.

My thyroid had not only overgrown, but nodules were also present. Because they were larger than a centimeter, a biopsy was needed. To me, this meant I was heading down a scary road. I felt my body had betrayed me. Up to that point, I'd not only been a nurse, I also was a baby-harness-wearing, invincible Crunchy Mom of five natural-born, breast-fed, cloth-diapered, home-schooled, well-mannered children. I'd been the one caregiving, not receiving care. This was a huge wake-up call for me to re-establish myself as a priority.

A few years prior, I'd cared for a female thyroidectomy patient (the suffix "ectomy" means surgical removal of a specified body part). Hearing my own diagnosis, my mind immediately went to the worst of possibilities—removal of my thyroid. At first, I had no feeling about this scenario because I'd shoved my emotions so far away . . . it was as if I was seeing myself in a slow-motion scene of a silent movie. I remained stoic and matter of fact.

Believing the ultrasound tech would have insider information, I boldly requested her recommendation of a good surgeon. I never forgot her answer, "I wouldn't go there if I were you." She meant that my assumption about needing a surgeon was unwarranted and premature. I'd already assumed a thyroid that big with nodules (tumors?) was surely dysfunctional beyond repair and possibly cancerous.

Up to this point, because of previous life experiences, negative thought patterns, and ineffective beliefs as well as blatant fear of the unknown, I thought I had the correct information . . . but I didn't. I'd asked the wrong questions and I'd predetermined a poor outcome. I'd assumed I was going to have to have a thyroidectomy, just like my patient years before. I believed my thyroid gland couldn't be healed and I probably had cancer.

My Wake-up Call

At that juncture, I was given a very clear choice; this came in the form of an inaudible voice speaking to my heart. God's words, penned by Moses in the Bible, would soon reframe my entire way of being.

"I have set before you life and death, the blessing and the curse. Now choose life in order that you may live, you and your descendants." (Deuteronomy 30:19)

The words of both the ultrasound tech and the Holy Spirit were examples of hearing from my inner wisdom. I heard and I listened.

The Revolution Inside Me

Hearing and responding to the words of God began another chapter in my life I call "The Overthrow." This is when living crunchy took on an even deeper, metamorphic meaning. I realized at that moment I had the power to choose. I had the power to be well and I had the power to be ill. It was my choice.

I chose life. And I chose not to "have" any disease, ever. I might be experiencing symptoms of Hashimoto's but I didn't "have" disease or dysfunction. Having something implies ownership. I decided I wouldn't claim anything that put distance between me and my destiny of fullness and blessing.

You see, I came to realize I was made for more than being a victim of how difficult life can be at times. My ineffective heart beliefs were robbing me of seeing myself healed. Prior to the Hashimoto's diagnosis, I was tired and heartbroken, working outside the home. As a single working mom, I sent my kids off to school when all I ever wanted to do in life was to be a faithful, happily married wife. I wanted to be a fantastic mom, home-schooling and raising amazing children to become amazing adults, making wonderful memories, and cheering loudly at ball games. When much of that ended with divorce, the resulting grief, failed expectations, and loss of peace played a role in the creation of dysfunction.

I had to take responsibility for becoming a priority in my own life. I had to speak to my circumstances and tell the truth, to acknowledge and soak in a different reality . . . that there was a call and a destiny in my life despite the past. When spoken with strong emotion, the creative work of the tongue has power.

"Life and death are in the power of the tongue." (Proverbs 18:21)

I'd come to understand that my own words and thoughts carried great power, and I was determined to use mine to serve the revolution that was taking place inside me. I knew this was a key piece for my body's healing and my transformation.

Words are energy, resonating with the vibrancy of creation. Words create physical reality. The words you speak, and even the words you think can manifest in physical form. Quantum physics explains this phenomenon in studying the behavior of matter and energy and how they interact. Dr. Bruce Lipton, noted biologist, epigenetic researcher, and author of *The Biology of Belief*, tells us, "Beliefs and thoughts alter cells in your body." If your thoughts and beliefs are powerful enough to alter the cells in your body, imagine how you can powerfully choose life and influence your healing with your own thoughts and words!

I learned to choose my words well, speak to the positive, and eradicate from my life words like: "need," "want," "hard," "stress," and "can't" to name a few. I became conscientious . . . limiting complaining, eliminating fear, and adding thankfulness.

I came to believe that a good outcome was my choice and within my grasp. I believed I had the power in me to create it. I set out exploring gratitude and expecting the good outcome I desired. I took responsibility and applied awareness to help manifest healing in my life through my imagination. I believed it was God's intention for me to be healed. Because I didn't see it occurring right then didn't mean it didn't exist in God's realm for me.

With curiosity fueling my energy and leading the way, I set out full steam ahead. I launched into the discovery of all the alternatives available to me for wellness. I did a deep dive into research. First, on how I could reduce the thyroid inflammation, and second, to find out what was occurring that generated the dysfunction in the first place.

On the medical front, I was referred to an endocrinologist, prescribed Synthroid, and a thyroid nodule biopsy was scheduled. While I waited to have the procedure, I also saw a naturopathic doctor who helped me understand thyroid function and the inflammatory process which caused the abnormal growth of the thyroid gland. She prescribed a supplement with cooling properties (Padma, a Tibetan herbal formula) and a treatment of cool packs of organic castor oil (using undyed organic cotton cloth) applied externally directly over the thyroid gland at least twice a day.

By the time of the thyroid biopsy, the nodules had already dramatically reduced in size. During the procedure, I got the idea to look at the microscope slide of my thyroid gland tissue that had just been biopsied. Right there, I saw microscopically what my abnormal cells looked like. I asked the medical provider what healthy cells looked like, and I created a clear mental picture to visualize my cells as they should be. (I held that vision and meditated on my healthy cells while I continued the castor oil compresses.)

Immediately after the biopsy procedure, I was instructed to hold a gauze pad to the needle insertion site and apply direct pressure for a few minutes. Intuitively, I sensed I was supposed to save the gauze for something in the future—for what I wasn't sure yet—and I embraced this opportunity for inner listening. I later used the gauze in an acupuncture energy healing session.

Within a few months, I had a follow-up appointment with the endocrinologist. I told him I was improving. He was doubtful and unimpressed. Without explanation, he rose from his seat, moved behind me, and got up on the exam table where I was seated. He then wrapped his hands around my neck and squeezed. I coughed. (And simultaneously swore under my breath because there was no breath to swear out loud!) When I coughed, he said something I can't remember, having just been choked. I felt violated, belittled, unacknowledged, and unheard. He made no recommendations to forward the healing that was already in process.

Perhaps you've felt like this before, like you were just a number or statistic, or worse, that your concerns weren't addressed, and you were rushed through your fifteen-minute appointment. For me, this was a turning point where I became convinced more than ever that I could, and would, find a better way.

How Hippocrates Helped Me

The thyroid medication, Synthroid, I was taking made me feel jittery and uncomfortable in my skin. While I don't recommend this to anyone, I sensed I should cut my dose in half. I did so and began to feel better. A different medical practitioner, a chiropractic naturopath, later confirmed I'd been taking too much Synthroid and that I'd reduced the dose to exactly what was right for me at that time. My body had told me so, and I began to trust what I was distinguishing as my innate wisdom.

Like Hippocrates, I believed that by strengthening and building up my body's inherent resistance to disease I could find restoration. For me, restoration continued to come through a myriad of crunchy, countercultural options that helped my body repair and heal: prayer and meditation, essential oils, kinesiology, bodywork, functional medicine, and true naturopathy. I chose the path of boosting my immune system instead of conventional medicine, which is more about treatment of symptoms in the presence of a crisis.

Some of the powerful tools I used included positive words and imagination, a low-level healing laser, a frequency generator, and high-magnification live blood analysis to observe the health of my blood cells. Each of these modalities and resources could be a chapter of its own. Suffice it to say, when I dared to inquire, answers appeared, and solutions seemed to find me.

Now I maintain thyroid health via Network Spinal chiropractic care, so my body isn't in fight/flight/freeze mode anymore. My autoimmune response to stress is melting away such that I no longer require medication to treat a disease. I also listen to what my Spirit calls for. If it's rest, I comply. Instead of piling more on to the endless duties of a single working woman, I honor the inner voice asking me to play and laugh more. I choose forgiveness and release whenever appropriate. And I continually allow God to lead me to wisdom each moment of my day.

Chewing on the Invisible Questions

My experience with the disease of thyroiditis is how I discovered so many of the things that qualify as the "getting back to nature" quality of living. These, regrettably, had been overlaid by woeful environmental conditions and my lack of awareness of the "Invisible Questions."

Invisible Questions are the ones begging to be asked. They may not seem obvious because they can be hidden or obscured by our own judgements and blind spots, our lack of insight and awareness, and our lack of education in complementary and alternative medicine. Cultural or medical norms may limit our view and perspective; cultural pressures and familial expectations may further limit us.

Yet Invisible Questions haunt you, urging you to wake up. They persist until you give them a voice and an audience. Your Invisible Questions urge you to take responsibility for your own healing process. They're your power partners in bringing about your personal transformation and empowerment.

While there's much for which we can take responsibility in our individual health and healing journeys, and many ways we can empower ourselves with awareness and helpful practices, I've learned that searching for the cause of disease may not be a simple discovery or exclusively an inside job. The cause of disease may not fall solely on our own shoulders or be our own fault. We were tainted from the get-go.

An Environmental Working Group study reports newborn cord blood contains over two hundred toxic chemicals before infants are even one day old. (Possible sources causing toxic exposure and obstructions in our bodies could be another chapter of its own.) The following compilation of contributing factors is by no means exclusive: food additives, artificial sweeteners, artificial colors, artificial fragrances, plastics, preservatives, pesticides, petrochemicals, fungicides, household cleaners, tobacco products, air pollutants, water contaminants, and electromagnetic emissions (EMFs)—a daunting list of detriments to our health, to be sure.

You consume. Everything you smell and breathe in, everything you eat and drink, everything you slather, spray, and drip on your skin, your hair, and your eyes must be absorbed, digested, and even detoxified in your body. Detoxification is a healthy living essential.

The Invisible Becomes Visible

The good news is that every thought, feeling, hormone, and cell in your body, everything you taste, smell, and hear, and every word you speak has a frequency signature. Which frequencies heal? Which ones don't?

What if you had access to this information and were empowered to prevent or overcome disease by making a few changes, now? If you had the opportunity to live differently, empowered with information to create a better outcome and future for yourself, would that intrigue you? What if you could have more energy and no brain fog, less fatigue, and fewer body aches? Would you want to find out how?

For years I'd picked up *Natural Awakenings*, a free magazine available outside my neighborhood grocer. This treasure trove of information also lists local holistic health practitioners. For months I was captivated by the advertisement for Digital Infrared Thermal Imaging (DITI).

I was reassured when I found Hippocrates was also the generator of the concept of thermal science. I felt DITI was something I could get behind. I was intrigued by the thought of a non-invasive, no-radiation option to be able to monitor thyroid health.

Not only that, but when thermal imaging (DITI) is used it can accurately detect most breast cancers years before a lump is even palpable. So, why aren't we women being told that with lifestyle changes, we can reverse problematic or questionable areas in our breast tissue? Why don't most medical professionals teach us that with regular lymphatic massage, we can eliminate breast lymph fluid stagnation to prevent breast cancer? What I came to find out cemented my passion for educating women and shouting from the rooftop, "You have options!"

Seeking Wisdom and Its Source

In my quest for answers to these and other questions, I studied thermal imaging and Emotional Freedom Technique (EFT), and I became a Certified Empowerment Advocate as well as a Regenerative Health Specialist. Everything I'd studied in nursing had to be questioned and turned on its head when addressing preventative health and sustained well-being. Rather than treating symptoms, my personal and professional goal had to become to repair and prevent them, and to manage well-being rather than disease. I began to ask for Godly wisdom—a call to my inner witness. (I love that I get to do that.)

"God said, 'You are intricately and wonderfully made.'" (Psalm 139)

The main doorway to eliminating disease and regenerating our bodies is through detoxification. Cleaning/detoxification and rebuilding our bodies require rest, reducing acidity, eating vital raw foods, and taking botanicals (plant-based supplements) when necessary.

Herbal formulas increase endocrine function, clean and rebuild tissues, and increase cellular metabolism. Pure water, a chemical-free home and work environment, and keeping active is also key to rejuvenating health. As I mentioned earlier, the fewer chemicals you are exposed to, the less work your body has to do to detoxify.

Our Earth has been toxified and the whole process of nutrition has been over-complicated. Our food chain has been bastardized and a large proportion of our diets are genetically modified (GMOs). Using the Dirty Dozen list, produced annually by the Environmental Working Group (EWG), is helpful to determine which fruits and vegetables should be purchased. Buying organically grown produce is important due to the overabundance of chemical residue present in or on nonorganic consumables.

A good rule of thumb is to avoid GMO foods when possible; if you can't afford to buy all organic products and if you're regularly consuming meat, milk, and eggs, then try to choose grass-fed meats, organic milk products, and eggs from pasture-raised hens. (The potential risk for a greater concentration of pesticides and herbicides is far more likely in these products than the amount in or on a single fruit or vegetable.)

"Let thy food be thy medicine and thy medicine be thy food." (Hippocrates)

Like me, you might have the Department of Health's outdated image of the food triangle forever stuck in your brain. They called it the Healthy Food Groups. Eating a well-balanced meal was important in my home, and my mom always prepared those triangle meals for me and my brothers. Her mom did the same for her and so on. I always wondered, though, why people in remote places with little means and no access to our triangle frequently had better teeth and better overall health, yet their diets looked nothing like ours following the so-called healthy food groups.

It turns out, when it comes to digestion, it's best to keep it simple. Who said it's okay to stick every food group on a bun and call it good? I know many of us ruggedly insist on having it our way, like the burger chain slogan, but what if our way is killing us slowly over time?

Keeping it simple means proper food combining. Carbohydrates with proteins are a no-go. They don't go together well. Separating starch and protein is important, otherwise they compete in the gut for proper digestion. Protein loses the fight because it's more complex to metabolize, especially in gut-compromised cultures.

The Whole is Greater Than the Sum of Its Parts

What is the purpose of eating anyway? Do you live to eat, or do you eat to live? Hopefully you eat for life and vibrant living. What foods are most alive and have the most energy? Choose fruit and other raw foods because of their digestive enzymes and electromagnetic energy not found in cooked food.

People tend to compartmentalize, but you're all one piece, one whole being—fearfully and wonderfully made, intelligently designed with interconnected biochemical, bio-electric, and bio-energetic systems, communicating with one another. Getting well and being well is a holistic endeavor. Making choices, such as eating raw, taking herbal supplements for regenerating and detoxifying, exercising/movement, meditation, breathwork, and using other non-traditional modalities enable us to rediscover our energetic body as a whole, not just its parts. Our emotional, mental, physical, and spiritual being are one.

It's Time for a Change

You can begin the change by asking questions. Good questions. Deep questions. As I write this chapter, life can seem overwhelming with continued threats of worldwide pandemic and pandemonium. Many are hunkered down in dread and trepidation amidst the chaos and confusion. When you give way to fear, you lose the connection between the heart and brain. You can't hear from God amidst the fear and scarcity thinking.

"Where there is fear, there is no faith. Where there is faith, there is no fear." (2 Timothy 1:7)

Your answers wait for you in the invisible space between fear and faith, when you pause, connect with your inner witness, have courage to ask the invisible questions, listen, and then act on the wisdom you receive. Your body has innate knowledge and you're made in God's image. How could that not be incredible? Living in that same incredibility is the capacity to be well in your body, mind, and spirit.

Trust Your Gut

In a world where we can drown in information and search the internet for anything in a split second, we can also be starving for wisdom. I think we forget to trust our gut, and to keep asking questions—the right questions, the "Invisible Questions" begging to be asked.

No one is coming to save you, so Be your own hero

Getting crunchy in life requires you to vigorously ask the right questions and not be quieted until you get adequate answers. You can do it like this:

- Ask for more information if you haven't gotten an adequate explanation.
- If something doesn't make sense, don't say you understand.
- Use *un*common sense. Ask the uncomfortable questions. The life you save may be yours.
- Here's my favorite question of all time, which I use to query any doctor, practitioner, or individual when I am looking for information: "If you were me, what questions should I be asking you right now?" (God bless the person who taught me this.)

Put another way, "As you are the expert and have the information I'm after, what else should I know?" And then just wait. You can almost see the wheels turning in the person's head. Once you get an answer, ask, "What else?" Every time you question in this way, you'll come away with pertinent, valuable gems you otherwise wouldn't have had. Brilliant! When living crunchy, you strip away the husk to get to the kernel inside.

If you struggle with health issues, you may be disempowered by thoughts like these:

- "It's in my family," or "It's just old age."
- "The doctor knows best."
- "I'm not responsible for my illness," or conversely "I *am* my illness—my arthritis; my depression; my diabetes."
- "I'm not educated enough to make that health decision."
- "I'm too old . . ." or "I'm too young . . ." or "I'm too (whatever) . . ."

I invite you to replace those disempowering thoughts with more empowering ones—thoughts of positive responsibility and healthy ownership.

Own Your Divine Wellness

I wrote this chapter to be a wake-up call. For some, it may sound like a deafening fire alarm. For others, maybe it's more like a favorite ringtone that stands as a reminder of an upcoming appointment. I hope you'll hear it as an invitation to begin or continue the journey of awakening to another dimension of Divine Wellness.

Question everything.
Choose Life Daily.
Be crunchy.

DEBRA MUSE WOLFF became a Registered Nurse (RN) at the age of nineteen and has cared for patients in many ways for forty-four years. She says she went into nursing by accident, having originally wanted to work with her father as a heavy equipment engineer.

She grew to love the engineering and mechanics of the human body and developed a passion for healing the whole person—body, mind, and spirit. Debra came to understand that many sick patients were not aware of other, better choices or more natural ways to live and be well. She became determined to speak the truth about the healthcare misnomer.

While raising, homeschooling, and climbing trees with her children, Debra encouraged new experiences and adventures. She believes in well-nourished and well-tended gardens of all kinds, allowing children as well as tomatoes to sprawl. She is committed to homes being safe havens by eliminating toxic chemicals and using environmentally friendly cleaning products and essential oils.

THE MOST BEAUTIFUL TAPESTRY EVER WOVEN

ADA IRIS JAIME

"We have to become still in the midst of the turmoil so we can observe clearly how our actions and the actions of others, past and present, fit together in the tapestry of life. In the timeless instant when we stop moving and simply witness the moment, the dust settles and the big picture emerges." ~ Alberto Villoldo, Ph.D

My Life. My first memory. My true memory. If only I could have replaced all others with this one. All the other memories that have negated who I truly am. I ask myself, *Why would I allow the world of victimhood to seduce me away from the moment I witnessed my gift of power and light?* Imagine being in a moment just before the unimaginable. A moment that will never be erased yet at times forgotten.

When Mami arrived from the hospital, she had me come close to her side and moved the blanket so I could peek at the bundle in her arms. Debbie wiggled and smiled at me. It was grace and love itself mirroring back. I gasped and swallowed all the energy we were transmitting to each other without knowing how or why—I simply did. I was three and a half years old.

Mami said to me, "Be still and I will put her in your arms." In that instant, something exhilarating happened in my body. I felt something inside was released and then danced joyfully in and out of me. I had to keep telling myself to stay still. It was a ticklish and ecstatic sensation, unknown and unforgettable. What I do know is that from then on, this instant was housed and sourced inside me.

I relive this perfect moment in my life when I say all is lost. I reclaim myself and breathe into this inner source in these moments of challenge and heartache when I abandon myself and believe myself to be broken. What I know to do is gasp inward and hold my breath as another inflicts wounds on my body, tears my confidence and self-love, and breeds in me a desire to quit and cave inward. When I remember, or as a last resort, I seek this unexplainable exuberant energy—this energy that is not from my body and seems to be my life force—to bring me back to life.

I pray, *I'm okay, it'll be okay. I seek you—I feel you, my Heart, my Spirit, and Great Spirit . . . walk with me through this.* And yet, I admit there are times I forget what I know there is to do and allow myself to suffer and unravel in the fear.

I have been a storyteller for as long as I can remember. I have retold my Debbie story a million times. I recall the struggle I had at three and a half years old to put into words what I felt. I remember making noises and moving my arms up and down. It connects me to how at times words are inadequate. I picture myself coming from a long lineage of storytellers, as I believe we all are, and in our dream of dreams we can remember what there is to tell. Those who experience my words will hear the origin from their heart. We all share this connection.

Through my veins four ancestral blood lines flow. Each giving the other its place to be and to express itself through me.

I am Taina of Arawak descent. The Red Nation blood of my grandmother flows in me, gifting me a gracious peaceful loving nature and granting me connection to my eternal creator mother, my Pachamama—Mother Nature—who guides my hands, heart, and thoughts to Life and Spirit.

The Black Nation that runs through my blood built my body with undulations, rhythms, and dance. Just like my grandmother, my form dominates a space with the sound of the drumbeats that can calm the fiercest beast and bring all of it silently into our hearts. I learned from her stories that a story requires sound and movement. That I have plenty.

My White Nation blood is of my grandfathers of the East. The Canary Islands is the birthplace of the Spanish song, language, poetry, and beauty that connects me with another. I express myself in the sun, the water, the nightfall, and the breeze as the islander that I am.

The Yellow Nation that runs through my blood brings me solace like the landscape of the Himalayas. With the Golden Rule of Confucius, the father of the art of teaching a way of life awakening. In the quiet I can get to my blueprint.

My blood flows inside these spaces of my grandmothers and grandfathers and I am grateful. This is who I am and who I am becoming.

And I am here to offer a glimpse of the inner journey available to you.

Kind Reader, I invite you to enter my story in the ways of years long forgotten. In this narrative, I will create with you and journey inward. It will require you to follow the instructions and enter the circle as I take you through a series of instructions. I invite you to allow the experience to happen within and without. Read and participate as you are moved to engage.

Join me in a beautiful, lush garden. Pass the Arcadia tree. Circle in a spiral and get close to the fire. Breathe gently. Dance, walk, drum, sing, breathe. Follow your heart as you take in the words. I pray you accept my invitation.

Very well. My heart smiles as I see you in our circle. Thank you for answering Pachamama's call. Our Mother welcomes you. She brings us the fire at the center of the circle. You enter from the South and find your place moving in the circle clockwise. Give yourself a comfortable place and sit. As you settle in your space, notice your body close to the ground.

Sit as if the ground is a part of you and imagine you have lined up your back like the trunk of a tree to the ground. Stretch your back and imagine a cord from above passing through your spine and penetrating the ground beneath you. The cord extends from above your head to the heavens and goes through into the ground as if it were a taproot sustaining you to the soil. This root takes voyage into the layers of the Earth. It doesn't stop its descension until it reaches into the heart of the mantle where you are now connected.

You can now source yourself in the very center, the golden light of the Earth's core surrounded by the fire that feeds all aboveground. Now imagine aboveground that your hands are reaching upwards. Stretch like the branches of a tree and source the energy in the sky and move to the wind all around you as your roots do the same beneath you.

You sit in bountiful light and receive love that comes from above as from below.

Close your eyes and find your place in her heart. Thank you. Listen to her heartbeat. Hear the beat of her drumming heart. Gently close your eyes and open your awareness. Take in a new deep breath. Notice how you breathe. Take in the air and feel how your chest moves upward. How your lungs fill with air. Now, let us practice breathing consciously and gratefully.

Bring in air for a count of four and listen for your heartbeat: 1 ⌁ 2 ⌁ 3 ⌁ 4 ⌁ and hold your breath gently in that space for two counts: 1 ⌁ and 2 ⌁ .

Now release your breath through your nostrils with a closed smile. As you notice you have no more breath inside, hold for two more counts: 1 ⌁ 2 ⌁ .

Hold your mouth closed. Inhale gratefully in the next heartbeat: four counts

1 ⌁ 2 ⌁ 3 ⌁ 4 ⌁ .

Breathe out slowly, deep into the beat. Hold and count: 1 ⌁ 2 Breathe.

Now inhale taking in all the blessings around you. Notice all the love that surrounds the circle. Feel your mind with one loving thought. Invoke it into your heart. Exhale softly on the next beat. ⌁ Take a deeper breath into the beat as you smile. Take it all in. Count as you inhale: 1 ⌁ 2 ⌁ 3 ⌁ 4 ⌁ . Hold for two.

Exhale slowly ⌁ ⌁ ⌁ ⌁ , breathe out all the thoughts that do not serve you. The ideas that are creeping in onto the beat. Say goodbye to them. Keep yourself intentionally in light and loving breath.

Let it all out. Hold for two once more. 1 ⌁ 2 ⌁ Breathe. Smile.

Open your eyes and find yourself in the circle. See the faces of your ancestors. Those you know the image of or know of their story. Salute them. All your teachers sit with you. All those you hold beloved. We are all here in the connected circle. We hear the drumbeat as one heart. ⌁ ⌁ ⌁ ⌁ . We are called to gather and unite. Thank you for listening. I salute you. I salute all you bring to the circle from the four directions. My heart smiles.

Very well. Our circle is ignited inside the fire. Our heartbeat is one under a sky lit by Grandmother moon and her sister stars. With the permission of my ancestors, I sit in the circle with my talking drum between my thighs. I shall speak the story of our Earth Mother. I surrender my voice to Mother. My voice is Yours. My only will is to transmit all you have me say in this circle. So be it and so it shall be.

I will play you a drumbeat. I will play slowly. Softly. Gently. I shall barely make a sound. My voice will disappear as it escapes past my lips so you can speak, Mother. Speak, Mother . . . speak silently into the shadows of light so it can be heard by all creation from the crawlers in the ground to the flyers up above in the starlit night.

My hands hit palm down on the canvas of my leather-skinned speaking drum and I rub my legs on the curves of its hourglass sides and set free my soul's voice that ignites.

Taa taa taa taa . . .

I lift my hands again and let it sing . . . Taa taa taa taa . . .

My heart hisses. My hands pound harder with a rhythm on a drum you can't hear without awakening my soul, Her soul, your soul, our soul. My voice! Her Voice! Your Voice! Our Voice! As I hit the drum with my hungry hands, all of us can hear the recognizable cadence that shakes and awakens the consciousness of our body. The heartbeat ⎯⋏⎯ ⎯⋏⎯ ⎯⋏⎯ ⎯⋏⎯ of many lives.

Here we are in a circle around a fire with Mother, Elders, young ones, men and women, and their little-footed ones. From the animal kingdom we are joined by the crawlers, the swimmers, the flyers, the two-legged, and four-legged creatures of our gracious home. Like we did then, we do now—we always have. Let us unite as one around the fire. Bring to the circle the oscillating question that carries so many mysteries, and especially the desire for discernment of how to live a life of light in moments of darkness.

Hear the crackling sounds of flames ignite the wisdom of the circle.

All humanity danced in the waters of our mother's womb. We danced with her to the heartbeat in the waters of creation. Remember its pleasurable sound. Silence the mind and listen. Can you hear it? My hands land rhythmically harder on the drum creating the pounding heartbeat of our first sounds of mother.

Taa taa taa taa . . .

Joy. Defenselessness. Gentleness. Awaken your listening as Mother begins to speak. The fire has awakened and sounds the rhythm. My hands respond and hit the canvas harder, and the sound gets louder. ⎯⋏⎯ ⎯⋏⎯ ⎯⋏⎯ ⎯⋏⎯ . Your heart pounds harder and my voice grows wider; Her Voice sweetly floats into your ear. We enter the womb, into the many wombs that are ours. We rest in the space of warmth.

Tonight, the story about to be told is the story of The Most Beautiful Tapestry Ever Woven. It's about the Weaver who wove it, the Black Dog who watched her weave it, then destroyed it, and about the heart that forgave Chaos. Remember, chaos is order waiting to happen and dogs do what dogs do.

Slowly, I tap and weave our connection with the drum. All of us in the circle's loom intertwined, connected in this story. Our heartbeats. One movement. One beat. Our Mother's voice . . . . . ⎯⋏⎯ ⎯⋏⎯ ⎯⋏⎯ ⎯⋏⎯ .

This timeless, ancient creation story is still told by the people who remember there was once a pathway to the Cave of Creation. A cave that today we cannot find. The great inventor of instruments, Galileo, did not find it. Marco Polo, the explorer and adventurer, did not find it. Nor could today's techies with satellites and GPS in their hands find it. A cave on a mountain facing all of Creation—we cannot find it no matter how hard we try. It is said the cave finds us and not the other way around.

Know that this cave exists even though no one in living memory has ever found it. There is not one Elder who knew of an Elder who knew of an Elder who had seen it themselves—none have touched its cavern walls of smoke and water. Regardless, I know the cave exists. As I also know there is a moon that eclipses. A sun that rises from the East. A tireless ocean that tides. The cave is there where it has been and will be forever.

It still houses a beautiful tapestry, a loom, a cauldron, a beautiful old woman weaving, and a black dog lying beside her. Only you cannot find it even though it sits in plain sight. Our ancient ones kept the story alive because at one time someone witnessed it and brought this story to us from Creation itself. I rest here knowing we are capable of remembering, even if we have forgotten the way we can find it. It is there awaiting your return.

You see, in this forgotten cave lies the source of the seeds of all the seeds for Creation. And these seeds, each one is all the seeds of all creation, and they are tended by the beautiful Weaver who stirs the seeds in the cauldron hour after hour, day after day, week after week, month after month, for years and years, millenniums past, since time immemorial. The Weaver who stirs and weaves tends to the seeds of all Creation with a deep breath, a present heart, and a smile on her face. She has stayed in the cave as she was asked to do, faithfully tending to the seeds by the fire in her cauldron, watching the smoke with a smile that only Creation can give.

Life itself is spawned and birthed from her breath moving the steam that arises above the cauldron, moving the wooden spoon and the beating of her heart, the glory of her beauty, and the grace of her smile. She sends to the world all the seeds, the flowers, the leaves, the trees, the bees, the butterflies, the hummingbirds, and all other pollinators. She smiles at the divine animals that eat the bugs that open the seeds that pollinate the entire world over—inside and out, as above, so below. All is alive. And the Weaver turns to the fire and stirs. Pause is required in all that is agitated, so the Weaver, having the sense it is time to rest the stir, turns away from the fire and goes back to sit by her Black Dog.

⌁ ⌁ ⌁ ⌁

Sitting by the beautiful threads surrounding the loom, with an open hand, the Weaver picks up an end or a beginning thread. And she says to her dog her most delightful thought, "I will weave the most beautiful tapestry ever woven." She starts with her heart full of joyful colors and sends forth her beloved declaration into the majestic loom of her vision.

Immediately the threads as she weaves take their place and bloom with colors and shapes. he Weaver breathes life into what she weaves. What begins to arrive on the threads are jungles and forests, water and streams, jaguar and eagle, hummingbirds and serpent, butterflies and sweet fruits—all woven harmoniously on the loom. And she weaves and weaves. And the Black Dog silently watches day after faithful day, weeks, years—as long as the Weaver weaves the dog can be found at her feet. A millennium, day after faithful day. The Black Dog witnesses as the most beautiful tapestry ever woven in creation comes to life inside the threads lovingly woven together.

All is quiet and peaceful in the cave. The dark spaces are dark. The cool places are cool. The light of the fire crackles and sets the hearth inside to the frequency of peace. The stove begins to bubble a cauldron of rich aromas.

The Weaver decides it is time to stir. She is completely covered in flowers and leaves and stems. Her beautiful black hair is braided with seeds. Necklaces and bracelets of ancient origins decorate her neck colorfully like a beautiful garden.

Beautiful Mother Weaver smiles and glances at her loom, completing her work of the hands, a tapestry of creation, a work of love. She decides to bring to its edge the finishing touch. The blessed quills of a porcupine will hem the rugged edges. So, she collected the quills that lay on her shelf and began to bite down on them one at a time to flatten them and have the colors expose themselves as a flat surface of light through the shadows. Finally, the moment arose when all the quills were flattened along with her teeth. The Weaver decided before adding them to the tapestry to tend her seeds and stir the cauldron to keep creation flowing in the world. Long forgotten was when she last stirred. She stirred and stirred by the fire and left behind her tapestry. The cauldron welcomed her as she stirred and agitated life into what is to come next.

The Black Dog, being the Black Dog, was silent and faithful by her side. When she moved, it awakened from its deep sleep. As the Weaver moved and stirred, so did the Black Dog.

The Weaver's attention was now fully given at the cauldron, stirring life into the seeds. As when weaving, her presence created the most beautiful images of creation onto her seeds. The weaver stood mesmerized, stirring, and breathing and stirring. Her gaze was captured by the beauty of the colors and the shapes of the seeds of all that is coming to the universe. She stirred with a smile by the fire that heated the black cauldron. And she faithfully stirred her creations and breathed life to each pod and seed. Giving rise to life. Her breath, deep and generous, filled the world with creatures and flowers, leaves and trees with the very water we swim in and the invisible air we breathe. The cave filled with flyers, crawlers, swimmers, walkers, and jumpers, and all of them did their dance out of the cave.

Satisfied with her work with the seeds, she moved back to her loom to complete her tapestry with the flattened spines that poked out from her pocket. When she arrived at the space of her loom, she found her Black Dog beside a mound of unwoven colored thread. Her loom stood naked. No more did the tapestry lie in it. The Black Dog had unraveled it all. All that was left . . . was Chaos.

⼼ ⼼ ⼼ ⼼

Breathe.

Silence.

You see, if there is a thread near a dog, the dog will pull on it. That first tug is inevitable. The unraveling happens thereafter. It is inevitable. And this is how the most beautiful tapestry ever woven was unwoven without consciousness of what was just unraveled.

Silence.

Are you ready for the rest of the story? Let us go to the Weaver and the Black Dog.

Well, what I do not know is how long the Weaver stayed staring at the pile of Chaos, the threads of multi-colors that no longer made a recognizable expression of lines and shapes—the forms of creation. What they say is the Weaver stared at the mound that once was ready for the finished brilliant spines of porcupine that she bit into shape in silence. She stood there as long as she did. This I know. Until, at some point, she stopped staring at the pile of chaotic threads and sat back down at her loom.

She lovingly picked up a thread that was poking out of the colorful mound and started to do what she knows there is to do. She began to weave the most beautiful tapestry ever to have been woven. The Black Dog sat down beside her. The seeds settled themselves in the cauldron on the fire in the corner of the cave bubbling patiently, waiting to be stirred.

I slow down the beat of the drum and bring softness to the hand. Taa taa taa taa.

You see, Chaos is order waiting to be threaded.

The fire can be activated or it can subside. We can create or destroy. It is all the same when you remove time. If you are like me, you have had the Black Dog unravel you many times in your life of woven tapestry. Black Dogs pulled on your threads. And, unlike the Weaver, you might be like me. You might have forced many unraveling mounds of Chaos throughout your life. Walked away angry, hurt, or even devastated. You may do as I did: I abandoned my threads of dreams and stopped stirring my cauldron. Like me, you may have sat on your Chaos.

I wanted nothing to do with starting over. I abandoned my threads and ran to a new loom. I did not see each thread in the chaos as a part of me. Instead, I believed the mound of my undoing are the parts I need to abandon. So, I would pick up the unraveled mess of threads and throw it all away. I did not bother to detangle and recreate. See, with the threads I see now I threw away my connections. I would take with me my Black Dog and leave my threads. And now, it is no wonder I cannot find the cave with my originating seeds of Creation.

. . . . ⎍ . . . I slam loudly on the drum . . . ⎍ . . . with both hands hitting true center, both at once . . . ⎍ . . .

I can begin to do what is possible, living my life as the beautiful, faithful Weaver. In times of undoing, I believe it is exactly as it should be. What happens between a heartbeat and a breath can be peace.

I, too, can pick up the unraveled thread from the pile of Chaos and there will be no loss to start fresh. I can weave and reweave a beautiful tapestry for all of Creation to unite in, despite the interlude of darkness that had me see this new light. I can bring order to Chaos. Experience light in darkness. I can use myself all up without losing a thread, and then do it all over again.

Discovering this new thought brings a pounding to my heart. It joins the rhythm of my hands to the drum. It feels alive . . . ⎍ ⎍ ⎍ ⎍ . . .

Aho. On behalf of all of us, I acknowledge you, Grandmother. I praise you for this teaching.

Your womb is now awakened, Kind Reader. Breathe into it the story of *The Cave, the Weaver, and the Black Dog*. Breathe it in. Allow life to open and begin to shift. It is now that you know you can choose to pick up the threads of the tapestry you have left behind. Collect the abandoned threads and begin to weave into the loom the most beautiful tapestry ever woven in your cave. Remember all of it. Go off and weave it into the loom—do not be afraid of the darkness.

Our woven and nonwoven pieces are alive. We are invited by the story to do as the Weaver did. Weave the most beautiful tapestry ever woven. Our tapestry is impermanent. It is the weaving that brings us life.

The cool breeze announces the moment to return is approaching. I invite you to listen to the last of our time together in a circle in silence. When ready, stand up, bring your hands to your heart, salute your beloveds, your guides, your teachers, and your Masters who sit here with you. They are with you at the fire of our gathering. Thank them and ask for their continual blessings. They invite you to return to the world knowing yourself newly. Your assignment is to keep this seed alive, awakened in your womb, weaving into the loom the most beautiful tapestry ever woven.

Now we exit the circle taking loving intentional steps in gratitude, spiraling in a counterclockwise direction as you allow inspiration to guide you. Dance and move your body to the beat of the birthing drum. Leave behind in the fire your story of sorrow and pain. Your losses and heartaches. Unravel any harmful thought or memory you hold as true. Release it and claim your innocence in each step. Believe in the miracle that you are. Take with you to the four corners of your nations the fresh new seed of your creation. Find your way out of the circle exiting from the South. Bow to the fire. Time to head home to your cave.

I will stay here and tend to the fire in your name. Sending you endless blessings.

My hands fall on the drum.

〰️ 〰️ 〰️ 〰️

The drum is now silent.

Keep your heartbeat beating 〰️ 〰️ 〰️ 〰️

ADA IRIS JAIME remembers vividly her grandmother's instructions to keep their traditions alive. The telling and retelling of stories and realities have always been faithful companions in Ada's studies and work. Stories flowed in the oral traditions of circle and fire as well as written historic fiction and Creation stories. Ada's first book, *Footprints,* brings to life the stories of her beloved ancestors of the island of Puerto Rico.

As the founder of *Awaken the Heart Healing,* Ada puts into practice ancient healing traditions from all corners of the globe. She conducts ceremonies long forgotten, tells stories, and gives lessons grounded in nature about the interconnectedness of all living beings. With 30 years' experience in the field of training and education of children aged 0-99, she honors the past and looks to the future, lighting new paths for people to explore. Ada plans to travel the world, bringing the stories of all time and spaces back to our remembrance.

Find out more and contact Ada for Spiritual Coaching, Alignment Bodywork, Sound Therapy, and Chakra Alignment:

　　　Email: lifecoachath@gmail.com

DIVINE AWAKENING

SUSAN JONES

Albert Einstein once said, "There are two ways to live your life. One is as though nothing is a miracle. The other is as though everything is a miracle."

Over the course of my life, I have found enough evidence to choose that second way of looking at things: spontaneous miracles line the path to God, right here, right now, on Earth. I also discovered it took the courage of surrender to find my way to that awakening.

I was born into this world as an empath with extrasensory awareness. As the youngest of four children by five years, my parents did not plan me . . . and then here I came, born under the sign of the fish, on the cusp of the Aquarian Age. From the beginning of my life, I have been inextricably connected to a source of love and magical imaginings.

In this chapter, I will share how I discovered my connection to the Divine Source of Life, and how my soul came to flourish in the Son's Light. This is about my life with all its messy discombobulations and the hidden truths discovered along the way. My quest has been healing from generational dysfunction, addiction, and abuse; this has led me down many paths. I have been guided by wonder and gratitude. I have been changed by faith.

As early as I can remember, I experienced life as unpredictable. My mom often said she could not tell whether I was laughing or crying. As an infant, I innately knew that smiles and pleasantness made things better. This innocent way of being kept me safe and offered abundant opportunities for love and affection.

I never questioned whether or not my family loved me, yet ours was a warring household. My earliest sense was that my role in the sibling order was to be the peacekeeper. I hated conflict and just wanted everybody to get along.

I remember my older siblings watching over me. I adored it when they played with me and took me places with them. Yet, when Mom and Dad were not around, my sisters and brother would quarrel, bicker, and shout at each other. My brother, the middle child, was five years older than me. He was usually the root cause of the conflict. My earliest anxiety was instigated loud noises and shouting.

By the time I arrived, the relationship between my parents was tense and at times volatile. Mom was highly critical of Dad's drinking as well as the time he spent away from the family, either working or at the bar watching sports with his friends. Arguments started almost every time he came home drunk. When my dad did not call or show up for dinner, my mom would get angry, stewing on it, waiting to unload on him the moment he walked in the door.

When I was little, my brother and I shared a bedroom together just off the kitchen. We frequently listened to Mom and Dad arguing late at night after he got home. One time, I stood trembling, peeking around the doorway, standing up on my toes as tall I could, straining to see what was going on. Then, suddenly, plates hit the floor with a loud crash. Frightened, I ran to my brother's bed and buried my head under his covers while he held me.

By the time I was four years old, I had found ways to interrupt the action when things got too overwhelming. I just shut down physically, sacrificing my own body to restore unity. I had bouts of intense raging migraines, which served to stop the action of whatever was going on. My parents would come together at my side, take my little hands, stroke my hair, place cold compresses on my head, and give me sweet kisses while my sibling looked on. They comforted me and assured me that everything was going to be okay. Having them together at my side was the right medicine. The headache's intensity would peak, I would vomit, and then pass out.

There was no medical reason for my migraines, and I assert that it was my intuitive response to uncertainty. The same was true about my nightly ritual of crawling into bed with my parents. Sandwiched between them was my perfect place, my source of comfort and safety. Several times they tried to break me of the habit, but I was relentless in my pursuit of comfort.

While my mom was the love of my life, my dad was the apple of my eye, and I was his. I never felt that I got to be with him enough, and I always looked forward to more. We saw him briefly at night or on weekends. Sometimes he worked out of town at job sites.

Going to church on Sunday morning as a family made me happy, as well as family get-togethers. My extended family of grandparents, aunts, uncles, cousins, family friends, and all their children would come to celebrate and socialize. The adults drank heavily while setting up family cookouts, then played card games, Scrabble, or croquet on the back lawn. The children played games in age groups, with the older ones taking care of the younger.

The most precious memories I have of my dad were those when he came home from work. I waited with anticipation to hear his footsteps on the porch, then listened for the doorknob to turn. As soon as the door opened, I would run up to him, waving my arms in the air.

"Daddy, Daddy! Did you bring me something?"

He always bent down to greet me with a twinkle in his bright blue eyes. Then with a great big smile, he would reach into his pocket and pull out a Hershey's chocolate bar! Sometimes he would affectionately tease me, holding it just out of reach. I would jump up and down giggling with delight. That connection with him made the smell and taste of the chocolate even sweeter.

By four years old, I had also come to know inner conflict. The strained relationship between Mom and Dad forced us kids to take sides at times. I felt that on the one hand, if I sided with my mom, then I would not be showing love to my dad. And if I chose my dad, I feared it would mean I was betraying my mom. I made up a childish superstition that not siding with my dad meant something terrible was going to happen to him. I worried about this in secret. Little did I know what would soon happen . . .

When I was in kindergarten, my dad came home unexpectedly early one day. I found him sitting on the bed in his room, pulling tiny chunks of shattered glass from his curly black hair. I was confused and concerned at the same time. I asked, "Daddy, what are you doing?" He told me he had been in an automobile accident.

I thought, *An accident? What's that?* At five and a half years old, I did not know what an accident was. (Much later, I found out that the collision had been serious, but my dad had decided to come straight home instead of going to the hospital.) Over the next two days, he seemed perfectly okay to me, and having him home to play with me was heaven. I wished it could always be that way.

The third day, I went to crawl in bed with my parents, as was my usual ritual, and found the door locked. I was told Dad was sick and not to be disturbed. Only Mom, the Doctor, Dad's adult siblings, and my two older sisters could see him for brief visits. Additionally, there seemed to be increasing conflict and tension around my Dad refusing to go to the hospital to get checked out, even though he was getting worse, not better.

All I knew was that I wanted to see my daddy, and I was not allowed. I pleaded but no one would listen to me. I thought, *If I can just see my daddy, then everything will be okay.* I planted myself in the middle of the living room floor, right outside the bedroom door, waiting for somebody to let me go in. Being appeased by well-meaning adults was simply not enough. Exhausted and bewildered, I finally did what I had conditioned myself to do when I was scared; I shut down and fell asleep.

When I woke up, it was eerily quiet. I noticed my mom's eyes were wet with tears. *Why is Mommy crying?* I wondered. As I carefully studied her swollen face for clues, a terrible feeling came over me.

"Where's my daddy?" I asked, but Mom was too choked up to answer. She just hugged me tightly and went out to meet people who had already started to arrive.

Something was clearly not right! Soon the house was filled with family and friends as I witnessed grown men and women weeping. Others brought in big pots of food and casserole dishes, the smell of which made me sick to my stomach. My sisters and brother seemed grim and desperately sad. I saw them crying, hugging, and talking with cousins and close friends. People were moving about speaking in hushed tones, and the whole scene was dizzying.

Adults grabbed me, hugging me tightly, saying, "I'm so sorry."

I just kept asking, "Where's my daddy?"

Mostly, I got an answer which I could not comprehend. It was the same answer over and over: "Your daddy has died and gone to heaven."

I did not know what they meant by that. I had no prior awareness of death, no reference to go by. I did not know where my daddy had gone, or how to locate him. I thought, *surely Daddy wouldn't go away without telling me!*

I desperately wanted to understand where to find this place called Heaven. For the first time, I did not intuitively know how to make things better. What I did know was that my daddy was missing, and I did not know where he was.

Next, my mother, sisters, and brother were all dressed up in their Sunday best and I was still in my pajamas. They were getting ready to go to something called a funeral. I did not know what that was, though I did understand it was about our dad and he would be there. It became clear that they were going but I was not, and I wondered, *Why is everyone else going to see Daddy, but not me?* I begged them to take me.

"You're just too young, little Suzie," they said to me.

I was heartbroken, and I cried in anguish as the door shut behind them. I felt lost and abandoned.

As my family went to the funeral, I was whisked away to stay with my aunt and cousins who lived a long way away. I could only talk to my mom briefly on the phone, as long distance was too expensive for longer calls back then. I felt I was once again being left out and all alone. After what felt like an eternity, about a week later they finally came to get me.

When I returned to school, I felt awkward and shy. I was uncomfortable with questions, and all I could say was that my daddy had died and gone to heaven. I repeated it many times. I had little ability express natural thoughts or emotion about it, and I held an almost angelic fairytale image in my imagination.

For a long time afterward, I was paranoid, and everything frightened me. I convinced myself that my dad was hiding from me somewhere. I was on heightened alert, afraid that he would pop up from behind the couch, from under my bed, or in the dark open closet at night. I hid frozen under the covers with only a peephole to breathe through.

Whenever my mom left the house, I became distraught and hysterical, fearing I would never see her again. I kicked, screamed, bit, and scratched my siblings, who were left to deal with me. They quickly grew weary of my episodes, as no matter what they said or did, I was inconsolable.

Even so, I was not the only one in pain. My three siblings were also dealing with Dad's death, and unlike me, they knew that he was never coming home again.

My oldest sister, at fifteen, had already had a lifetime's worth of being responsible for the three of us. Yet who was nurturing her? Out of necessity, my mom had to work full time. After many years of child rearing, she became the sole breadwinner. That left my oldest sister as substitute parent. She was also mourning a significant loss; our dad was the most cherished part of her life and now that was over.

My second oldest sister, who babysat me as well, shared with me years later that she would have preferred not to go to the funeral. She was horrified when she saw the dark makeup stain on her glove from touching Dad's face. She had been very close to our dad as well. In our childhood I did not know how much sadness she had, nor that she visited his grave every day after school to talk with him.

My brother had lost his father right when he needed strong parental guidance the most. Highly hyper-active, with a learning disability, my brother was already prone to troublemaking. His way of coping was to become defensively louder, more obnoxious, and more "in your face" than ever.

In the months to come, I became hypersensitive, such that I could no longer trust my senses. The movement of shadows from passing clouds, echoing whispers of wind, and the cracking, banging, and hissing of an old house settling all scared me. I was on heightened alert, listening and looking for anything that might be coming for me or coming to visit me in the night. I saw colors and shapes moving around in my room. I had mental and verbal conversations with ghostly figures which I thought were angels or beings from another dimension.

No doubt, I had an overactive imagination. However, this also was the beginning of my relationship with the supernatural.

The first year after Dad died, the holidays were mostly depressed and somber. Everything seemed dull and unsettled. Then, Santa brought me a special gift, a beautiful battery-powered doll named Tippy Toes. She was ivory skinned with big blue eyes, perfect pink lips, and curly blonde hair. Her legs moved in a walking motion. Much to my delight, this enabled her to ride a little pink and blue bike along with a festively adorned parade pony.

I instantly fell madly in love. I played with joyous abandon. It was as if happiness had been restored in an otherwise bleak existence.

Tippy Toes and I were inseparable until one spring day. I had been across the street, playing with my dolly in our neighbor's huge backyard, when I heard my sister shout my name to come home for dinner. When I walked through the door, my family noticed that I did not have my favorite doll.

"Susan," Mom said, "where is your baby doll?"

I remember feeling a cold wave wash over me—I had left my dolly at the neighbors'. In that moment, I told my first big lie.

My answer was a coy, "I don't know."

I gobbled my food as fast as I could. I asked to be excused and ran out the door at the speed of wind. I needed to retrieve my baby doll before dark.

A sickening feeling knotted my stomach as I looked down at my doll. I knew I that had left her on top of the picnic table, and now she was lying face up on the ground. I quickly picked her up, wiped her off and tenderly kissed her face. Then, when I turned Tippy Toes over, I saw her back cracked wide open.

"She's broken!" I yelled with fury at the neighbor boys who were out in the yard. "What happened to my dolly?"

They all started to laugh. One of them, who was particularly mean, imitated a cartoon character's voice in response.

"Your dolly walked off the end of the table."

I shrieked and began to cry. The same older boy continued to laugh and mock me. He called my doll "Tipsy Toes" and mimed drunken staggering. Then he blamed me for leaving her there. I felt angry and violated. Hot tears stung my face as I walked home.

Incredibly, instead of telling my family what had happened when I got home, I walked up three flights of stairs to the spooky attic. I held my broken doll and cried quietly in the dark. Then I hid her in an old baby stroller, padded and protected. Again and again, I snuck back up those steep stairs to be with her.

Every day, my mom and siblings asked me, "Little Suzie, where is your baby doll?"

Each time I shrugged and said, "I can't find her."

My family knew that there was clearly something odd about this. None the less, they searched with me to find the doll I had hidden in secret. Crushed and embarrassed, I continued to tell that lie until I was caught by my middle sister. As I recounted the full story of what had happened, she listened with compassion.

"It's okay, little Suzie," my sister said. "We'll fix Tippy Toes and make her better than ever. You can always come to us."

Well, why I didn't think of that? Nobody had told me I would get in trouble for the mistake of leaving my dolly. But by that time, I already believed that everything was my fault. I was broken like my dolly.

Although I did feel shame and guilt for the lie, it became easier, not harder, to withhold the truth and keep secrets.

In the immediate years after my dad died, there was little comfort for me. I just wanted to feel okay. Then somehow, in between the spaces, I found a way to do just that.

I have only a vague memory of what was probably the first time I had a clitoral orgasm. I think it happened riding a mechanical horse outside of a grocery store. Maybe it was the rhythmic back and forth, up and down motion. I was certainly not expecting *that* to happen. I had discovered something I had not known about my body, and I liked it. Soon I began to figure out ways to repeat that eruption of feelings, which somehow calmed, comforted and consumed me.

When I was seven, after what seemed like an interminable amount of time living with insecurity following Dad's passing, Mom started dating a most wonderful man. He was an incredibly handsome, blue eyed, mild-mannered Irishman—a bachelor who, at forty-two, married a widow with four children.

This man came at the perfect moment and was an absolute gift. He was my hero, and their wedding took place on my eighth birthday. (For the next forty-five years, we celebrated that special day together.) That event restored hope back to my life.

Shortly after the wedding we all moved to a larger three-story house. During the packing, I experienced an uncomfortable event. My brother caught me pleasuring myself with a little handheld vibrator I had found in a box in our room. I knew it was his, but I had helped myself to it anyway. His loud laughter and teasing mortified me, especially when he called over my sisters to make a spectacle of it.

This was a pivotal moment for me. My private precociousness had become public, and this unwanted attention led to secret-keeping and being inappropriately sexualized. I felt like I had no boundaries. Essentially, I had lost the freedom to discover my body naturally. From then on privacy was never assured, so my pleasure became the new secret to protect.

This incident left me shrouded in shame and disrepute, which my brother perpetuated with his insinuating smirks, covert gestures, and inflammatory insults. Although I loved my brother, and I knew he loved me, it was also true that our relationship was complicated. Sometimes he was the only one I had to play with. At times he was my protector and at times my tormentor.

Moving into the new house meant making many adjustments. Some of these adjustments were not easy for me, like having a bedroom of my own for the first time. I was on the second floor; my brother was now on the third next to the attic.

At first, I was relieved to have some space from him. But that proved to be short-lived as I immediately began to have night terrors. Upon moving into the new house, I discovered that I was locked out of my newlywed parents' bedroom. I would knock on the door, rattle the knob, and call out for my mom, but there was no answer. This was not okay for me. My sisters did not want me in their room either. I felt that I had no other choice but to walk up those narrow stairs to be comforted by my brother.

This was both a lifeline and a problem, as it required my dealing with my thirteen-year-old brother's newly emerging hormones and hard-ons. The mystery of what was happening behind my parents' locked door also fascinated me. I adored playing house in the attic for hours on end. Unfortunately, there was no hiding from my brother or his mind games. It seemed that he could always find me and assert himself into my play.

One day, he manipulated me into a most unwelcome encounter. He convinced me to get naked under a sheet, which he said was just like our parents would be doing. Then he pressured me into putting his flaccid penis into my mouth. It was totally gross and highly upsetting to me. I have a vivid memory of staring intensely at the open attic window, its curtains blowing gently in the wind. After that, dissociation became my method of escape.

A short time later, when he was being bossy and dominating in his usual manner, I threatened to tell. He retorted by saying that if I told Mom, I would be the one to get into trouble. His threat was so convincing that I bought into it. To avoid potential humiliation and conflict, I kept it to myself. That decision would dictate what I was and was not capable of saying for a long time to come.

A little over a year later, our family relocated to Phoenix, Arizona. By that time, I was deeply self-conscious. I had a hard time adjusting, and the neighborhood kids made fun of my Maine accent. Most of my new friendships did not seem to last very long, and I could not figure out why. I deeply craved acceptance and approval. When I did make a friend, I would cling like Saran Wrap. As a result, I developed a reputation for being intense, dramatic, and sometimes inappropriate.

In the third grade, I had a new friend who invited me to sleep over. I was especially looking forward to swimming in her large pool with a slide. After her parents went to bed, my girlfriend suggested we skinny-dip together. Although I had never done that before and was uncomfortable, I wanted her to like me. So, I took off my bathing suit. We were having a good time in the secret of the dark until I saw her big brother lurking behind the bushes.

Later, she and I were watching TV in a dark den-like area when her brother joined us. Like my brother, he was probably five years older than me. I got up to go to the bathroom. When I returned to the TV room, my friend had gone to bed. I felt awkward and uncomfortable without her, but her brother insisted that I stay to finish watching the end of the movie.

He kept inching closer and closer to me on the couch. I began to feel even more uncomfortable, so I shifted to sit on the floor. Then he got up off the couch, pushed me onto my back, and pinned me down, his hands forcefully roaming my body. In dismay I resisted and struggled, yet the harder I tried to get free, the more pressure he exerted. My heart pounded wildly, and my ears rang with alarm. I said no over and over and demanded that he stop, but I was too petrified to scream.

It was horrifying—my body was hot with shame and humiliation, while cold waves of fear made me shiver. Finally, I escaped. I still shudder to think how much worse it could have been.

My thoughts and feelings were muddled and confused. I questioned myself and puzzled over why this had happened. I felt betrayed by my friend for leaving me alone. Then I wondered whether she might have invited me over to be an offering for her brother. Still, I ended up keeping everything to myself, settling on never going near that girl again.

During those years, between the ages of four and twelve, I was bullied, mocked, taunted, teased, harassed, manhandled, and sexually violated. Because I blamed myself, I hid it deep inside me. I could not see my own innocence.

Due to the lack of boundaries growing up, I grew to have a distorted view of my body. My relationship with boys paralleled my rapid physical development. I looked mature for my age, yet I was stunted in my mental and emotional maturity.

I found that the safest place was the private world inside my head. There I could imagine all sorts of adult endeavors: my wedding, my future love life, my children, and my career. I also visualized my sudden-death funeral. I obsessed over every detail, imagining what that drama might entail. When I was particularly morose, I wondered whether my family and friends would even care. I did not really want to die—just escape the pain of the moment.

When I was in eighth grade, my first real boyfriend fully ignited my sexual awareness along with a burning desire to experience the pleasure of heavy petting. I was excited and curious, even putting pressure on him to go further. From then on, I fell into seeking validation through offering up my body.

This was a double-edged sword. I often found myself in situations where my boundaries were threatened or compromised. This happened not only with boys, but also with men in authority with whom I should have been safe.

It was as if I showed up on a particular kind of male radar indicating, "This girl is weak, needy, and vulnerable." I tried to understand what I did to deserve the attention of those men with whom I did not want to engage. Afterward, each encounter played out over and over in my mind. I would visualize and re-create the memory to play it out differently: adding new evasive maneuvers to get the upper hand, saying just what I wanted to say to defend myself, and pushing those guys around with my ninja moves. (If only it was that easy.)

Additionally, somewhere along the line, my brain got cross-wired. Excitement equaled fear and fear equaled excitement. If it felt good it was surely bad, and if it felt bad it was because I was bad. I was a walking beacon for that certain type of guy. This pattern would follow me through my teenage years into adulthood, where I continued to attract codependently abusive and addictive relationships. This ultimately led me to pursue spiritual answers.

During my teens, my parents had moved away from formalized Christian religion and started to explore Eastern religion. From there, they explored Metaphysics. I went where they went. In their friendship circles, I met the most interesting people and often engaged in conversations that stimulated my interest in spirituality.

We attended a delightful Metaphysical church where I met the man who would become my first husband. He was five years older than I was, and he was a lot more sexually adventurous. After we got married, he informed me that I needed to expand my sexual horizons. He wanted to invite other people into our bedroom. I resisted every way I could until finally I succumbed to persuasion. My expanded horizons started with watching porn. Later, I figured out that I could have things I wanted if I used sexual performance as leverage. This became a twisted, painful lifestyle and I completely lost whatever remained of my self-esteem.

Then I got pregnant and had an abortion. In my warped thinking, I believed that having a baby would cause me to lose my husband. I had no way of knowing the physical, mental, and emotional impact that decision would have on my life. Although I agreed to it, I immediately experienced overwhelming remorse.

In retrospect, I realize my choice was completely inconsistent with my values. Paradoxically, it reflected my low sense of self-worth as well as my self-centeredness. It also represented straight-up self-punishment. I neglected proper medical care for many years after that, which further sentenced me to needless suffering. As time went on, I grew angrier about the agonizing abuse that I had endured as the victim of men, not yet realizing my responsibility and the impact of my own self-treachery.

Fortunately, God had other plans for me. I began the process of surrendering my brokenness. Still married, I started group counseling for sexual abuse survivors. In this program I learned what sexual abuse was and identified common characteristics that most survivors shared. I also discovered that sexual abuse covered a broad range of boundary violating behaviors within an unbalanced power structure.

Part of my recovery required abstaining from all drugs and alcohol. It was not easy, but I finally sobered up. As my head cleared, it became evident that to grow, I needed to own the bankruptcy of my marriage. Thereafter, we mutually agreed to call it quits.

After the divorce, I moved back to Arizona, and in my grief I quickly went adrift. You could say I relapsed on unhealthy relationships—I just could not be alone. Finally, I hit another bottom, this time with financial bankruptcy.

Thank God I chose to go back into twelve-step recovery! It was there I found the humility, courage, and willingness to embrace Jesus Christ as my Higher Power. Through recovery, I started to pray and connect with other women. I could hear the essence of my own story through other recovering addicts. In the program, this is referred to as experience, strength, and hope, or the therapeutic value of one addict helping another. Ultimately, I learned to love and heal with Twelve Steps and a great big hug.

Twenty-plus years of recovery experience allows me to say this with certainty: God shows up before I do, always waiting with open arms, and in any given moment, all my brokenness can be made useful to another.

My journey of recovery over the years has been truly magnificent. In one way or another, it endures endlessly. To this day, I maintain that God offers special dispensation to addicts and survivors of abuse. In addition to abundant grace and mercy, surrender to God includes gifts of hyper-amplified intuition, empathic insight, ultra creative resourcefulness, and even precognition.

When I had been clean for a little while, I met a man of faith who loved the Bible and believed in praying in Jesus's name. He taught me many things during the time we were together. I got more familiar with the Bible and went crazy over contemporary Christian music.

We entered a business venture together that expanded in the Southwest. One of our retail locations was near Las Vegas, Nevada. Over eighteen months, we drove back and forth from Phoenix to Las Vegas many times. It was a six-hour drive each way, and I loved every minute of the natural desert scenery.

One particularly gorgeous spot captured my attention and imagination whenever we passed. It featured gigantic red rock boulders. I envisioned the blue sky opening and plopping those boulders straight down from heaven. This was a blink-of-an-eye spot in the middle of nowhere, literally between two dots on the map called Nowhere and Wikiup. I was fascinated by that part of the vast desert, and my heart had determined to stop there one day. Finally, on our last trip, we did just that.

Pulling off the road, I got out of the car and stretched. I looked around, becoming aware of an impending urge to relieve my bladder, but there were no services at that pull-off. So, I grabbed some tissues, found a small opening in the fence, and stepped through. Then I climbed up between the boulders to find a place to do my prairie tinkle.

Once I finished, I became completely mesmerized by the beauty of the late afternoon. I was immersed in the moment and flooded with gratitude. I turned to the west and spontaneously raised my arms to praise God.

There I was, in the beauty of the natural desert, audibly praying to the God of my understanding. Then, out of the corner of my eye, something shimmering caught my attention. My eyes came to focus on a little brittlebush. To my surprise, on this bush hung two necklaces blowing gently in the wind.

Wait! What?

I was stunned. My heart began to pound, and an inner ear frequency resonated with a high-pitched ringing tone.

I leaned in to take a closer look. One of the two necklaces was a handmade, beautifully woven, finely braided, black jute cross with tiny gold beads. Right next to it hung a slightly broken silver peace sign on a humble, black silk rope. I stood there trying to comprehend what I was seeing and how I could have found these necklaces. What were the odds, after all?

I questioned myself, *What is happening here? What does this mean? Are these for me, and should I take them?*

Then a clear, resonant voice arose in my mind and spoke, "Peace be with you, I am here!"

I stood there, in the moment, dumbfounded. The sunset illuminated all around me. It felt as if I was in a transparent bubble of light, expanding to become one with the desert. Both calmness and vibrancy surrounded me. The natural desert came alive, and its essence rested within me.

I lifted the necklaces off the bush. I looked up to the sky, raised my arms and started to laugh and cry at the same time.

I realized that the symbol of the cross had been too big for me to really comprehend, yet in that moment its essence said to me, "Surrender." Then and there I fully received my connection to God through Christ. Further, the peace sign necklace represented the universal truth of peace, inclusion and belonging. Finding it alongside the cross was another direct message to me: "My Peace resides within you." I felt that I was finally free, embraced by the natural world around me, created by the God that I belong to.

My experience in the desert solidified my connection to God the Father, the Son, and the Holy Spirit within me. It also illuminated my divine connection to the earth and the natural order of life. Further, I understood that God, the Creator of Life, really does know me as if I am the only one in the universe, and that He is always present to communicate His unconditional love and acceptance anywhere, anytime. And finally, He will always create opportunities for Divine Awakening … even where those opportunities are least expected.

In truth, I could never have discovered any of this if the events of my life had not unfolded exactly as they did, including all the struggle and strife.

This realization has not been characterized by a one-time event. It is an unfolding, in every moment. Even more, it is knowing everything has been for a purpose, and nothing has been wasted. For that wisdom I am deeply grateful.

In the moments of experiencing this awareness, I am filled, thrilled, and exhilarated. It is akin to free-falling into complete forgiveness, acceptance, and renewed hope for being alive. This is as powerful a miracle as I have ever known.

My journey since then has been one of learning to trust God for the restoration of my body, mind, and soul. This has been a rite of passage, taking me through unknown territories, with beautifully woven intersections and astonishing interconnectedness.

In my experience, true miracles often reveal themselves in totally unexpected ways. Key among these is the story of forgiveness, reconciliation, and healing of my relationship with my brother, which I will leave for another chapter.

Life might not always look like we imagine or expect, yet with an open mind and heart, we can always find our way home to the miracle of the moment. I am convinced that it is our recognition of the possibility of miracles that gives us ongoing access to them, including when they are not readily apparent.

Whether big or small, gloriously obvious or disguised in the mundane, they are there, awaiting our awareness and acceptance. The breath, depth, and scope of ongoing miracles electrifies our senses, and encourages us to come alive again and again.

I often say that we are witnesses to a Living Revelation, unfolding exactly as it should in the present. Spirit always meets us right where we are versus where we think we should or should not be. Miracles also are not limited by any condition we place upon ourselves in order to be worthy.

In my experience, Divine Awakening is an invitation to come as you are, no conditions required.

SUSAN JONES is an empathic visionary and spiritual healer, creating partnership and community throughout life. She uses her broad range of training to teach others how to activate their natural empathic gifts to create powerful clearings as magical miracle generators in their own lives.

Susan is also a coach, author, workshop developer and business collaborator. A Founding Member of the Empowering Women Alliance, Susan is a mentor to women discovering their authentic self-expression and personal power. She guides them in developing and sharing their unique voices through published authorship.

Susan has cultivated her unique vision for leadership through advanced graduate coursework at Landmark Worldwide and Coaching Certification with Codebreaker Technologies™. She is presently studying ancient healing traditions and practices through *Awaken the Heart Master Series*.

Find out more and contact Susan for speaking engagements, coaching, and empathic training:

    1blessedgirl.com

WHAT I DIDN'T KNOW COST ME PLENTY!

KATHY PEAKE

I bet you've heard the proverb, "What you don't know won't hurt you." The idea behind this old saying is that by remaining ignorant or uninformed, you won't have to worry about it, feel responsible for it, or get upset by it. Sometimes people use variations of this phrase to justify not telling someone about a problem or a situation, or to try to remain oblivious to certain realities.

In my life, I've learned some difficult lessons the hard way. Learning this proverb is untrue was one of the biggest and harshest lessons in my life. I found out that being ignorant and uninformed ultimately leads to more worry, more responsibility, and more upset, not less. Sometimes the reality of what you don't know has a way of getting unpleasantly up-close and personal . . . especially when it comes to finances.

This is a cautionary tale.

You'll begin to see why as I take you back to certain periods of my life, or to situations relating to my family members. In my experience, ignorance and lack of information did hurt, and the resulting lessons cost me plenty, either emotionally or monetarily. I want to share my hard-earned lessons with you, so you won't need to make the same mistakes or have the same poor outcomes that I did.

This is an encouraging tale.

Eventually I came through these difficult financial lessons intact; empowered by what I learned. I even became a financial professional. So, I'll also lay out some of my top financial insights for you and give you a few key pieces of information that may benefit you in your own life.

Let's start with a bit of my family history.

My grandfather was a powerhouse who lived a remarkable life. He'd come to America through Ellis Island as an immigrant in the early 1900s. A hard worker, he was also smart and good with people. He put down roots in Chicago, and eventually owned his own real estate and construction company. He achieved the American Dream through hard work, smarts, and making connections.

In the early 1950s, Granddaddy heard about plans to build a new airport which would be called O'Hare. He bought land surrounding the airport site and built commercial and industrial buildings. He leased the land rather than sell it, for a good ongoing investment. Prior to his death in 1978, he'd set up all the leases to transfer to Grandmomme and continue in perpetuity. Grandmomme and future generations were set to live a good life thanks to his financial acumen.

Unfortunately, a family friend introduced Grandmomme to a scheming financial advisor who only had his immediate best interests in mind, rather than hers, convincing my grandmother that, at her age, all those checks from multiple leases coming in each month were a bother. He advised her to sell all the land (ending the leases generating money) and put that money into an Irrevocable Real Estate Investment Trust (REIT). And regretfully, that's what she did.

This action resulted in a very hefty commission for him. His advice was based on taking advantage of her declining mental acuity to earn that commission rather than for her benefit or the preservation of my grandfather's legacy. Since the REIT performed poorly, and nothing was done to preserve the original principal, fifteen years before my mom passed away, the REIT Trust, which Mom inherited, ran out of money leaving nothing of Granddaddy's legacy. I wish I had my granddaddy around now to ask all the questions I didn't even know to ask when I was still in my early twenties before he passed.

Maybe that's why I eventually became a Financial Advisor. I wanted to find out how I could prevent something like this from happening to anybody again. So, I vowed to always act in my clients' best interests and to always make sure they were able to make sound decisions after being well informed. (It burns me up to know that some people can prey on the elderly and still sleep at night.)

Now let me tell you a little bit about me, personally.

In some ways I was just like every other girl next door. My early childhood was spent in a suburb of Miami, where my grandparents lived across the street, my elementary school was just around the corner, and families of those working at the Air Force Base lived nearby. Ours wasn't a fancy neighborhood. My father was a commercial pilot, low on the airline's totem pole, earning about the same as a military pilot.

I've always been inquisitive about how the world works and why people are the way they are. Yet often I was so naïve that I ended up the butt of many jokes. I was always a gullible girl and tended to learn my lessons the hard way.

From the time I was young, I always wanted to teach. In fact, some of my earliest memories are of setting up my stuffed animals and dolls in rows on my bed, classroom style. I had my class list, and I took roll call: Elephant, Suzette, Bear, Piggy, Buster, Lilly, Raggedy Ann, etc. My list had places marked off for grades for each lesson. I'm not sure what I taught to this collection of sweet faces, but I'm guessing teaching was part of my DNA. (My mom had taught grades three to five when I was in preschool.)

I've also known from a young age that I'm a seeker of knowledge; I manage to learn things at every turn in life. Along the way, I've learned to embrace each lesson as something that happened for me and not to me.

I graduated from Mary Washington College and used my degree in chemistry and a minor in math to become a teacher in a private high school in Virginia for a time. Later, I was blessed for some time to be a wife, and a stay-at-home mom for three precious and rambunctious kiddos. That was my only dream at the time, to be a wife and mother, the best job I've ever had.

Years later, my dream turned into a nightmare when we divorced. I didn't have a clue about managing money, and suddenly I needed to find a way to support myself and the kids. I had to pay the bills plus raise two boys and a girl as a single mom.

My life hasn't always been easy, but I consider myself very blessed with a wide range of experiences. Over my lifetime, I've had menial, hectic jobs that taught me how to breathe and stay calm. I've taught school, which required another set of stress-management techniques. I was co-owner of a seminar company which coached people and businesses in high performance psychology. I developed a successful direct sales business which still generates residual income after nearly thirty years. I also worked under contract in the information technology industry.

What I really wanted, after all these various experiences that spanned decades, was a career where I could use all my talents and expertise to serve others and make a difference in the world. When my last contract was coming to an end, I prayed for months, since I was the sole support of my family. I wanted something with a flexible schedule so I could still go on field trips with my kids, something that would have the potential to make good money, and something that would challenge me. I wanted a long-term career I could be proud of.

God answered my prayer when I saw an ad for a management position with the potential of a six-figure income. I had no idea what the industry was at first, and even after I found out, I didn't know much about it. But I felt drawn to it. I began my new career in a starting position in a financial services office; there they would train and assist me to become a licensed professional. At that time, I didn't know the difference between a stock and a bond.

I soon discovered this was more than a profession, this was an area in my life which had been missing. I really liked learning all about it. Sometimes it blew my mind—there was so much I didn't know. However, that first year, I was number one in my office, and as they say, the rest is history.

Now I'm an experienced independent financial advisor. I've owned my business for more than twenty years. But I'm so much more than that, just as you're so much more than your position, title, job, or career. We're women, with all that entails, and we have the internal and external scars to show for it.

As I grew my business, my kids grew up, too. They moved out and went away to the military or college, and then on to adventures of their own. Now they're adults with jobs, kids, and puppies, all living their own lives.

Over the years, I realized that more and more of my clients were either divorced or widowed. I think this gravitational change happened naturally at first. I listen to them, woman to woman. I empathize with them, and I want to help them with their transitions in life. I also want to give them the knowledge they would need to make informed decisions.

I've been divorced for many years, so I can relate to the single women I work with in my financial practice. I also get a chance to flex my motherly muscles and be a teacher, two of the things I do best. After some time, I knew I'd found my best-fitting niche. I bring empathetic listening, expertise, and life experience to the table, and I provide what women in transition need in the financial realm. Much like a doctor who specializes, I've become a financial specialist. Even more importantly, I introduce something else to our conversations: Money Mindset.

The Distinction of Money Mindset

A Money Mindset is your distinctive and specific set of core beliefs about money and how money works in the world. It's mostly an unconscious set of concepts and ideas—you're usually not even aware but this mindset is running the show. These core beliefs shape all your attitudes about money and every aspect of money.

A Money Mindset dictates how you deal with money, or shy away from dealing with it. It determines how you understand money, embrace it, or reject it. It rules how much money you feel you're entitled to, setting limits on what you're "allowed" or able to earn. It calls the shots on how you "should" spend money, and whether you give it away or stack it up for a rainy day. It controls what you think about the rich and the poor.

This quiet, mental dictator colors how you interact with the haves and the have-nots. It regulates your monetary confidence or lack of it, and it determines whether you can keep your money, grow it, or are successful managing it. The set of beliefs that make up your Money Mindset act as your own covert Money Commandments, underlying everything in your life that has to do with money.

If you've never thought about it this way, perhaps it's time to figure out what runs your ideas about money. Maybe now's the time to reveal the filters through which you see anything money related. When you're aware of your Money Mindset and your filters, you have the option of taking back control of your life regarding money.

People who are successfully wealthy aren't smarter, luckier, or more talented; they just have a certain mastery over money. Money isn't a mystery. Anyone can learn to master it by first discovering and understanding their Money Mindset. If you want to shift your relationship to money, first you must discover and understand your core beliefs about it.

Here are just a few of the basic Money Mindsets I've encountered:

The Ostrich—An Ostrich keeps her head down and buries herself in being busy in order to not deal with money. If learning about managing money is on this gal's to-do list, it's usually at the bottom. I call this "Someday-itis," but someday never comes. Are you an Ostrich, too busy to be bothered with money?

The Scarlett—Scarlett O'Hara, an iconic fictional character, was strong and determined, controlling everyone and everything around her. She was brave and tenacious, except when it came to her blind spots. When Scarlett encountered something she preferred not to deal with, she would say "Fiddle-dee-dee! I can't think about that now. I'll think about that tomorrow. After all, tomorrow *is* another day!" Is money one of your blind spots? Are you a strong woman like Scarlett until it comes to dealing with money?

The Noble Nelly—Nelly generally believes making/having/keeping money is *wrong* because . . .

a) She isn't worthy, so she has trouble asking for a fair wage or charging enough for her products or services. She might think others are more deserving or better suited to handling money matters for her (such as a man in her life). She might be comfortable volunteering but uncomfortable asking to be paid.

b) She's moralistic, so she believes there's something inherently principled, honorable, or righteous about not being rich. She thinks money is tainted, corrupting, or even sinful (i.e., "Money is the root of all evil"). She thinks those who have a lot of money probably did something disreputable to get it.

c) She's concerned about being selfish, so she thinks that wealth and selfishness are somehow linked. She believes that using, enjoying, or keeping money for herself is wrong, but giving away money to others is noble. She has a "give until it hurts" philosophy, being overly charitable or beggaring herself through philanthropy.

Do any of these Nellies sound like you?

The Hippie-Dippy—This gal is carefree; convinced that all she needs is to go with the flow and money takes care of itself. Life is meant to be easy-breezy; dealing with the nitty-gritty of finances just isn't cool. For the most part, money matters are a buzzkill. Are you a Hippie-Dippy when it comes to dealing with money?

The Squirrel—She saves money mostly, *just in case*, knowing all the money is hers because she gathered it. "Give it away . . ." the Squirrel scoffs. ". . . Are you nuts?" All her money is safely tucked away in the bank because it's safe there, but she hasn't considered that the value of her pile of nuts is being eroded by inflation. She usually lives below her means, feeling out of harm's way because she has more than enough for that fateful rainy day, or she may feel ever panicky because whatever she's saved is never enough. Are you a Squirrel?

The Peacock—Do you strut your stuff looking pretty on the outside, but inside you're just another chicken? The Peacock spends her time and energy "looking good" at the cost of just about everything else. Inside she hides her insecurities, fears, brokenness, and what she perceives as her failures. Outside, she surrounds herself with whatever is beautiful, popular, or exotic, often blowing her budget or living beyond her means to keep up appearances. What she really wants is to be accepted for who she truly is. The Peacock hasn't yet learned to live authentically. Maintaining her facade drains her energy and her pocketbook, ultimately stealing her greatest riches. Do you see any aspect of yourself in the Peacock?

The Queen—A Queen is just like she sounds—magnificent—the queen of her financial scene. She's the gal who's "large and in charge" of all aspects of handling her money. She knows what's happening with her income, outflow, and investments. She's savvy about finance and understands the language of money. She's also a smart monarch—she knows enough to consult a trustworthy Financial Advisor, surround herself with loyal experts (such as a lawyer, broker, banker, CPA, or insurance agent), and delegate the day-to-day management of her financial kingdom to her minions. She's free to reign over her domain, and she doesn't live to serve her money because her money exists to serve her. Are you the Queen of your finances?

There are many more types of Money Mindsets because, just like fingerprints, no two women's mindsets are exactly the same. You might recognize aspects of yourself in these descriptions; perhaps you identify with some of their listed beliefs. Maybe you're asking yourself, where did those beliefs come from?

Most of our Money Mindsets came from the messages we received or observed when we were children, usually from our parents or other family members. We've collected our experiences around money, made what we thought were rational judgements and decisions based on those messages and experiences, and then added those results to our (mostly unconscious) set of beliefs. We've done this throughout our lives; not only about money, but about everything.

These beliefs become a sort of top-secret guidance system which filters how money and life appears to us. It colors everything we think, do, and feel, and then directs the actions we take going forward. Nothing is inherently bad or good about any of these beliefs; however, they affect how life goes. Once we become conscious of our beliefs, when their top-secret nature has been declassified, then we can choose them again or discard them for a better way of being. Our responsibility is to recognize them and choose anew from an informed adult viewpoint.

Is your mindset generally one of scarcity or abundance? Or maybe you're somewhere in between? These mindsets don't necessarily determine how much money you have, but they do affect how you respond to or deal with that money. For instance, you could be very wealthy but have a scarcity mindset—you hoard all you have, constantly worrying that it might disappear at any moment. Or you could have very little money, even be what some might consider poor, and still, you're happy, have close personal connections, and never worry about how much or little you have because you choose to live fully in joy.

Noticing how you think and feel about money is the first step to unlocking any limiting beliefs. How does money make you feel? Are you jealous of people who have lots of money? Do you disregard people who aren't well off? Do you like to shop because it makes you feel a certain way, or do you avoid spending money because of the emotions evoked? Do you believe you're no good with numbers, or that only rich people can have financial advisors? Do you avoid conversations about finances or money in your marriage because it always ends in an argument? Do you create a mask that shields you from dealing with your brokenness and robs you of true beauty? Do you find yourself getting angry at a friend who's spending money by going on a trip to the Bahamas for a week?

As I grew up during the 60s and 70s, somehow, I didn't get the money memo. You know the one . . . the memo summarizing that special facts-of-life talk about money, outlining all the things a kid needs to know before becoming an adult. The secretly circulated memo about money, finances, investments, insurance, and savings. What's that, you say? You didn't get that memo, either?

I suspect that being a girl, the adults in my family expected I would grow up, get married, and be a homemaker. The unspoken assumption was that men were better money managers. So, sharing the money memo with me wasn't necessary, since that knowledge was best left to the man in charge of the family. (Unfortunately, the men I married must have missed seeing that secret memo, too.)

I certainly didn't have any clue about what I was missing out on until my early forties. Though I didn't get the money memo, I did learn several other lessons about money while I was growing up, including some my parents weren't even aware they were teaching.

Dad was an airline pilot from the late 1950s until the early 80s. He was dedicated to his profession and eventually made exceptionally good money. Lack of money wasn't an issue in my formative years; I think my childhood was fairly normal, upper middle-class, and suburban. My dad was in the air and away from home half of the week doing his job.

Because she was a single parent half of the time, Mom was strict with us. I don't know for sure why; maybe she felt if she let us have free rein, we'd become spoiled brats. She ruled with an iron fist. Mom wasn't mean about it. However, we all knew who was in charge when Dad wasn't home.

While growing up, money was simply never discussed, especially about retirement. Sixty was the mandatory retirement age for commercial pilots, so Dad's post-sixty future was entirely dependent upon the company pension.

As a result, saving or planning for the future wasn't a topic at the dinner table in my family.

Mom was a homemaker who eventually built a prosperous direct sales business in the late 1960s. She worked diligently to build that business when most middle-class women weren't expected to work. I now understand how remarkable she was, and I'm even more impressed by what she accomplished. Especially since back then, drop-shipping was not yet a thing, and the internet was decades away.

I was aware that Dad had a job that paid very well, but Mom had a business with the potential to bring in an unlimited amount of money. It sparked my interest. Mom took me along to some of her business training sessions, and I remember one speaker telling us, "Never let anyone steal your dreams." That stuck with me, especially when Mom let her dream be taken away.

She had continued to grow her little home business until her income rivaled Dad's income as a pilot. Then one day, Mom stopped her profitable business cold turkey. I didn't understand, but I remember sadness and uneasiness during that time when Dad was around the house. Later I found out that Dad's ego couldn't deal with Mom's success. He'd put his foot down, saying, "I won't stand for my wife making as much money selling soap as I do as an Airline Pilot!"

I appreciated my dad for many things, but not for his controlling and jealous ways. Mom acquiesced to Dad's demand because she put the family first. I didn't know what was going on behind the scenes, but it seemed some part of her died along with that dream of her business. A bit of her life spark got snuffed out, and as a child I certainly wasn't in a position to advise her.

I think part of her gave up on the future in general, too, when she gave up her business. I realize now just how much she'd sacrificed. That residual income would have provided millions of dollars when she was ready to retire. Instead, Mom ended up divorced anyway, and when she retired, she was dependent upon a meager Social Security check, and me.

Within the family dynamics of my childhood, what happened around money gave me mixed messages as well as several direct and indirect lessons. These messages and lessons could be viewed as positive, negative, or neutral, depending on how they impacted me, even if I wasn't fully aware of them at the time. Some were true, and some were later proven to be untrue.

Here's a sampling of the hodgepodge of messages I absorbed:

- Don't talk about money.
- Women don't need to know about money and finance because men are supposed to take care of all of that.
- Money comes from having a good education and a good career.
- If you have a good job, you don't need to plan for retirement or the future because your company will pay you a pension and take care of everything.
- You can create your own wealth by starting your own business.
- Money can create freedom and lifestyle.
- Money is good and gives you options.
- Money doesn't grow on trees (Dad).
- Money comes from giving people what they want or providing a service (Mom).
- Women can have a cute hobby business, but they shouldn't take it too seriously.
- Wives are never allowed to make more money than their husbands.
- If a woman's work or income threatens a man's ego, she should stop what she's doing immediately.
- Money is the source of either happiness or grief.
- Sometimes you must choose between money and relationships.
- Watch out and be careful about what kind of a man you let into your life.
- Freedom comes only when it's granted.

Now what does all of this have to do with my Money Mindset? Well, all those messages and lessons were recorded in my subconscious during childhood, and they informed how I dealt with money and what I thought about wealth (and relationships) well into adulthood. These true/untrue, helpful/unhelpful thoughts and beliefs, along with many others, were tumbling around in my head as I moved into college, marriage, and then the business world.

Emotional triggers offer clues about your Money Mindset and are indicators of your core beliefs.

What's your mindset about money? When you hear the word "money," how does it make you feel? What images does it evoke? Is money a good thing, or not? Everyone has a relationship with money that started at an incredibly young age—you do, too. You may not have been aware of it at the time, and you may not be fully aware of it now.

Did you overhear your parents or family members argue over money? Did they discuss bills or finances, or was all of that handled behind closed doors? Were you taught to save money? Was tithing a part of your upbringing? Or have you never heard of tithing? Did one or both parents stress about having/not having money? Was money scarce or plentiful? Where did money come from? What did money mean in your family? Who controlled the money in your family's household? Did anyone ever say that money gives you choices? Did you get the message that money is a problem?

Once you understand how you think about money, and once you comprehend how money makes you feel, you're on your way to knowing your Money Mindset. With a grasp on that, you're in a good position to examine where you are now. Then you can start to reconfigure your beliefs about money, picking and choosing which beliefs will serve you best.

What went into creating your Money Mindset?
I invite you to take a moment now to write down your own memories involving money. What messages did you receive? Were they spoken or unspoken? What were some of your lessons around money? What are the components of the mindset these messages and lessons created? Write down all your thoughts and feelings . . . you might begin to see a pattern.

Here's another good exercise to help you reveal your Money Mindset: visualize Money as though it was a person sitting across from you at the table. Imagine what Money looks like and sounds like. What would you say to Money if you had a chance? Would you ask questions, or would you make pronouncements? How would Money respond?

Take a few minutes to try this out. I know it might seem silly, but please try it. This can be an enormously powerful and freeing exercise. Maybe you can have a close friend (who might not think you're too crazy) stand in for Money. That might make it easier to have Money talk back to you. The other person must get into character and take on being Money as you interact.

After the exercise, write down what you felt, discovered, or noticed. What did you learn? What does this have to do with your Money Mindset? Did you uncover something you didn't know before?

How can you shift a Money Mindset?

It's possible that I've shaken you up by now. If so, I'd like to offer three alternative ways of thinking about money for your consideration. You might find one or more of them to be comforting, thought provoking, or door-opening. I invite you to try on one or more of these concepts as a way to begin to shift your Money Mindset, if you so desire.

1. God always provides.

I mostly went through my life never really thinking about money. It wasn't something for me to deal with; I just figured that being concerned with money was up to someone else. Then I became responsible for making my own money, managing a household's money, supporting my family with money, and finally advising others about money.

When I was in my twenties, I stumbled onto an affirmation which has served me ever since. God always provides. I have hung on to this belief during good times and bad, and I genuinely believe it. The timing of God's provision doesn't always correspond to my liking, but God always does provide, and often in the most unimaginable ways.

2. Money is energy.

Money is a value of energy, just like a calorie is a measure of a unit of physical energy. We call money "currency" because it flows like a current of energy. It also can be either attracted or repelled depending on how our magnet is calibrated. That magnet is found in our core beliefs and in limiting beliefs about money. Our thoughts and emotions can be positive or negative like the poles of a magnet, so they can attract or repel, either blocking or pulling in money energy.

If the current of energy is cut off, then the flow is stopped, which is what happens when you harbor beliefs of scarcity. On the other hand, if you cultivate beliefs of abundance, then the current can flow in your life, money is attracted, and growth is the outcome. That's why tithing (or giving a tenth) as gratitude for what you receive is part of life's natural flow of abundance. Gratitude is essential for more. Giving allows for confidence in abundance; your belief in the energy of money allows its current to flow abundantly. When you hang on to money too tightly, you dam the flow of the ever-renewing supply of what you need. Giving part of your money away encourages that current or flow of energy.

Give and receive. Both are important to the flow of energy and the flow of abundance, and therefore to the flow of money.

3. Money is a tool.

To quote Ayn Rand: "Money is only a tool. [. . .] It will take you wherever you wish, but it will not replace you as the driver." Just as a hammer can be used to build a house, it can also be destructive if in the wrong hands. The hammer is a tool, but how it's used is up to whoever holds the tool. Money is a tool of exchange. Money's value only exists if there are goods or services produced and others are willing to exchange something for those goods or services at that value.

Our ancestors experienced a different world than we do now. Money was synonymous with power. Those who had money owned (literally and figuratively) or had power over those who didn't. This held true all over the world. Many stories and history lessons down through the ages have shaped our collective consciousness concerning money; however, money itself has no power.

Whoever holds money holds a tool, and whoever wields the tool is responsible for the outcome of what's produced by wielding that tool, whether for good or evil. Viewing money as a tool also offers a barometer of a society's virtue. The value of money is determined by what the society agrees, or economics demands. Either money can serve you or it can destroy you. Your view of money can do the same.

Become The Queen of your financial scene.

Let's assume you've seen something about your Money Mindset you'd like to shift. Perhaps, like I did, you've noticed that something has been missing in your life regarding money or your finances. Maybe you'd like to take steps to further shift your Money Mindset to being *The Queen* regarding money. If so, where can you start?

Learn the basics. Maybe you're already familiar with or have mastered one or more of the following categories. If not, do some research on your own by reading books, taking a class, or consulting a qualified and reputable Financial Advisor. Concentrate on these four categories:

1. **Save.** Start small but start. Create a savings account to handle emergency situations like needing new tires or replacing a refrigerator on the blink. Be consistent growing it.
2. **Plan.** Create an investment plan which beats inflation and avoids excessive taxes beyond your basic savings. Someone once said, "Failing to plan is planning to fail." So, for whatever you do that requires money, you'll need a plan. A good Financial Advisor can help you plan, by working out the details of implementing your plan.
3. **Diversify.** You've probably heard the phrase, "Don't put all your eggs in one basket." What that means in terms of money is this: don't rely on one source of income or have all your money in one place—one stock, mutual fund, bond, sector, or stream of income.
4. **Insure.** Life insurance is meant to be used to recover the earning ability of a loved one when they're no longer here to provide it. It also allows loved ones enough time and money to grieve. Best to speak with someone who's both Securities and Insurance Licensed because they can give you more well-rounded choices.

I've intended this chapter to be a cautionary tale as well as an empowering glimpse into money. I hope I've given you some things to think about while encouraging you to take money seriously, and I hope my simple suggestions will enable you to shift your mindset, and future, with money.

All of life is tied to money in some way. Whether money is used for living expenses, paying bills, buying a home, raising kids, retirement, a vacation, or giving to your church or the charities you're passionate about . . . you need money. That's a fact of life.

Now you know there are only four essential building blocks to financial freedom: saving, planning, diversifying, and protecting with insurance.

It all begins with your Money Mindset. Have you found that you have beliefs that stop you or limit you? Then now's the time to remedy any stops or limits by shifting your mindset! Are you The Queen of your financial scene, or have you discovered that something's been missing which you now can put into place to allow you freedom?

What I didn't know over the years cost me plenty. Now that you know, you have a chance to avoid pitfalls and live a life of financial ease and security. I pray what I've shared has been of service for you, and you'll enjoy an abundant life while you keep the current flowing.

What you've been reading is mostly my story along with some general information and my personal opinions. Since I'm a licensed Financial Advisor, I'm required to add this **Disclaimer:** This chapter is designed to provide general information on the subjects covered. It is not, however, intended to provide specific legal or tax investment advice. You are encouraged to consult with your tax advisor, attorney, or investment professional on these subjects.

KATHY PEAKE enlightens and empowers women in every encounter. Whether advising about finances, mentoring in business, or coaching for success in life, her essence is teacher and mother.

Kathy earned her BS degree in Chemistry from Mary Washington College and taught high school chemistry for several years. While owning multiple businesses, she expanded her education and training over a forty-year period with Werner Erhard, Tony Robbins, Wayne Dyer, Sandra Yancey, Brian Tracy, and Jim Rohn.

In addition to her business successes, Kathy is enormously proud of her three children, their counterparts, and her four grandchildren and three granddogs.

For over twenty years, Kathy has enjoyed teaching, coaching, and caring for single moms, divorcées, and widows as a licensed, independent financial advisor. A founding member of the Empowering Women Alliance, Kathy also loves connecting people with one another and has developed an extensive network around the world. Kathy is active in eWomenNetwork, BeeKonnected, and FUNancial Freedom For Kids and Teens, as well as in her Tucson, Arizona community and church.

Find out more about The Peake Financial Group:

>   tpfinancial.net

THE WAY OF THE HEART

UTE VAUGHN

We're all connected. We all have stories to share, and what you're about to read is part of mine. As you read this you might see yourself in my story as I might see myself in yours.

I still remember it like yesterday, one of those moments in time that shapes everything. I was barely four years old, lying on my stomach on my top bunk. I shared a small room with my brother in Germany, where I grew up. Both of my parents were angry. I can't remember why they were mad, but my dad started to spank me. After the first hit I decided to cry very loud and sure enough, the next hit was much lighter and stopped after the next. Then it was my brother's turn.

As I watched the fury and emotional uproar, not knowing why, what I'd done wrong, or what to do differently, I was confused and afraid. It frightened me to see my parents in this state of anger and it hurt me seeing the terror in my brother's eyes.

I remember hearing a voice coming from within me: "I don't like this. I don't understand it—there's got to be another way."

That moment sparked my thinking, questioning what was happening. It was also the first time I heard my inner voice . . . the voice of my soul, living in my heart. Of course, I was too young to comprehend all of this, but this experience was the beginning of my heart speaking to me and guiding me in many lessons to come.

Unfortunately, the spanking continued, only teaching me to be afraid, to hide, and to lie. No matter how hard I tried to be good, I didn't know what "good" was and kept getting into trouble. The continued punishments left me convinced I was a bad person.

The next lesson took place when I was a little older. My mom forgot something in the house and told me to wait outside. My brother was across the street and kept calling me to cross over to join him. I had no idea how to do that. One car passed and I ran. A second later I found myself lying on the street.

The woman who'd been driving the car that hit me happened to be a doctor. She was right by my side, saying, "I think your leg is broken."

The hospital confirmed. To my additional disadvantage, the children's section of this hospital was under construction. I had to stay for six weeks in a large room with adults, in a crib (what an insult to an almost-five-year-old) wearing a cast from hip to heel. The hospital's rule was that my parents were only able to visit me on Sundays for two hours.

I don't know how I got through that time. I couldn't move, I had no one to play with or talk to, and I couldn't yet read. There were no TVs, smartphones, or video games, etc. Thinking back, I was lost, terrified, hurt, and left to myself.

One Sunday, when I was desperately waiting for my parents, a young man visiting a relative asked me why I was there and what had happened. After I told him, he asked me if I knew now how to cross a street? I'd never thought of it, but no, I didn't. Using two beds, pretending they were parked cars, he showed me how to approach the street and look to see if it was safe to cross.

Later I realized that angels, guides, and teachers come unexpectedly and in many ways.

Most of us don't realize when this happens. This was the first instance I remember, with many more to follow.

I don't know how I made it through the weeks in the hospital, but I did. I didn't know at the time that it was the hospital's rules that kept my parents away. They weren't there, so I was deeply convinced that besides not being a good person, I was clearly unworthy and unlovable.

Not able to satisfy anybody, I learned to listen to my own thoughts and my own sense of how things worked and what made me feel good. I began to develop a sense of self independent of others' pronouncements. I learned to rely on myself, recognize my own voice, and trust and listen to my heart.

When I started school a few months later, it turned out I wrote with the wrong hand (I was left-handed). After being hit with a large ruler on my hand, over and over, I finally learned to use my right hand.

In art class, my heart suggested drawing with my left hand. There I was safe, and nobody cared. Art became a trusted and fun activity. I didn't know at the time how important it would be for me, and that art would become one of my companions for the rest of my life.

When I was eight, we moved to the outskirts of another town, and I was given two lifelong gifts: the healing power of nature and the experience of unconditional love.

The first gift occurred the moment I stepped into the woods and farmlands behind my house. I felt safe; my heart opened. I felt the magic of trees, heard the whisper of grass, felt the wind caressing my hair, listened to birds singing their songs, tasted the sweetness of wild strawberries, and smelled the scent of wildflowers. I felt free. I sang. I laughed.

Nature welcomed me, and so much made me feel like I belonged. No one was mad at me, criticizing me, shouting at me, or blamed me for anything. Instead of pushing me away, everything in nature accepted me. There was so much to explore, and all of it seemed sacred to me. It still does to this day.

The second gift came in the form of puppies: Minka, Hasso, and Trixie, all born at a neighboring farm in three different litters. I found my way to them by meeting a young girl pushing a baby stroller full of newborn dogs. I was delighted, never having seen puppies before. I spent every minute I could for the next few years with these exuberant and loving creatures. Their unabashed love and enthusiasm seeped deep into my heart.

Minka was in the first litter. I loved her sweetness and affection, but when she was about eight months old, I watched her being adopted. This was a tremendous loss for me—I had suddenly lost my best friend. I took shelter in an old trailer, sobbing.

Hasso came along a few months later. This pup was very smart, and we literally played games of hide and seek. When it was time for me to go home, he had to be locked up, otherwise he'd always find a way to follow me. The farmer's wife told me he was getting too old for adoption, and it was costing too much for them to keep him. I wanted to take him home, but my parents wouldn't allow it.

One day, when Hasso was a little over a year old, I went to see him as usual. I was calling for him, but he didn't come. The farmer's wife told me they'd just shot him. I was shocked. All I wanted to do was get away, so I started running.

I ran into the forest. When I finally came to rest, I checked in with myself. *Am I okay?* I still remember listening to see if I was still breathing and whether my body was still functioning. Would I be swallowed up by the grief? Was I still alive? To my own surprise, I was. My heart was still beating. The sky was still blue. And everything around me was still the way it was before. Then a deep knowing came over me.

My heart told me I was okay, and I realized the deepest part of me could never die or break, no matter what happened.

Trixie was the next dog I fell in love with. She, too, wanted to stay with me, and it became harder and harder to leave her. Her gift to me was her unconditional love. When we were together, nothing could distract her or take her focus off me. Even though I knew she wanted to stay with me more than anything, she'd never stop loving me when it was time to leave.

Raising these dogs taught me about love—what it felt like to be loved, and giving and receiving love, unconditionally. It also gave me my first practice in teaching without the use of punishment, violence, or force. People were amazed at what I was able to teach these dogs. I'd found a way to train by showing them, rewarding them, and loving them. This was something I wished that people would do for me and for one another.

School was taking more time, but I loved learning. Then two things happened.

First, the school board decided to change the school calendar. That year, all German grammar schools had to combine the study content of two grades into one. My grade combination was the third and fourth grades, which required me to learn and master twice the material in one year.

Second, my city was part of an experiment for gifted students. In Germany at that time, all children started in grammar school. After that, students had three education options: one was to stay in grammar school until graduation, but not be able to attend college or a trade school; a second option was to attend trade school and college, but not university; and the third option was to attend "Gymnasium," a program for gifted students (similar to gifted and talented programs or advanced placement in other countries), which was the only way to be accepted at university. During the city-wide experiment, students were sent a year early to the high-level educational Gymnasium to see how they'd do. It turned out they didn't do so well; out of thirty students, only two succeeded.

I was one of the twenty-eight. At twelve years old, I found myself away from my friends and overwhelmed by new academic subjects. All of a sudden, I had to learn Latin, French, and English as well as Chemistry, Physics, and Advanced Math. When I started to show signs of stress, my parents decided to force me into succeeding by taking away the activities I enjoyed and different punishments. I became more afraid and froze during exams, not remembering anything.

I tried so hard. On a previous test I'd gotten a D and decided not to show it to my parents. I had to do better on the next one. If I got a C, I could show it along with the D and maybe my parents wouldn't be so mad. But again, the moment I took the test, I couldn't think straight. Now things were worse; I had two bad tests, plus I'd lied.

My mom and dad were invited to a social with the parents of one of my classmates. I knew they'd find out. I waited in front of my house to see the look on their faces to help me determine whether to stay or run away from home.

I still see their faces in my mind: my mom was angry, but my dad wasn't. I decided to stay. I don't remember exactly what happened, but it was all finally over. I think my parents realized that no matter how much they hit or punished me, it wasn't going to make me any smarter.

Since I'd failed, I had to leave the advanced school and complete the lowest level of academics. This was a very sad time for me because I loved learning. Luckily, one of my previous teachers (another angel in disguise) stepped in and arranged for me to be accepted to a higher level of education. I'd never be allowed to study at a university in Germany, but at least I'd be able to attend trade schools and college.

Becoming a young woman was next. I was careful, timid, quiet, and polite. I was also fearful and easily intimidated. However, I also trusted myself more than I was afraid.

Violations came from all directions.

The first came from the farmer, where I visited the dogs. One day, he sat down next to me in the barn, put his hand between my legs, and asked me if I wanted him to play with me there. I just got up and walked away. I wasn't frightened. I was disgusted. I think he sensed that and didn't pursue me ever again.

But I also felt betrayed. This farm and its dogs had been my sanctuary. He'd taken that away. My mom could tell something was up and asked me what was going on. I hesitated, in fear they would forbid me to go back to the farm, but I finally told her. My mom listened, and then nothing happened. Some part of me wanted my parents to go and defend me, but they never had before. I did go back to the farm a few more times but the place didn't feel the same. Eventually, I just stopped going.

The worst intrusion came from my dad. It shattered the last of my respect and hopes for him to love and protect me. It started with him trying to engage me in inappropriate sexual conversations about masturbating and how my breasts felt. Remembering this still gives me the creeps. Then he'd come into the bathroom while I was taking a bath and ask me to show myself to him. I never cooperated. I hated what he did. I hated it just as much when he pretended to want to hug me, but his hands would slip, trying to touch my breasts.

I very quickly became adept at avoiding any situation where I might be alone with my dad. I locked the bathroom door, which I wasn't supposed to do, but did anyway. I also started spending more and more time away from home

My brother continued the intrusions. He was three years older than me and tried to get me to play "doctor games." I was a strong "no" to my brother. I told him "no" enough times that eventually he gave up. Next was one of his friends. One day, this friend pulled me behind some bushes and pinned me down, trying to slip his hands into my pants. I told him, "Stop right now or I'll scream." He knew I would and stopped. That was the end of the attempts at inappropriate intrusions in my life.

The voice in my heart had gotten stronger—I'd learned how to protect and to stand up for myself.

After high school, I chose to become a teacher, which was a career possible within my academic limitations. Teaching was perfect for me. It provided me with the fundamental knowledge of human behavior. My family's teaching method used punishment and force; I was determined to discover and use other means of educating my students. This became my personal quest. In addition, teaching gave me an outlet for my creativity and the heart-level communication I preferred to use.

At my local grammar school, teachers and parents noticed the difference. I was loved and appreciated by the children in my class and their parents. But it became a problem for the teachers and other grade's parents. I was asked by my principal to lower myself to the "normal" standard of education. But by now doing anything that wasn't from my heart would never be an option for me.

Meanwhile, the city had a project no one wanted to take on. My principal had noticed the difference in my classroom and, looking for a solution, recommended me for the directorial position of the city's experimental project.

My city desperately needed a playground. However, no empty lots were available. So, the city bought a narrow, three-story house to be converted into a kids' playhouse. The location was in a poor neighborhood with a lot of conflict, fueled by many guest worker families from Turkey, Greece, Italy, Spain, and Morocco, etc. These families were forced to live in close proximity with each other. , They did not speak one another's languages and were being rejected by the German families of the neighborhood.

My job was to design the space and come up with a program, as well as train assistants and find supplies. The biggest challenge was to integrate these different groups of people. This was the next step for me—using my heart and experiences to make this project work and bring people together in peace.

I love children. Children sensed this intuitively, and their curiosity was quickly sparked. The kids designed the different levels and spaces. They cleaned, painted, and worked hard. Materials and equipment were donated by businesses and the community, and this remarkable space soon became their "House." I never had to worry about things getting stolen or broken because it was already theirs—all of it.

I began integrating by having the children share different games from their various countries. Everybody wanted to learn more about one another. We exchanged foreign foods and recipes, and the children taught each other their languages and helped each other with homework. It was a fantastic environment. As I'd hoped, the kids became friends and the parents got to know each other as well.

I was twenty-two years old, and this project was all I'd done for two years. Being the director of an educational facility was the highest level of achievement with my level of education. My project was running successfully, but I began to wonder what would be next for me.

I also had a boyfriend who couldn't make up his mind whether he loved me or not. It seemed that there should be more than this for the rest of my life.

Of course, my heart had more plans. I'd always had a fascination for the United States. I was intrigued with the saying, "It's a land of unlimited opportunity." So, when my boyfriend suggested we travel for a bit together to see if we wanted to stay together, I took a sabbatical and was ready to go.

We started in New York in a station wagon and traveled for several months. We went down to the Gulf Coast and up to Northern California. It was an incredible experience, mostly because of the extraordinary generosity and friendliness of the many people we met on the way. When we came to Mendocino, an artist village on the Northern California Coast, I instantly fell in love. Heaven on earth.

Everybody knew everybody else—creative idealists, free spirits, musicians, spirituality seekers, and artists—a large eclectic family deeply connected to nature. Everyone welcomed me with open arms. No one was interested in what I did for a living, how much money I had, or what kind of car I drove. They related to me, heart to heart. I felt at home for the first time, and it became my most intense learning period. I was supported by an unwavering, powerful path of expanding and healing for the next twenty-five years of my life.

My boyfriend went back to Germany, and I fell in love with Matt, a charismatic artist. We both wanted to have a family. We got married and I got pregnant. Both of us were very excited when I gave birth to a healthy baby boy we named Sam.

One day, when Sam was just four months old, we put him down for a nap. Matt and I went into the bedroom ten minutes later, and when I looked at Sam, I knew immediately something was wrong. He wasn't breathing. The ambulance came very fast, but it was too late. At the hospital, we learned about a children's disease called SIDS, Sudden Infant Death Syndrome.

Sam had died.

Darkness landed upon me. The pain was excruciating—in my heart, mind, and body. It isn't possible to describe the devastation, sadness, pain, and hopelessness I was feeling. I was also overwhelmed with endless questions and fears. I remember being terrified to walk around any corner, scared of what I'd find. I'd been breastfeeding and even my breasts screamed with pain.

I don't think I would have healed if it hadn't been for this extraordinary community. We grieved together. My husband and I were surrounded by a constant stream of love and emotional, mental, and physical support. Everybody around us was making sure we wouldn't get lost in the darkness.

During this time, I searched deep into my heart. I looked at my life . . . so much pain, so many difficulties, so many challenges. I asked myself, *Was I that bad and unlovable to need this level of punishment?* It didn't make sense. As I looked around at my strong community, seeing the loving hands and faces amid the beauty of this place, I remembered that I don't believe in punishment.

Somewhere there was light and goodness, even in this darkness. I became aware of how we're all here on this planet to learn, every single one of us. And all our lessons are designed to strengthen gifts we carry in our hearts. Some of us make slower progress and some make huge jumps, but all of us are never given more than we can handle.

The biggest lessons source the biggest transformations.

I could see how being spanked had started me questioning things, and prompted me to look for love, versus hate. My time in the hospital as a child had taught me to think for myself; I'd learned to rely on myself and to be my own best friend. Losing Sam, I learned I could survive even the worst. I started to look at every incident throughout my life and saw the common thread of growth with each lesson. Everything that had happened had been an essential part of the whole; one thing couldn't have happened without the other.

I started to see my life as a blessing, with everything in it—good and bad—and how it was supposed to be exactly the way it was. Everything that had happened made me the person I am, bringing out my gifts and offerings to this world. I realized I trusted this path of becoming the best I could be. I could feel compassion for others, even for the people that brought me my biggest challenges.

So, I looked at Sam's life. I wanted to honor him. I wanted to think of him with love, not sadness, and wanted to find his gift.

Some of us get to live for a minute, some for a hundred and eight years or more. Sam's life was only four months, yet he'd made a difference on this planet. I wanted to see the miracle of his life in this world. It didn't take me long to figure it out, once I knew what I was looking for.

His gift was threefold: to remember not to take life for granted, to leave nothing unsaid minute by minute, and to share love as much and as big as possible, always. Sam strengthened me to live the way of the heart. The heart unconditionally loves; it's compassionate, kind, forgiving, understanding, and it has discernment and great reverence.

The heart is never against anything; the heart is always for something.

Being against something can't bring forth healing or goodness, because being against exists in the same energy as whatever you're against. Therefore, being against will only feed and grow whatever you're against.

But here is the secret: behind everything and anything you are against, there is always something you are for.

When I started looking for those pieces of gold, I found the things I'm wholeheartedly for. I looked deeper to find it in my interactions and my encounters. I was amazed at what I found and what doors opened. Looking at what I was for showed me where to direct my energy, ideas, love, and time.

The Way of the Heart became my life.

With this new outlook on life, I began to heal. It also became the basis for the extraordinary miracles and blessings all around me.

One of these miracles has been my extraordinary relationship with my two now-grown daughters. Their births followed a few years after Sam's death. I'm very clear that our relationship is beyond what I could have ever imagined if it hadn't been for the gift of Sam's life and death. Learning the way of the heart allowed me to love them and teach them about love. I love them unconditionally, and they love one another unconditionally. I look at their lives now, carrying forth Sam's gift while creating families of their own. I feel great joy. This feeling is immense, and it gives me hope for the world.

Sam's gift also revealed itself in my beautiful paintings. My joy connects me deeply to my heart and translates into my art, appreciating the magic all around me.

Almost a year after my oldest daughter was born, my parents wanted to come to visit. I was excited. However, I was also dreading being around my dad. Even then, his hand would sometimes slip over my breast, and I avoided being near him. I couldn't bear the thought of that happening in my safe environment, in my own home, or around my daughter.

I don't know where I got the courage, but shortly after my parents arrived, I took my dad aside. I told him clearly and calmly that he could never, ever do any of those inappropriate things to me again. He didn't like me talking to him that way; he was angry. He told my mom I was extremely rude to him, and he wanted to leave immediately. He didn't explain, and she didn't ask. I was scared, but I stood firm.

I learned another huge lesson that day, this time about secrets. Secrets are there to intimidate, keep someone quiet, or imprison them.

The moment a secret is out in the open, its power is broken.

Because my dad couldn't explain my "rudeness" to my mom, he couldn't justify leaving in a huff. So, he stayed. It was very awkward, but I let my dad deal with it. I'd said what I needed to say. Dad stayed angry, but he left me alone. Two weeks later, my parents left at the end of their scheduled visit. I was relieved.

A few months later I was listening to a woman speak in a personal development course. I was participating to learn more about why we are the way we are, and because I still had issues with fears, feelings of abandonment, and intimacy.

The woman was talking about her relationship with her dad. She'd had a wonderful childhood and loved her dad deeply. He'd supported and loved her all her life, and they'd shared beautiful experiences together. He'd recently passed away, and she was dealing with her grief and inability to express so many things she'd never told him. As I was listening, it made me sad that I'd never had that kind of relationship with my dad. I was imagining what that kind of relationship would have been like, when it all of a sudden it hit me.

A feeling of expansion came over me. I felt my heart beating. Warmth radiated all over my body.

I thought, *My dad isn't dead; my dad is very much alive.* Unlike this woman, I still had the opportunity to talk to my dad. In that moment I saw the possibility of having a loving relationship with him. I knew it was time to close the gap.

The moment I got home, I called my dad. I told him about the experience I'd just had, and how I wanted more than anything to have him back. I told him how devastating it'd been to grow up with him being sexually inappropriate with me. I told him how I couldn't trust him, couldn't get close to him, and couldn't understand why he'd do something like that to me. I said that doing those things made me think he didn't love me. That was why I turned away from him.

I said all of this in the context of love—no blame, no judgment, no righteousness, and no making him wrong. I was speaking directly from the heart. I told him, tears running down my cheeks, that we still had time—we could create a loving relationship with each other for the rest of our lives. I also told him he could never be inappropriate with me, ever again. If he agreed, I would love to rebuild our relationship. I said I truly, deeply wanted to get to know him.

There was a long pause . . . It seemed like forever. Then I realized my dad was crying. He told me he remembered the moment I was born. He'd held me in his arms, envisioning our relationship and what it would be like. He told me that he, too, had been sad that it hadn't turned out the way he'd wished for. He promised I'd never have to be afraid of him being inappropriate again.

I was adamant that what he'd done would never be okay. But because what had happened was in the past, I wasn't willing to keep it alive in my present or bring it into the future—neither my future nor my family's. I knew if I gave us a chance in the present, we had an opportunity to have a new future together. My heart understood the difference.

The impact was bigger than I could have imagined. I'm so much like my dad in so many ways, and I'd been rejecting even the positive parts of me that were like him. Now, I was able to embrace all those parts. I look like my dad, and like him, I'm very handy and can fix anything. I also have my dad's strength, silliness, and humor, along with my creativity. All these parts of me could blossom now.

I love my dad deeply. We now have so much fun together. It blows me away how much respect he has for me. We were able to tackle other issues in our conversations, and the bond we have now is profound.

A couple of weeks after that phone conversation with my dad, my mom called, thanking me for what I'd done. She said my dad hadn't been the same since. He was so happy, as if years had disappeared and loads had come off his back.

This was an opportunity to ask my mom if she'd known at the time about the inappropriate things he'd been doing, and if so, why she hadn't done anything to protect me. She said she'd known. Then she told me she hadn't known what to do, and she hadn't wanted to go against my dad.

Although I couldn't agree with her choice, I could understand it. The ability to ask with an open heart and to get an honest answer made a huge difference for me. It allowed our hearts to connect.

Unconditional love means loving someone the way they are and also loving them the way they are not. To unconditionally love is to choose the Way of the Heart.

Looking back, letting go of the past with my dad was certainly an unconventional and controversial way to create a new relationship. Many people told me they were concerned that I was making it too easy for him, or they shared their conviction that certain things are unforgivable. Some asked, "What if it happened again?" None of those issues were my concern. My dad had suffered in his own way, I'd grown up, and I'd become a strong and self-reliant person as a result of my experiences. My heart was willing to take the risk. Our new relationship's been one of my most satisfying and impactful experiences.

Throughout my life, I can see how every part is an important piece of who I am. There were things I needed to learn in order to grow and make the impact I'm making.

My heart always looks out for me—my heart always loves me.

I've made it a practice, no matter what happens, to ask the question: *How can this be the best thing that ever happened to me?*

Sometimes the answer takes a little time to reveal itself, but it always does. Even if I can't see it at the moment, maybe because I can't see the whole picture, I've learned to trust that I'm being divinely guided. I know from experience that any "wrongness" I may sense is actually part of something bigger/better that's going on.

The Way of the Heart healed and impacted many more relationships and situations. I found it far more powerful than any force or retribution. To this day, I honor my heart's guidance as much and as often as possible. My love and compassion has grown in all areas of life. Including in my world of painting, which always gives me great joy, connection, and comfort.

I continue my studies of human nature, energy medicine, and spirituality. I've had many wonderful opportunities to bring people and hearts together. I uplift people and situations, and guide people out of their worries and concerns by reacquainting them with their gifts and strengths. Over the last thirty years, I've full-heartedly shared my learnings and teachings in my life coaching business.

How to listen to the voice of your heart:

1. Shift from thinking with your head into experiencing your heart's truth and intuition. Find a quiet place to sit or lie. Focus your attention on the area of your heart. (You can even put your hand on your heart to shift your attention there.)
2. Imagine your breath flowing in and out of your heart. Begin breathing a little slower and deeper than usual for about a minute. (If it helps, you can breathe in for a count of four and out for a count of four.)
3. Now, recall an uplifting feeling, such as appreciation, love, or caring for something or somebody in your life (a special place, someone you love, a pet, an accomplishment, etc.). Stay connected to that feeling, breathing in and out of your heart for another few minutes. Deeply recall that feeling.
4. Ask a question or inquire about something—then listen. Answers always come—sometimes right away, and other times days later.

Answers often come in mysterious ways: a dream, a message someone sends you, words on a billboard, lyrics to a song playing on the radio . . . you'll recognize your answers when they come. That is the way of your heart.

5. Finish by sending love. Send love through your whole body, to every part and through every cell. Then radiate love all around you, throughout your house, into your neighborhood, and out into the world.

You can practice the Way of the Heart anywhere, at any time, and in any situation. The more you practice, the deeper and clearer your connection becomes to your inner voice, your heart's voice. Beautiful coincidences will begin to appear. Your natural state of happiness and enjoyment of life will expand, giving you even more to be grateful for.

The more you practice the way of the heart, the more you can rely on it—the more you trust yourself, your heart, and your life, the more present you'll be to love.

UTE VAUGHN naturally attracts people interested in being powerfully in love with life. A Life Coach and teacher for over forty years, Ute has been seeking, studying, and living her true passion which she calls "The Light Side of Being."

Earning her degree in Early Childhood Education led to continued studies, teaching, and coaching opportunities. Ute has certifications by The Coaches Training Institute, The HeartMath Institute, The Rhys Thomas Institute of Energy Medicine, The Science of Self-Empowerment, and Landmark Education. She was a founding member of the Empowering Women Alliance.

Combining her studies with her creative gifts as artist, illustrator, entrepreneur, theater producer, construction contractor, and writer, Ute developed a new empowerment paradigm. This coaching method is not based on changing, fixing, getting better, or working harder. Instead, Ute focuses on bringing out your given strengths and abilities, and she encourages play, caring, enthusiasm, and falling in love with your true self.

Visit: artbyute.com

FEELING YOUR WAY TO FREEDOM

VERA KNIGHT

What if weight loss isn't about dieting? What if it's not about food at all? What if weight is a symptom of something more complex than the entire food system?

So, if it's not about food, then what *is* it about?

I've come to believe it's really about fears, emotions, wounds, and things of the heart, and what we need is to feel all those things to understand what our inner self is really hungry for. Denying our deepest truths keeps bringing us back to trying to fix ourselves with more dieting. In my sixty-three years of life, five decades of dieting, and twenty-three years of experience in the fitness industry, I'm now one hundred percent certain that food (or any other way we use to numb our pain) is not the answer.

So, what is?

Answering that question became the story of my life.

Although we were well cared for as children and wanted for nothing, the dysfunction of my childhood family went beyond our four walls. My tightly knit, extended family played a huge role in my life. I believe my family's dysfunction helped ruin both me and my brother Frankie but in entirely different ways. While I could never measure up to him, he could never measure up to who they told him he was.

Frankie was the golden child. He could do no wrong, and he knew it too. He wanted me to be quiet and go along, but I couldn't. Instead, every day I screamed and cried and carried on.

"Why are you crying, Vera Ann?" my mother would ask with all the patience of a saint. But at three, four, five, ten, fifteen years old . . . I couldn't verbalize why I cried.

I cried over everything, and I stood up to injustices. For me, Frankie was one big injustice in my life. I felt overshadowed by him all the time, even on my own Holy Communion Day. But he was also my only sibling, my soulmate, and he had debilitating demons to fight that I didn't know about. At that time, I was in no position to understand or help him.

Decades later, and after working harder on myself than anything else, I now know it was my inner child, my baby girl self, who was crying to be heard.

My mother had been a dutiful, long-suffering, Catholic Italian girl who didn't talk much about herself. It saddens me to know that she never married the love of her life because her father forbade it. I can't imagine what fear kept her under such control, or how broken she must have been. At twenty-six, she married my father who was older than her by seventeen years. We affectionately called him "Oldie."

I believe Mother tried to do better for me than she'd done for herself. Her favorite words of encouragement were, "You can do anything you want, Vera Ann," and "You can grow up to marry John-John Kennedy." But her actions communicated something else. What she meant was: you can do anything, as long as you do it while staying attached to my ass, where I can see you. She reminded me often, "The world is a scary place," and "Don't talk to strangers."

She drilled these things into my young head, and as I grew, I wondered what was wrong with me. I was afraid of people, places, and things. I was terrified of the dark and prayed hard every night for God to keep me safe. I peed the bed because I was afraid to get up at night. I was also terrified of dead people, though my mother always said, "It's not the dead you need to be afraid of, Vera Ann. It's the living!"

I know she meant well, but wow, talk about cementing fear into a young child. The barrier of fear she imposed on me from birth was invisible and impenetrable. She justified the contradiction between my independent yet clinging behavior by saying, "Vera Ann hears a different drummer."

But I didn't want to hear a different drummer. I prayed, "God, make me be like everyone else." I tried hard to fit in, yet I never felt like I did. I never remember a time being comfortable in my own skin.

Through the years, I got good at living in chaos: relationships, school, money, jobs, religion, shopping, drama, drugs, and food. Ahh, food. Food was my escape. It was my earliest friend, my comfort. It ultimately became my drug of choice. When I was eating a big bowl of ice cream loaded with peanut butter, cookies, or whatever was in the kitchen, I would go into a trance, and for just a few moments, I would forget myself and the chaos within me.

Inevitably, as soon as I was done licking the bowl, I would start berating myself. *Idiot, why did you eat that? What's wrong with you?* I would shudder in disgust and think about throwing up; the few times I attempted it just made me hate myself all the more.

Born into a food-obsessed family, I went on my first official diet at the age of eleven. Eleven! My cousins and I promised to write down what we ate every week. But as our next visit approached, I felt ashamed knowing I hadn't dieted at all. That's when I started stealing Mom's doctor-prescribed diet drops.

My mother—"Chubby" as she was called—was always on a diet. She weighed three hundred pounds. I believe her biggest fear was that I would become like her. Now I wonder if she left the drops out for me to find.

In 1969, my mother moved us from Queens to Long Island to escape street drugs. That move magnified my fears. The link between my weight and my worthiness was already established, and I continued to fight for my place in the world. I hated the idea of moving, but Mom said I would make new friends, better friends.

Of course, I followed Frankie, who quickly became the leader of the pack. I was Frankie's sister; there was no getting away from it. In our new small town, all the girls wanted to be my best friend to get near him. My countless insecurities, need for approval, and fear of being left out grew stronger by the day. I finally figured, *If you can't beat 'em, join 'em.*

I started the seventh grade hiding behind my sassy Queens-girl attitude; I developed a loud, funny, and persistent personality. I began smoking pot and drinking beer in the woods with my new friends. To be self-supporting, we grubbed money on the street corner . . . "Got a dime, mister? I gotta call my mother." My parents had little control over Frankie and me; their resolve crumbled easily. Between the two of them, they enabled us nicely. Their love language never said "no."

By the time I was seventeen, I'd found my own diet doctor. Getting a steady supply of pharmaceutical speed was easy. I survived by eating sliced carrots and drinking a few cups of coffee each day. And though I'd pig out every few days, I managed to stay at an acceptable size.

God, how I hated my body.

When Dr. Greco got busted in 1979, there was no way I could downgrade to street speed. It made me jittery and sick. So, if I couldn't be skinny, then I would be stoned.

At twenty years old, after reaching an all-time drug-related low, I had a come to Jesus moment. This was the first time God saved my life. I high tailed it off of Long Island quickly after that.

The first thing I did when I arrived in California was to get a tattoo. I decided I was a rebel now, and that tiny red heart tattooed on my wrist proved it. I told myself, *I'm leaving all my fears and shit behind—I'm starting over, making new friends. I'm gonna do it right this time!*

Eventually, I adventured to Houston, Texas. There I met David. We fell in love, my parents gave us a beautiful Catholic wedding on Long Island, and soon after, we started a family.

I was twenty-eight years old and just shy of two hundred pounds the day our first baby was born. Four months later, I was pregnant again and still fifty pounds overweight. I was disgusted with myself and terrified. My mother's three hundred pounds didn't seem that far away.

I felt immense guilt when I miscarried. *Did I cause this because I'm so fat? Or because I'm miserable? Is God punishing me for my past?* I couldn't stand any of those thoughts.

"Please, God," I begged, "Don't let me have lost my baby in vain. Help me lose this weight."

I'm not sure what happened, but willpower washed over me like never before. I didn't put a morsel of food in my mouth that wasn't weighed, measured, or counted. I remember fixing dinner one night and spitting out a piece of not-quite-done-yet pasta instead of swallowing those two calories. Within a year, I was down to my lowest adult weight and feeling mighty proud of myself. I was a dieting goddess.

And bam, just like that, I was pregnant again. My insanity loop began to circle back the other way.

By the time I was in my thirties, I'd spent my whole life fighting with food, my body, and myself to deny my feelings. I kept going strong with a solid mission—to not be like my mother. I knew I had to protect my children. But protect them from what? My inner critic smirked, *Why, you, of course.*

Desperate to do better for my own kids, I rejected the weakness I perceived in my parent's parenting style. I decided to do the exact opposite. There would be no weak or mixed messages coming from this mama.

I had to be in control, but maintaining this strength was hard. I didn't trust myself, my feelings, or my emotions. Over time I disconnected from them and from myself. I became a high-level silent sufferer. And I thought if I could just get my food under control, maybe I could feel better.

I knew all the tricks. And every time I put something in my mouth that didn't fit the diet of the day, I'd just confirm that I was a loser. After shame-eating for a few days, weeks, or even years, I'd eventually muster up the willpower to try another diet. Then I'd cross my fingers and hope for the best.

I wrapped a happy fat lady persona around my defensive, controlling behavior, hiding a belief that nobody took me seriously. I was never comfortable in groups like the PTA or Bible studies, afraid to offer ideas because all eyes would be on me if I spoke. I was sure others were judging me because of my weight, and I despised the sound of my voice. To top it off, I secretly feared my husband was going to leave me.

And food, as always, was a readily available, socially acceptable drug that I used to numb my emotions. By the time David and I had two babies, we'd bought a house. I wasn't working, money was tight, and food was still my escape.

At that time, we visited a new non-denominational Christian church. I could feel God alive in that church. I'd never felt that before, and when the pastor gave an altar call, I was compelled to stand up. I accepted Jesus as my Savior right on the spot.

Still, I felt constant concern about my parents living so far away and I worried about my brother Frankie. Loving a drug addict is hard. Every time the phone rang, I would pray before answering it.

"Please don't let this be bad news about Frankie."

Then one day my worst fears were realized. Frankie's death by drug overdose destroyed me. When I returned from Frankie's funeral, I appealed to my husband's kindness.

"We can't leave my parents alone," I said. Dysfunctional as we'd been, we were still family. Within months we'd sold our home and moved across the country to be near my parents.

My mother died shortly after we arrived, and my father followed three months later. I was devastated. Six weeks later, on the first anniversary of Frankie's death, I vowed never to feel pain again. That decision almost killed me.

When we left Long Island for another cross-country move, I was utterly exhausted and gaining weight by the day. Shortly after arriving in Tucson, Arizona, I was diagnosed with prediabetes and given an inhaler for weight-induced asthma. My doctor warned me that my next visit would be for medication.

I was desperate, and I needed help. God apparently wasn't helping me anymore. But when I thought of help, I meant drugs. But I no longer allowed drugs in my world—no alcohol, no cigarettes, and no cursing either. Nevertheless, I'd been secretly waiting for a new weight loss miracle drug to be released—Phen-Phen promised to be a game-changer.

"God, I hope so," I prayed. "I need a miracle now more than ever."

However, I was ashamed about going to the diet doctor and even more afraid that my kids would find out about my past drug abuse. I hated being a hypocrite, taking Phen-Phen while preaching NO drugs to them. After a few weeks, I couldn't take agonizing over it anymore. The pills had to go.

And almost like magic, my willpower was back. It washed over me as it had after the miscarriage six years earlier. I could do no wrong. I lost seventy pounds.

I was pretty close to "skinny," but this time I didn't want just to be skinny. I wanted more. I wanted to be healthy and feel good about myself, and I wanted my clothes to fit. I had a lot to learn.

Then I had this bright idea: *I'll become a personal trainer!* Never mind that I'd never been in a gym before, and I had no idea what a personal trainer really did. Honestly, I didn't care about those details. I just thought it would help me stay skinny. My family and friends didn't know what to think when I announced I was going back to school. I got a degree in sports science and got a certification in personal training the year I turned forty.

With my sights set on some abstract vision of dieting perfection, my wall of protection felt complete. For the first time in my life, I had control . . . As long as my ass looked good in those black Nike pants I wore every day, I was good.

"What the hell is wrong with you?" I said out loud to myself after scarfing a leftover meatball that caught my eye when I opened the fridge looking for something—something I would never find in there.

No one knew what a hypocrite I was, presenting optimism when I felt defeat. Ten years into my career, I was disillusioned with the diet industry and the hype that went with it. I questioned my sanity while reassuring my clients, "We'll get it next time, for sure."

Meanwhile, I bitched, "Why God? Why do I keep winding up in the same place? What am I frigging missing?"

By my fifth decade, I was heavily into personal development and determined to figure out a sustainable lifestyle for myself and my clients. I prided myself on being on the cutting edge of the fitness/weight-loss industry. I added Certified Life Coach to my resumé and continued looking for the answer.

I was deep in the diet illusion, managing to maintain my weight, yo-yoing only a few pounds up and down at a time. Living like this was exhausting. No matter what I was doing in my life, it seemed hard. I hid the anxiety and fear I was experiencing. I had no idea of the depth of emotional suffering I was in under the mask of vibrant energy I manufactured.

The industry gurus I trusted said it was hard because I hadn't identified my Big Why. They said, "Once you identify your 'Why,' nothing will stop you."

How can that be? I snapped at myself. *I've been at this for years, decades—I knew my why.*

So, if I knew my why, maybe the real question was "What." What was actually getting in my way?

I was willing to do anything to get my weight under control once and for all. I worked harder on myself than ever before. But somehow, harder never resulted in sustainable effectiveness. I wondered, *How is it possible that I'm still trying to fix myself by dieting?*

I hated corporate fitness, so I left to open a personal training studio where I believed I had the freedom to do my own thing. Nevertheless I was burning out, and it was becoming hard to fake it. I sold my studio seven years later.

I wanted to believe that my body knew what it needed when it needed it. I wanted to listen to my body, to trust myself, but my head had no intention of giving up power. My inner critic, judge, and jury were right there, as always, to trip me up. I entered into a new phase of diet distraction, or maybe it was diet depression or diet desperation.

Of course, I understood the power of food in our lives is right up there with people, places, and things closest to our hearts. So, when I began playing with my food, adding things back into my diet that I'd long ago forbidden, my clients thought I was a genius.

Suddenly, I was back on top and in control. Not the old willpower kind of control—this was different. My clients dubbed it "Food Freedom: The Game." I was having a good time going to my favorite local restaurant where they'd indulge my request for five to six French fries, on the side. They accommodated me, always amused by the clever ways I ordered my food. For me, playing with my food became my Game of Life. People invited me to lunch so that I could teach them how to order the way I did. For a while, it was a nice little side hustle.

Eventually, though, old patterns resurfaced again. One night, mindlessly eating French fries off David's plate, my momentary trance broke. *WTF?!* I spit the fry into my napkin and sighed deeply in disgust.

And with a long, slow exhale, this truth came through me . . .

If you're breathing, you're playing. You may not be playing well, but you're still playing.

Play on, Sister, I cheered myself. But I didn't need a cheerleader, I needed a miracle. I didn't want to start over with another diet, another food game. I was sick of it. I was sick of everything. My clients, my family, my friends, my food, myself . . . I couldn't have another conversation about any of it.

"I don't care what you do!" I wanted to scream at people when I ran into them in the grocery store. "I don't care what's in your cart—don't worry, I'm not looking—and I don't care what you think about the stuff in my cart either!"

I desperately wanted to quit everything. And yet, I continued to hold on with both hands to this identity that I despised. I had no idea who I was.

I felt like I was stealing money from my clients. I had nothing left to give them. I had nothing left to give myself. It was taking me hours to do things that used to take minutes. I labored to write the simplest of posts for my client groups. I would shut down by six or seven p.m., falling asleep in front of my laptop with the TV on in the background playing whatever mind-numbing sitcom was on.

I literally could not keep going. I was burning out but too headstrong to admit it, and I was killing myself slowly. And then, endometrial cancer.

I went straight into survival mode, Vera style. I vowed to fight with every fiber of my being. My brain went into overdrive. I spent hours researching anti-cancer diets, supplements, treatments, survival rates, and all the what ifs while forbidding any conversation about it.

"I will tell you what you need to know. Got it?" I would say, in my I-mean-frigging-business tone (that my family and friends were all very used to).

My world was crashing down around me. Endometrial cancer was the proverbial straw that broke the camel's back. The war inside me had raged out of control, and there was no stopping it this time. I couldn't deny this. There was no stuffing this down.

Four weeks after a total hysterectomy, I did the unthinkable. I quit. First, I canceled all recurring payments from every one of my clients. Next, I emailed them stating that it was my honor to have worked with them, I'd taught them all I could, and I was done.

My thinking was chaotic. Nothing seemed to satisfy me. And what the hell was going on with my appetite?

I hated being distracted in so many ways, and I had to remind myself often to breathe. My brain remained on overdrive, overwhelmed by a crisis decades in the making. I had nothing left. I was going under. Most of my available energy went to pull myself back from the brink. I tried to take control by pretending I was okay. But I wasn't okay. I was dying, and not from cancer, either.

I began negotiating with myself. I wondered if I could let my hair go gray, gain a few pounds, pretend I was on a diet, and offer cake from my secret stash to any visitors coming my way. I could do this while I waited to die. Then I'd think, *My mother was sixty-three when she passed. That's my age now. I'll be damned . . . there's no way I'm doing that!*

The night after my second radiation treatment, I was watching mindless TV when I started feeling weird. My mouth watered. I stiffened up a bit, took a deep breath, and swallowed. I could feel it coming . . . I was queasy and beginning to feel dizzy. I stood up and ran to the bathroom.

The moments that followed were more intense than anything I'd ever experienced before, ever. I didn't know what was happening. I tried to call for David, but I had no voice. My brain and my body were screaming, demanding an audience with each other. My limbs started to shake. *Do I need to throw up? Do I need to sit down?* I was sweating, suffocating as the oxygen seemed to be sucked out of the room. I ripped my clothes off as the last of my energy drained from me. My whole body shook violently as I fell to my knees on the bathroom floor. I felt shattered into a million pieces—naked, drained, and broken. I couldn't move.

I have never been so scared in my life.

But I had a strong sense that God was with me, just as He always has been. I could feel His presence right there with me on the bathroom floor. He held me as He spoke directly into me.

"Enough, Vera," He said. "Enough."

I shook my head. "What does that mean, God?"

I willed myself to stay present. Inwardly, I screamed at myself, *Stay here, Vera!* It was a primal life-or-death command. I felt like if I let go, I would die. David would find me draped over the tub, naked and dead.

What's happening? My head swirled. *Have I reached the end of my road?*

I was powerless. My soul felt pierced all the way through. My body continued to shake uncontrollably. I had no choice but to surrender as I felt myself splinter into a million more tiny pieces. I wasn't sure of anything at that moment, except that I'd never been so terrified. My body was not my own. I don't want to sound overly dramatic, but it was dramatic.

I cried out, "Is this where I die? Why did you bring me here, God?" I begged to know. I pleaded, "What am I not seeing? Show me what I'm not seeing!"

I don't know how long I stayed on the bathroom floor before gathering enough strength to stand up—holding onto the door jamb for a long time before taking a breath and exhaling myself out into the unknown.

I went to bed, blaming the radiation. *I don't think I'll be doing that again,* I said to myself as I drifted off to sleep.

I was up the next morning at the crack of dawn, ready for a busy weekend babysitting my three grandbabies. I didn't give the bathroom floor event the night before any thought until the oncologist's office called on Monday to change my radiology appointment time.

"I'm glad you called," I said. "I almost forgot, but I had this wild frigging reaction Friday night. It was off-the-charts crazy. I was dizzy and weak; my body shook violently. I thought I might die. Bottom line, I think I'm going to pass on this last treatment. I can't go through that again."

"Ooooh . . . okay," the nurse said. "Hang on, let me run that by the doctor." She came back with a message from Doc B: "I don't know what that was, but it had nothing to do with radiation. You need to finish the treatments."

I promised the nurse I would be there for the final treatment, which was thankfully uneventful. But the days, weeks, and months following what I came to believe was a near-death experience, were anything but uneventful.

I felt like I was in a strange new land. I found myself marveling at ordinary things. Colors seemed brighter, sounds were crisper, and food tasted better. I remember looking up at the sky early one morning and thinking, *My God, I've never seen the sky so blue!* I couldn't stop looking at it. I even called out to David to come take a look. Moments later, I remember tipping my ear up to hear the birds sounding extra cheerful. This was strange since birds usually annoyed me before I drank my first cup of coffee.

My experience caused an awakening—a shift in my perception of the present reality, and of the past. I felt vulnerable, and at the same time empowered. I wanted more. It was a rollercoaster of emotions.

Curiosity set in. My mind was exploding with questions about everything in my life. Then I wondered, *Exactly when did I abdicate my personal power? Was I twenty? No, it was earlier than that. Was I eleven? Was I five? Three?* It made me sad.

And that's when it hit me . . . *Did I ever know my personal power?*

That question struck deep. Sadly, I wasn't sure. I wondered if it was actually possible for my mother's fears to have passed right into my DNA. Did her fear suppress my personal power before I even had a chance to own it? I had to think about that.

But that's what I'd been doing for a very long time . . . thinking. Telling myself what to think, what to feel, what to believe. And all that thinking did, was cause me to crave more thinking.

Only this was different. My body was pushing back, no longer willing to retreat from the bully that lived in my head. It was as if I'd been baptized right there on that bathroom floor. That event changed me. My body had a will of its own now. My insides trembled almost constantly. I was different. I felt different. People even said I looked different.

My family, friends, and those closest to me didn't know what to think. It was obvious I was going through something. I could see their sideways glances at each other wondering if I was losing it. But I didn't care. I wasn't hiding this authentic self-expression. This new perspective had me feeling euphoric. At times I felt like I was floating.

My husband, concerned for me, would ask our grown children, "What the hell is going on with your mother?"

I assured them that I was good—more than good. But I could see why they would be concerned. I was exhibiting symptoms that seemed like heart attack, stress, anxiety, and physical pain. For almost two years I was in and out of doctor's offices. The tests all came back negative, and the medical community pooh-poohed when I would mention energy. But I was present with these intense feelings pulsing through my body.

I was living in duality. Right out in the open for everyone to see. On one hand was sickness, and fear, on the other was connection, truth, and love.

I felt alive.

Trust the process. How many thousands of times did I encourage my clients with those words over the years?

But what is this process, Lord?

My mind was still trying to make it about food, while my body was wild with feelings I couldn't yet name. But I wanted answers, damn it.

The answers began to show up when God nudged me to explore myself deeper.

"It's okay to use all the tools," He spoke directly into me. "I gave them to the world. Don't be afraid."

"Wait, what?" I protested. "Don't be afraid?" What the hell, God?

But the truth is, I knew what He meant. He meant it was time for me to stop being afraid, to stop hiding, and to stop looking outside for the answers.

Soon after teachers and guides, in both human and spiritual forms, started showing up everywhere in my life. I found myself being called to energy work, meditation, somatic, and breathwork. I was like, *Damn, God, you are serious about this!* My body knew not to try and fight God. He began downloading the process right into my being.

So, what is the process?

In a nutshell, it's your ability to call yourself back to your body, back to safety within, to give yourself what you need. It's being present in the moment, connected to your personal power, and able to easily access whatever you need. It's noticing whether your wounded inner baby girl needs reassurance or compassion. or your inner critic needs acknowledgement or a hug. Or maybe you need to surrender, and release, or you need movement, or music. Whatever it is, you get to give that to yourself.

The practices don't stop there. One of my favorite and most potent practices is to give old energies back to their source. This frees me to connect to the soul I was born to be. This practice lets that girl inform my personal power.

But even more than that, the process which has changed me one thousand percent for the better, is ongoing, flexible, and ever evolving in my life. I am proud that I never gave up, even in my deepest dark struggles. I am thankful knowing that I won't die, as my mother did, with my personal power unrealized.

The best part is I'm still me. I have the same sense of humor, convictions, and values as before. On this side of all that fear, pain, and shame I found my voice and my truth. I want to shout from the rooftops, "You're not too old, it's not too late, and you won't die doing this work."

This experience brought out the best in me, and my soul desires to stand for, and with women who might need a little support breaking through to feel their way to freedom.

I am most grateful for the loves of my life. My grown son, who's been a confidante throughout my transformation commented, "Damn, Mom. I'm a little jealous I didn't grow up with this version of you." I assured him, "You've got me now, my love. You've got me now."

My daughter, who's always been my most intense relationship, is softening as I get to know and share my heart. I can now hug her tight and tell her, "I didn't do this enough when you were a kid."

My husband, God love him, is slowly opening up to conversations involving healing and transformation.

And my relationship with food—ahh food—is as it should be. Today, I eat for hunger, health, and happiness!

I'm humbled by the journey God has given me to live and share. I believe in the process. I believe in connection. I believe in God and His perfect timing. I believe in myself. And I believe in you! All love, sisters. All love.

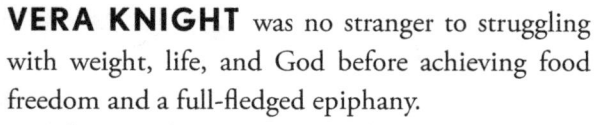

VERA KNIGHT was no stranger to struggling with weight, life, and God before achieving food freedom and a full-fledged epiphany.

After Vera's spiritual awakening, everything changed. She now connects on a much deeper level and helps women to heal their relationship with food, body, and self.

She founded Vera Knight Fitness in 2005 and is the creator of Food Freedom: The Game. A founding member of Empowering Women Alliance, Vera is also an author, speaker, and workshop developer and leader. Vera combines experience, knowledge, intuition, and humor in her workshops and retreats. She teaches virtually and in-person, with limited one-on-one coaching availability.

Vera's mission is to spread the idea that true freedom is only a breath away. When she's not challenging the status quo of traditional dieting and teaching, she's exploring personal growth. She spends her time with her husband, kids, and grandkids. Vera likes to cook, read, and serve in the community.

Find out more:

veraknightfitness.com

Contact Vera for speaking engagements, coaching, or training:

Email: vera@veraknightfitness.com

CULTIVATING WISDOM

KATHLEEN WESTWOOD

It's said that wisdom is the ability to think and act using knowledge, experience, understanding, common sense, and insight. It is the culmination of lessons learned. Wisdom cannot be imparted as knowledge can. We can find it, live it, do wonders as a result of it, but we can't teach it directly. In the words of Albert Einstein, "Wisdom is not a product of schooling but of the lifelong attempt to acquire it." It's received only when we love and trust ourselves enough to open our hearts and minds to it.

Wonder is the awakening that allows us to open ourselves to the beginning of wisdom.

Wonder is curiosity—the curiosity to discover what's out there or wondering what else is available. Wondering allows you to look beyond yourself, beyond the limits of what you can see. Wondering opens your eyes to recognize potential. There is no wisdom without being open to wonder.

So, when are we ready to cultivate wisdom—to hear and learn from the teachings of life? Everyone's lessons are unique to themselves. Knowing oneself is the beginning of all wisdom. So, to better understand who we are and what we have become, we must better understand our beginnings—the foundation upon which we mold and sculpt ourselves.

What were my life's lessons? When and how did I first start to open my heart and mind to make it possible to receive them?

My hand slipped into his. I felt secure, protected, safe. His strength and power could be felt in his grasp. I felt important. People noticed me only when they stopped to greet him on the street. But that was as short-lived as the happiness I felt. With each of his reprimands, "Look at people when they address you!" or "Speak up when spoken to!" I shrank back into my six-year-old body to take refuge.

It didn't matter that he was a well-known and well-respected surgeon, because I knew him differently as a father. I wished I could idolize him as his patients did. But that wasn't possible; I didn't see him as they did. As a child I failed to understand the different facets of his personality: professional (work) and personal (home). At home, he wasn't able to show the patience and understanding I longed for. I needed validation and received dissatisfaction in return. I didn't measure up to his expectations. He expected me to strive for intellectual excellence and demanded perfection. I couldn't deliver it.

He had a brilliant mind; he was a rational thinker who felt there was no reason for emotional displays. Unfortunately for me, I had an emotional temperament. I felt things deeply in my young heart. My sensitivity wasn't well received, so I found myself trying to bury it deeper and deeper inside where tears and feelings might have a chance to survive without being seen.

I have few memories of my younger days. Perhaps in some ways that's a gift. But it also prevents me from recalling the good moments, because I've learned from others that there were many.

I grew up in a blended family of seven children where I was the middle of the pack. In an attempt to bring us together, we had family meetings on Sundays when my father was home from work. I was young enough to be in a highchair when these meetings started. I'm told that the meeting was a time for each person to describe how he or she had contributed to the household (chores) that week so that they could earn their allowance.

We were taught the value of a dollar from a very early age. If my brothers earned their seventy-five-cent allowance, they always returned twenty-five cents to my father for household expenses, ten cents went to Boy Scout dues, twenty-five cents went into the bank as savings, and fifteen cents was theirs to spend. Saving was more important than any immediate gratification gained from spending it on oneself.

One Christmas Eve, I went with my brothers to deliver gifts to relatives and friends. My oldest brother was driving. I, at age six, was very excited to know that Santa was to visit our home that night. The excitement was shared with my four-year-old brother sitting next to me in the back seat of the station wagon and my two-year-old brother kneeling in the front seat looking back at us. There were no seatbelts at that time. An approaching car took the corner too wide, causing us to swerve to avoid hitting it. We hit a tree instead.

All three brothers were hospitalized for their injuries and were released within a few days. My impact was more severe. My face hit the metal panel on the seat in front of me, leaving me in a coma. The emergency medical response dealt with the visible physical damage, which was severe enough to require facial reconstruction. What wasn't considered at the time was the head trauma that occurred from the impact. This included a rebound shearing effect of the brain shifting within the skull.

I was left with an undiagnosed TBI (Traumatic Brain Injury.) My face and body healed, but my brain was left with residual damage. No one realized the long-term and serious implications of this injury, which changed the way in which I processed, stored, and retrieved verbal information. It also caused me to become scatterbrained, easily distracted, and unable to stay focused.

However, because neither medical personnel nor my family ever understood the extent of my brain injury, I was expected to function as I had before the accident. My father demanded it. I felt it was my fault whenever I heard condemning comments like, "Why can't you remember what we told you?" or "Can't you ever remember where you put things?"

The trauma of the accident also caused me to revert to bed-wetting. This was unacceptable to my father who felt that, since continence was once within my control, this incontinence was now a choice I was making. Therefore, he felt that he could punish me into making better choices. In the morning, as I was getting out of the bath, he would enter the bathroom and spank me. "This is going to hurt me more than it hurts you" wasn't believable to me. Avoiding punishment became my purpose. I felt if I was not seen, I might avoid being hurt.

I no longer have memories prior to the time of the accident, although family members have helped to fill in the blanks. I still grieve for the loss of those memories. To this day, many new and old memories remain lost until someone helps me to retrieve them. It took years for me to fully realize and understand the existence and nature of my brain injury and the impact it would have on my life.

Knowing how important education was to my father, I worked very hard to compensate in elementary and secondary school. I was only an average student. This was a disappointment to my father. I would feel proud of a perfect grade, knowing how much effort it took to achieve it, only to be made aware of other grades that were less than perfect.

I began to realize how much I wanted and needed to be accepted for who I was. I had to create my own sense of self-worth. Lying in bed at night, I often imagined that I had died, and people were gathered around the casket commenting on how I would be missed. Strangely enough, that brought a great sense of comfort to me.

Love existed in our family but none of us were sure of how to share it. We were all separate in our pursuit of emotional survival. We often had to pay for each other's offenses. If the guilty sibling didn't own up to it, we each received the belt, one at a time, chronologically. I cried when I heard the distress of the others as I waited for my turn to learn what was supposed to be a lesson.

My older sister and I shared a room but that was all. Instead of finding shelter in each other's understanding, we fought for our own right to be noticed and accepted. I now know that I wasn't easy to get along with. I must have felt entitled to the same attention that I had received when hospitalized, and she rightfully resented me for it.

I later learned that my sister turned down a rare and fabulous opportunity to go to the ocean with a friend because it meant kissing me goodbye when she left. Goodbye kisses were my mother's attempt to demonstrate emotional connectedness between us, but we siblings were emotionally polarized. My sister was so set against showing me any affection, even to this superficial degree, that she denied herself the pleasure of this ocean trip.

Things of an emotional nature were never discussed in our home. It was seen as a sign of weakness to ask for help. We were taught that "everyone has a cross to bear," so we were never to burden anyone with our own problems. "What happens at home stays at home." We were told to "pull yourself up by your bootstraps and move on." Self-indulgence was not tolerated. Crying wasn't an acceptable means of expression. It took years to learn that tears are my strength, not my weakness.

My mother was different from my father. She was kind and compassionate but, like the rest of us, she wasn't allowed to demonstrate it. My father forbade it. She was devoted to my father and honored his wishes, not because she agreed, but because she "had to live with him," which wasn't an unusual philosophy of their times. She never used physical punishment, but the fear instilled by the statement, "Wait until your father comes home," was often worse. Once, in frustration, I dared to reach out to her for understanding. When I told my mother that I was afraid of my father, she said I was never to say anything like that again.

I had no compass to help me navigate emotions I was told I should not have. I felt alone in trying to understand my feelings. No one was there to help put words to what I felt. I slammed the door shut to my emotions so that no one could see what was inside my heart. Unfortunately, this closed me off from learning more about what potential I might have or from any wisdom that could guide me. I was adrift with only my father's compass to guide me—not a match for my emotional needs.

I wasn't intelligent enough to sustain positive attention from my father. Any accomplishments faded in the light of my shortcomings. I was aware that he believed college education was wasted on girls. However, after my older sister fought for her right to attend, he was less resistant when it was my turn.

I had been so controlled and micro-managed as a child, I found myself lost when I left home for college. Walking through the mailroom on campus one afternoon, I saw a poster advertising an upcoming lecture: "WHO ARE YOU?" I remember being confused, thinking, *Who wouldn't know that?*

I didn't realize at the time that I had no idea who I was. I was a replica of what my parents thought I should be, but I didn't yet know how to recognize myself. All that I knew was how to shield myself. I was painfully shy and lacked self-confidence. I was unsure of how to establish friendships because I didn't know enough about myself to have any idea of what I could bring to others.

I chose to minor in theater as a way to gain some confidence in front of others. I was successful because I was told what to say, where to stand,

and how to express emotions. It was safe but it still didn't teach me how to understand who I was apart from the measured scripts I eagerly learned. I became involved in children's theatre and found that it combined my love of children and of teaching.

For the first time, I began to feel the stirrings of a potential that I didn't know I had. My brain injury came to play an important, positive role in the career choice I made. I began to learn more about speech pathology, which led me to a course of study that culminated in a master's degree.

Speech pathology allowed me to learn more about the memory systems we use to receive and understand language, store it into memory, and retrieve it upon demand. My memory was impaired, so I had already developed some accommodations to hide this weakness from others. While I had devised some creative solutions on my own, my studies provided additional insight, information, and strategies for functioning more successfully with my disability.

Most people have "clothesline" memory systems. For them, information is hanging in their memory as if on a clothesline: it's suspended in an organized way, easy to find and readily available when needed. Thoughts can be retrieved fluently, at any time, in any logical sequence.

My memory is a "clothes basket" memory system. When one thought is completed, it's discarded into the clothes basket and a new or associated thought takes its place. Soon the mental clothes basket is cluttered with random or related thoughts, piled one on top of the other. If I need to respond to a previous thought, comment, statement, or question, I have to rummage and sort through the disorganized collection of items that have been covered up in my basket. Digging frantically, I can only hope to find the information I need in a timely fashion, if at all.

During my education, I learned many retrieval strategies besides frantic searching, such as mnemonics, first letter association, repetition, associative coupling, and categorization to help me access the information needed. External memory systems are also helpful, like using notes. (I am a Sticky Note Queen!) Other external systems like calendars, daily planners, and phone reminders also help me to regain focus when other competing thoughts or events usurp my attention.

Although I am now better able to manage my disability, for most of my life I tried to keep it hidden from others. The memory challenges that resulted from my brain injury continue to plague me, having a negative effect on my overall confidence and self-esteem. Becoming a speech pathologist allowed me to better understand and accommodate my own limitations and, more importantly, it has helped me to see beyond myself. I began to believe I could make a difference in the lives of others who might also be searching for confidence in the face of their own personal challenges.

My father made it clear that I was only in college to get the job done, to make something of myself. So, my life on campus focused on studying. As a lingering result of my brain injury, I wasn't able to learn as easily as others. While others were out enjoying a social life, I was in the dorm or library developing strategies to help my brain learn and retain new information. My reward was graduating with honors and gaining a strong sense of purpose.

However, when it came time to demonstrate self-confidence to others, I was still shy and insecure. How could I convince someone else that I was worthy if I didn't fully believe it myself? Fortunately, at my last interview, I learned that a recent hire had just withdrawn, and the school district had to fill the position immediately. Right place, right time—I was hired.

For the first time, I felt independent. I could make my own decisions. I could also make mistakes and learn from them without suffering an incapacitating fear of failure. I realized that, as Eleanor Roosevelt had said, "No one can make you feel inferior without your consent." I was empowered. I started to break the bonds that tied me to an old sense of self. I began to listen less to my fears and more to my dreams. I grew under the nurturing care of others in my department. Success and validation were new to me. It opened me to the belief that I could actually find happiness on the road to self-discovery.

Happiness is an inside job. It's also a journey, not the destination. We are life-long learners and happiness is an ongoing process.

I'm so blessed to have a husband who loves me unconditionally. We met when I was thirteen and he was eleven years old. We were friends first, through all my faults and insecurities. Though we weren't able to spend much time together during high school and college, he saw me as I wanted to be seen and provided me with a new compass to help navigate life. Later, I became successful as a professional but was still insecure personally. His love gave me the confidence I needed to unlock my heart and dare show more of who I really was. It amazed me to learn that I could be loved. Our early years together helped to establish a deep trust and understanding that has served us well for our fifty years of marriage.

Starting out, we worked hard but had very little money. We were homesteaders, which means we self-sustained on all that we raised: cows, pigs, lamb, chickens, ducks, turkeys, fruits, and vegetables. I preserved all that we grew to last us through the winter.

My vegetable garden was my joy. I deeply appreciated all that it provided for us. The cultivation of each seed provided me with much needed food but, more importantly, the whisperings of a relationship with God. I began to understand that I was not unlike the seeds I planted.

The seeds all looked the same before they were planted, then changed as they grew. I knew I had started out as undifferentiated cells that looked the same as everyone else's. But I also knew that, as humans grow, we develop qualities that make us individual and unique—there isn't another person, anywhere, who is exactly like each of us.

We start out similarly, as one in God's handful of seeds. Who we are, what we become, and how we grow, depends upon how we are cultivated. How enriched we can become is the result of learning and taking to heart the lessons put before us. Learning this, I began to thrive in my garden with the nurturing of a budding faith and a loving husband.

However, there were many rocky patches to deal with and weeds to pull in the life we tilled together. When conflicts arose, my own insecurities often resurfaced, leaving me unprepared to help my husband with his own challenges. I had never learned how to be emotionally demonstrative, which often left him feeling alone. His occasional drinking became more frequent in his attempt to soothe himself. Alcoholism was in his family. So, it wasn't long before my husband became a practicing alcoholic. He was never physically abusive, which made it easier to make excuses for his failure to be a supportive part of the family.

I became skilled at compartmentalizing my life: professional and home (a seed that had been sown by my father). I had been taught that it was a sign of weakness to ask for help, so I put on a facade that convinced anyone looking, at least at a glance, that we had a perfect life. Along with my ability to separate home from work, I began to cultivate another necessary seed of my father's wisdom: inner strength. Therefore, at work I was able to appear confident and self-assured. However, at home I was unraveling while I enabled my husband's self-destruction. At first, his "social drinking" was easy to excuse and overlook as I looked for other ways to help love bloom at home.

One way was to take on motherhood. I took classes to learn how to become the perfect mother. (Do you recognize it? I was still striving for perfection.) I had learned so much from my own childhood that I knew I would never repeat. I vowed to demonstrate and express love frequently and unconditionally; any punishment would be provided with respect and administered through logical consequences, never to be inflicted physically.

I had three girls within three years of each other. They were my world. I found that I was now able to demonstrate and express unconditional love. And their love filled my heart. It gave me strength to confront the financial stress our family was under. I worked hard to make ends meet, understanding the value of a dollar (another seed of my father's wisdom taking root).

As I rolled pennies to buy enough gas to get to my job, my husband was spending dollars we didn't have on his beer. Only once did we argue about it in front of the children, and the frightened little voice that asked us to stop convinced me then that I had to make a change, for them and for me. I knew our minister was involved in alcoholic interventions, so I arranged to meet with him.

Fortunately, my husband chose to attend this meeting, and our lives changed. He recognized and took responsibility for his addiction and allowed himself to be admitted to a facility. He became a recovering alcoholic. AA (Alcoholics Anonymous) tells us to believe in a power bigger than ourselves, a higher power. God's hand was on us that day. My husband's newfound sobriety gave us an opportunity to rediscover who we were to each other and our children. We were given a second chance to be a functional, loving family, and my husband never drank again.

I tried to embrace AA's teaching, "Let go and let God," but I wasn't ready yet to relinquish my control. I fell back into old patterns. While my husband was rediscovering his place back in the family, I was hesitant to give up the reins. I wanted to maintain full control of my children's well-being and happiness.

I never anticipated what could happen outside my supervision. I believed my children were safe in the carefully chosen after-school care of their babysitter, my best friend. Instead, my sweet eleven-year-old daughter was being sexually abused by the babysitter's sons.

My daughter, who was threatened by her molesters, didn't tell anyone what was happening. When I sensed my daughter distancing herself emotionally and saw her becoming depressed, I knew something was wrong, but didn't at guess what was happening.

I finally learned that she had been molested and raped, and I got lost for a time in my rage and guilt. I hadn't been there to protect my daughter. What or who could I call upon to save me from my overwhelming sense of failure? I couldn't ask for help. I was never taught how to ask for help. My childhood teachings told me I had to rely on myself to stay strong. God waited patiently in the shadows.

Not able to ask for help for myself, I was able to set aside my own reactions and failures to ask for help on my daughter's behalf. I demanded help for her from her pediatrician as well as a counselor and a therapist. Still, she withdrew from us. She wouldn't allow herself to be vulnerable in any way. When I could sense we were in danger of losing her to self-destructive behavior, I enrolled her in a therapeutic program.

While in this counseling program, my daughter began to process her emotions, something I hadn't been able to demonstrate for her. She turned her once trusting, innocent eyes to me and said, "Where were you? You were supposed to protect me!" I painfully agreed that she was right. I did everything in my power to make things right for her, but I knew that everything I did from that point onward was after the fact—too little, too late. I hadn't kept her safe; I had failed at the fundamental purpose of being a mother.

I slowly, finally began to realize that perfect mothering wasn't possible, and that being a mother was only a part of a greater purpose. I wasn't comfortable in the role of victim, and I didn't want my daughter to be further victimized by my inability to be strong for her. I began to cope. My sense of failure and emotional self-indulgence was unbecoming to the principles I had been taught at an early age. I started finding strength that I didn't know I had.

Where was this strength coming from?

Surely, some was from the ongoing support of a loving husband. Some was from lessons learned in childhood. But there was more. This was an "aha" moment in my life. I found it was safe to draw strength from deeper within once I opened my heart—I opened my heart to God. I could allow myself to be vulnerable in His hands. I could draw on His strength. My emerging faith gave me strength and reassurance and the wisdom to know that I was never alone. God had been waiting for me to ask for help.

I accepted the realization that challenges are continually put before us in our life. We can do nothing to avoid them. That realization helped to release me from the crippling guilt I felt.

Things happen for a reason; there are no coincidences.

Only when we overcome obstacles can we gain some understanding of why they were there. I realized my emotional pain was necessary to cultivate a deeper understanding of myself and the life God has given me. So, I embraced it. I realized that pain is a part of living, a part of life. It brought with it a lesson to be learned that left me changed as a result. I was grateful for the emotional strength I was now able to call upon. I began to trust my inner voice, God's voice, so that I now felt safe enough to unlock more of the teachings of my childhood, to open myself up to the voice of wisdom.

I began to look at my father through a new lens. Until then, I couldn't accept that he could be the source of great wisdom. I believed it wouldn't be possible to learn and benefit from his teachings, his wisdom, while my heart remained closed. I understood that he had done the best he could with what he knew at the time.

I no longer viewed him as callous and uncaring but, instead, as one who worked so hard to prepare me for the many challenges I was to face in life. He had expected me to put my sensitivity aside in order to have the strength to face the unimaginable sorrows to come. I began to understand that growing up is all about getting hurt. In his wisdom, my father taught me not to indulge the pain. You get hurt, you recover, you move on. That is the strength he gave me, and it has served me well.

I found that I was now able to love him. I wanted to better understand him and the tomb that housed his heart. I needed to discover what made him the man he had become.

My father had been born an identical twin to a cold mother who didn't want children. She resented him when he married because it took his attention away from her. She also had no love for her grandchildren. My father had been very close to his twin brother. They went through medical school together and shared the same practice as surgeons. His twin, my uncle, died of ALS at age fifty-five. It was the only time I saw my father cry. Once, years later, as I watched him try to calm his mother's rage, I was shocked to hear her say that she wished he had died instead of his brother. That provided me with a window into his heart and a better understanding of his need to protect it.

Forgiveness came. I had light and love in my heart. I felt it necessary to share this new gift of love with him. I now could openly express my love for my father. Each time we parted, I hugged him and told him that I loved him. At first, he remained stiff and voiceless. It took many times before he dared mumble it back to me. Finally, his quiet, "I love you, too," and the strength of his hug revealed the appreciation he felt in being unlocked. Love brought him home.

Aristotle once said, "Knowing yourself is the beginning of all wisdom." I believe this. It involves the intelligence gained from learning about others and the wisdom that comes from knowing ourselves. I had been measuring myself with the yardstick of potential perfection, which I attempted to demonstrate as a professional, a spouse, a mother, and a friend. My striving for perfection had been shutting down my receptivity to others' voices and shutting out their wisdom. But, with the help of God and my loving family, I broke down the protective barriers shielding my heart and allowed more vulnerability to surface. I became less rigid and more receptive.

As a result, I have given the initials of AA a whole new, personal meaning: Accept and Adjust. I learned that I must be willing to let go of the life I planned (control) so that I can know and embrace the life that is waiting for me. I have gained much from the wisdom of the many voices I was once unable to hear, and I continue to trust God's message to me in learning my life's lessons. This is the life that continues to unfold before me—this is the wisdom I work to cultivate: love and faith give me purpose.

To this day, it saddens me to recall my dear ninety-five-year-old mother saying she had outlived her usefulness. We never outlive our purpose. My father's purpose was to prepare me for life and my mother's was to teach me about the love I needed to make myself a better person. Unfortunately, in her final days, my mother failed to see the importance of her knowledge and wisdom.

True understanding most often appears in the rearview mirror.

How I wish I could have helped my mother realize her importance and the gift her teachings and wisdom gave me. She didn't encourage me to wallow in my misfortunes or complaints. Her belief that "nothing is so bad that it couldn't be worse" helped me realize that others carry far heavier burdens in life. This helps me to maintain a positive perspective. I also continue to fight off negative thoughts about others with her frequent reminder that lives in my heart: be charitable. Each time we parted, Mom would sing, "Good-bye, good-bye, be always kind and good." These are truly words to live by. Owing thanks to my mother, my heart is open to this message.

Time has given me perspective and a willingness to be open to other messages as well. For example, I now can recognize the times when I became so engulfed in negativity that I was ineffective in dealing with situations that arose. Fortunately, I don't harbor or dwell on these bad memories. This is partially due to my memory issues, but it's also due to choice. I choose not to store negativity in my memory system. I have learned to discard the clutter of bad memories, which gives me more room for love.

I deliberately choose to hold onto love, joy, faith, and appreciation—I cultivate memories that serve this purpose. I am happiest dwelling in the positive world these generate. When necessary, I can access painful memories to be able to empathize, but otherwise, I seek the only memories that serve me. I choose to revisit only the memories that allow me to be positive and to learn life's lessons.

In writing this, many memories and lessons have resurfaced. They remind me of the importance of holding onto what is most important in life, to be persistent, and to never give up.

When my daughter emotionally struggled after her abuse, I wouldn't give up on her, even when she was pushing me away. Despite my memory problems, I had to be the keeper of the true vision of her—that she is beautiful, sensitive, and kind. When she blamed herself for being vulnerable, I had to be persistent in holding onto the truth that she didn't deserve to be hurt. I held onto what was most important for her until she was ready to see it, and believe it, for herself. She is loved and valued.

In holding onto these things for my daughter, I discovered them for myself as well. I also learned to recognize the seeds planted by my own parents. I had started out as a new parent just wanting my children to be happy. Then, like my parents, I wanted my children to survive, to come through intact, and to thrive. Eventually, I wanted my children to see and appreciate their true value. The wisdom of both of my parents lives on in me, and now my children are cultivating their own gardens of faith and knowledge.

I'm the product of my own harvested seeds of wisdom planted, cultivated, and nurtured into who I have become: my inner strength in the face of adversity, living simply, and appreciating everything life has given me. I still have much to learn about myself and my partnership with God. But the wisdom gained in my journey has made me a better person for myself, for my family, for others. I just need to use my knowledge wisely, to bring love to the hearts of those who need it.

I am so blessed to see the beautiful women my girls have become. I watch as they navigate their way through life, too. I wish I could protect them on their journeys, but I know they will need to learn their own life lessons and cultivate their own wisdom. Hopefully, my undying love and faith will be a beacon of light to guide them through the darker moments in their lives.

My hope for you in reading this is that you, too, will be guided to cultivate wisdom through positivity, love, and appreciation. You may be informed by adversity, but you aren't defined by it. Who you are is revealed by your persistence and your desire to continue to learn and grow. I also hope you will be kind to yourself. You, more than anyone else, deserve your love and affection. If you share your life lessons and cultivate your wisdom with an open heart, then love will take you home . . . to a place where you can know faith, peace, and joy.

KATHLEEN WESTWOOD has used her life-long struggle with Traumatic Brain Injury to create one-on-one intimacy and connectedness with others struggling in life.

She earned a master's degree in Speech Pathology to make a personal, positive impact. For fifty years, Kathleen addressed the needs of students from preschool through high school. Her extensive training encompasses memory systems, auditory processing, Visualization/Verbalization for Language Comprehension and Thinking, and autism spectrum disorders (ASD).

As an adjunct professor, Kathleen taught Early Childhood Language Development to adults seeking a degree in Education. She mentored under Michelle Garcia-Winner in California. Kathleen provides social thinking methodology to private clients who have difficulty navigating our complex social world. Though retired from the school system, she continues providing respite services for young adults with developmental challenges.

Kathleen and her husband happily winter in Arizona, returning to the East Coast every summer to enjoy their three daughters and twenty grandchildren.

Find out more about Traumatic Brain Injury:

> National Institute of Health: Traumatic Brain Injury Information
> Mayo Clinic: Traumatic Brain Injury Symptoms and Causes

THE GIFT OF BEING SEEN

ANASUYA ISAACS

> "I believe that appreciation is a holy thing—that when we look for what's best in a person we happen to be with at the moment, we're doing what God does all the time. So in loving and appreciating our neighbor, we're participating in something sacred." ~ Fred Rogers

Appreciating someone, acknowledging them for no good reason other than that they are there with you and it matters, I call The Gift of Being Seen. This simple act of kindness fills the holes in the soul as only unconditional love can. Whether we are successful and accomplished or still finding our way, so many of us feel invisible. We strive to be better, smarter, richer, thinner, something *other* than who we are in the moment for the hope of being seen for who we truly are by those that matter to us: by our parents and significant other, by our children, by our boss, and by our community.

I bet giving the gift of being seen is something that many of you give freely as an act of love and encouragement to those around you. Maybe some of you are like me. You give and give and give to others but have no clue how to give that same gift of being seen to yourself—or worse, you don't think you deserve it.

As a Teaching Artist and Workshop Facilitator, I made a career out of seeing people. I hugged the teens who had the courage to write essays about the sexual abuse they were enduring. I listened to women who had left their abusive spouses for the umpteenth time, terrified to go back and even more scared of trying to make it on their own after being repeatedly told they were worthless. I cried with survivors of rape whose stories mirrored my own in so many ways. I listened to my sisters and brothers in Kenya and South Africa who were suffocating under the heavy weight of guilt, shame, and fear of dying because of their HIV+ status, and helped them to remember their innate lovability.

Whether they were in the inner cities, the tony suburbs, the rural areas, or in other countries, the gift I gave to each person was the gift of being seen. This meant they were being seen, heard, and fully known as the beautiful, amazing souls they were born to be and still were despite their current, traumatic circumstances.

What I didn't know before, and what I learned on this book-writing journey, is that I had not really allowed myself to be fully seen, heard, and known. Unbeknownst to me, I was still hiding in plain sight because of the hurtful things people had said and the harmful things people had done to me. Though I faced them and even spoke my truth to the perpetrators, I was still hiding those broken parts of me, believing that if people knew the truth about me, they'd know I was unlovable.

I didn't realize how much I was trying to not ask for too much, not need too much, not take up too much space, to keep hidden. I shrank so that others could shine, and I didn't even see it. I put the spotlight happily on others who saw themselves as not enough, and whose greatness I saw without effort. I was blind to the fact that I hadn't offered the life-affirming gift of being seen to myself.

That was until I could no longer take care of others. I could barely take care of myself. The mask of not needing anything from anyone fell and shattered. That was when I had to either suffer alone and stay in agony so I wouldn't be too much of a burden on anyone or I had to let in the love and support offered by others.

I chose the latter and learned how to rise like a phoenix from my own ashes.

Every woman who co-wrote this book had a hand in supporting me to rise. They came through for me when I couldn't be there for myself. They became my sisters. They deserve so much love and praise.

So, I acknowledge you, my sisters. My near-fatal car accident in the middle of our writing journey together showed me who I could count on;

that I wasn't alone in my suffering. You all lifted me up, encouraged me, and prayed for me, making my long and arduous journey to recovery much sweeter and less overwhelming.

You all taught me to embrace the me that I am now, while letting go of the me I used to be before I crashed my car and my life. My resulting Traumatic Brain Injury made it clearer and clearer that I just didn't have the capacity to participate with a fully developed chapter as I'd intended when I started this journey with you. Nevertheless, you never once looked at me with pity. You held my space in our sacred circle, keeping the lights on and the food warm in the oven for my return. I could receive no greater gift than people seeing my magnificence when I was at my lowest point, and then reflecting it back to me.

For each and every one of you, I'm so very blessed to have spent almost two years with you in the warm womb of creativity, nurturing the book we would give birth to one day. The courageous vulnerability that you brought to the writing and rewriting (and even more rewriting) of your chapters revealed the indomitable spirit in each one of you—which is inside each of us. I read your stories, each so completely different from my own, and got the surprising opportunity to know myself better. I also accepted the invitation to have as much compassion for myself as I did for you. We blessed each other with tenderness and kindness as we became friends for life.

You, my soul-stirring writer-sisters, gave your all with great transparency and deep love, making the world so much better because you did. You gave yourselves the gift of seeing yourselves truly as you are and are not. Then you gave that gift away to each of us. The gift of being seen is a gift that keeps on giving. May we spread it far and wide.

Being ongoingly involved with each of you and your stories, honoring your life's most transformative lessons, motivated me to remember my purpose and to be healed enough to keep on fulfilling it. I learned that Sisterhood is Medicine—the very best kind.

I am blessed to be seventy-five percent healed. I am again able to offer courses to participants in many countries who dare to speak the unspeakable and heal themselves through art, theater, and creative writing. I was invited to speak at World Unity Week, an annual global conference fostering unity through peace. There, I shared that expanding our hearts and minds to the

Divine Feminine within invites her much-needed wisdom and guidance to solve humanity's biggest challenges.

I have been able to return to myself with a clearer focus and love because of the many sisters around me who kept speaking life into me, who kept giving me the gift of being seen when all I wanted to do was hide my many broken parts. I learned how to "be the gift" of being seen for myself, which changed my relationship to my body and my mind. I am discovering newly who I came to Earth to be: an advocate for women's and children's voices as contributions to be honored and valued.

"Women hold up half the sky" is a quote I remember. It reminds me just how amazing women are. When I see women being treated unfairly—when we're paid much less despite having the same education and experience as our male counterparts, or when we're being denied access to education and opportunity, as so many girls are all around the world, I get angry, and then I do something about it.

We women are taught early on to not be too much—not too loud, too sassy, too fresh, too much of a know-it-all. Despite this, we still struggle to be seen and heard, to take up our rightful space . . . but not too much. We're forced to shrink, hide our light, and be self-deprecating, or to be constantly sorry for whatever is wrong around us (which always seems to be because of us).

This makes so many of us second-guess ourselves, even to be at war with ourselves—with our bodies, our minds, our looks—while being beat up on the inside by imposter syndrome. We constantly apologize for not being enough—not quick enough, pretty enough, strong enough, thin enough—in a too much world.

Simultaneously, we're told to stop being too much—too sexy, too smart, too fat/skinny, too qualified, too bossy, too emasculating—in a very not enough world. If we're ambitious, independent, stand out in a crowd, voice our opinion with no doubt in our voice, or when we stand up for ourselves or for a defenseless being, we're being too much and pay for it in some form or fashion. We may later pay for our boldness by being overlooked for promotions, belittled, taken down a notch, put in our place, or having our ideas stolen.

Then we have to shrink to try not to provoke sexism, misogyny, and physical harm by a date, spouse, boss, or stranger. We apologize when the insecure are unable to be with our expansive and powerful life-giving nature which is our greatest superpower.

I salute and honor you who persist and go on to break the rules and the glass ceilings, who go on to lead, build, fly, and get what they say couldn't be done, done. You who have the courage to be bold, who have the audacity to do the very thing you were told you couldn't or shouldn't do, who dared to dream and go after it, and who missed the mark or succeeded. I see you.

I also see all of you who are timid and hiding. I see those of you who doubt yourselves and your worth, who don't have the force to speak up or fight back because the backlash is too great. I see all of you who think you are just ordinary, nothing special, not important . . . I see you. And if nobody has told you yet, you matter.

Beautiful soul that you are, blessed reader, you give me hope for the future. You give me light in these times of great despair, sorrow, and uncertainty. It's because you are here beside me, with me, around me, and, sometimes, even for me that I know that we—humanity—can make it. I know because women are life. Because women have problem-solving skills (running a household, being part of a team at work), can manage limited funds (a mom on a budget), and are masters at conflict resolution (ever separate children or best friends fighting?). Our compassion and empathy are so very needed right now.

We, women, bring forth the light of hope. We expand faith. We make the impossible possible. We make a way out of "no way." We are the Mothers of Invention; we see a need and we fill it. We don't even need to know "how," we just do it.

> "When she hears the cries of the world, she reaches out and grasps the hands of her sisters, gathers up her children and asks the blessings of her elders, kisses her lover and turns the kettle to simmer, and rides straight into the arms of the mystery where she will wait until it is clear what needs to be done. Then, together with her companions, she will do it." ~ Mirabai Starr

That's how I see you, Woman—that's how I see women . . . as phenomenal. "Thank you, my sister."

Thank you for all that you are and all you do to make this world a better place. Thank you for all that you do to make life better for children, for our parents, and for our elders. Thank you for all that you are and do to make life better for those who can't do for themselves; for the environment; for animals. Thank you for all the things you are and do to make joy where there is such despair and a sense of hopelessness.

I see you. You move me. Shine on, my glorious sisters. Shine on!

You:
Beautiful Sublime
Amazing
You.
You are
absolutely magnificent.
You are extraordinary.
You are sparkles
of great joy.
You are connected to
every human being who ever lived.
You are your very own galaxy.
You are creativity itself.
You are a goddess.
You are my
Sister.

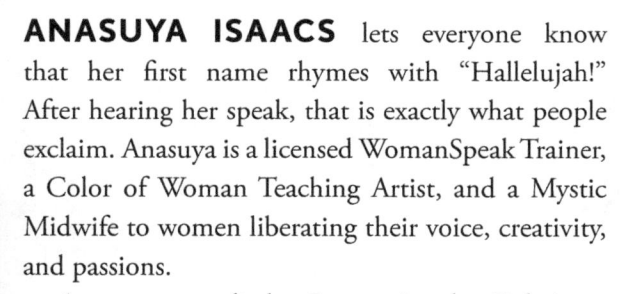

ANASUYA ISAACS lets everyone know that her first name rhymes with "Hallelujah!" After hearing her speak, that is exactly what people exclaim. Anasuya is a licensed WomanSpeak Trainer, a Color of Woman Teaching Artist, and a Mystic Midwife to women liberating their voice, creativity, and passions.

Anasuya studied International Relations, Communication, and French with the intention of joining the Foreign Service. She lived in Paris and studied at Sorbonne University, discovering that the arts could unite people and facilitate social change.

She became a working performer, writer, editor, translator, healer, and motivational speaker. As a teaching artist in schools, homeless shelters, and community centers, Anasuya used art, writing, theater, and spiritual teachings to create a safe space to speak the unspeakable and discover the golden gift available amid trauma.

This experience helped her create Let Love Lead healing workshops in Italy, South Africa, Kenya, and the United States, setting people free through the power of voice. Anasuya is a founding member of the Empowering Women Alliance.

Find out more about Anasuya and Workshops:

>hallelujah-anasuya.com

THE POWER OF CREATION

RHONDA PEOPLES

Women give birth. There's no greater power in the world.

As you've probably gathered from reading the previous chapters in this book, we women have many strengths. Sometimes we don't know our own strength until we're forced to use it. As we mature, we eventually make the discovery that everything we need is already within us. All we have to do is bring it out into the world, to birth it. God gave us the ability to birth—so use it!

Bringing out your greatness has been the stand we've taken for you. Regardless of whatever stories we writers created from our childhoods, we all used the resources available to us to become the women of power we are today. We've shared with you that you have this power within you, too. You have the built-in ability to get up out of the place you are in now and create what it is that you want. You can do this with the words from your mouth.

It's so important for women to stand for one another—to hold onto that vision of greatness we all have—and to remind each other of our greatness. There are times each of us gets in her own way. Our minds lie to us about our worthiness. We spend a lot of our lives trying to prove we're worthy, proving it to ourselves and to others. Competing and comparing ourselves with others immediately obscures and diminishes the power within us.

Power is our inherent right. It comes with being a human being. Some of us have forgotten that, so here's a reminder:

Women give birth. God made the choice to give that ability to us. God had a choice and God picked us.

Some of us give birth to babies. All of us have the ability and responsibility to give birth to something good. This can be love, light, encouragement, support, inspiration, possibility, joy, grace, patience, and forgiveness.

Often, we watch others, thinking they have more ability or power than we do. We might think so because they have more money, nicer clothes, or a better life than ours. We think, *If I had that, then my life would be better.*

Stand tall and know you're working hand in hand with the Creator. Now's the time to stop trying to prove you're worthy and know that you are. It's time to sort through the head trash you rely on to prove yourself, and instead focus on the power of creation that you are.

We women naturally, without practice or an instruction manual, grow, house, and deliver human beings into the world. We have, quite literally, birthed the world.

So, I invite you to take a moment to wrap your mind around the concept and depth of that power. Accepting the truth of just that idea alone is enough to free you of what you tell yourself on a daily basis about your self-worth, and about what you think you need to do to be worthy. You hold the power of creation, and whether you are a woman who physically gives birth, or not, is irrelevant.

You are a woman; you are worthy.

Giving birth, we women create by our very nature, but we also create in many other ways, just as naturally. We create when we manage and care for our families and our homes. We create each time we answer our children when they ask us about life. We create every time we plant the seed of an idea. We create every time we learn a life lesson and then share it with someone else. We create every time we encourage others to get up and do something positive, and each and every time we call women into action to be, do, or have something greater in their lives.

I'm a powerful woman. I create. I don't need to prove myself.

I had to learn these important facts for myself, the same way you do . . . by distinguishing fact from story. Stay with me as I walk you through my journey and share with you ways of releasing your Power of Creation.

I worked in the automotive industry for twenty-two years. That industry was designed by men, for men. For the most part, that's still how it's run today.

I acquired a lifetime of learning from the automotive business; I'm grateful for experience in it. It served me well for where I was in my life, when I was proving myself, and proving that I could do anything a man could do, and better. I'm also grateful I eventually learned to be successful another way.

When I started out, I felt like I needed to be a certain way to survive and succeed. That industry mostly follows the masculine way of doing business: there is work, and there is home, and the two do not meet. Everything about the car business was testosterone-charged. Most of the men had wives at home to take care of their family and home life. I was a single mom competing in a man's world, and I didn't have someone at home to take care of anything.

I created my bitch-on-heels persona working there. I'd been looking for someone to be, and that's where I found a role I could step into. I made fabulous money, lived in an impressive house, had fancy clothes, and collected shoes galore. My child was in private school. I paid people to do all the things I needed to get done at my house, and I watched football, baseball, and race car events from box seats. My dinners were at high-end restaurants, and I rubbed elbows with the richie-rich.

The owner of the dealership would always say to me, "That's right, straighten 'em up, Rhonda. Let 'em know how it needs to be done." Yet I had no training on how to manage or lead people, and I often felt like an outsider. No one else was dealing with the things I had to deal with at home, so I ran things like I ran my house, tight and efficient.

I would watch the guys interact with each other. The things they said to each other and the way they acted with one another surprised me. They'd be mean to each other, but then they'd go out for a beer together after work. So, I told myself, "That's what I need to do, too. If I act like them, then they'll accept me and take me seriously."

Well, it didn't work out that way. When I acted like them, when I acted like a man, I started having the experience of being with the group but not part of the group. So, I worked harder at proving I was worthy of belonging.

I gave up everything for my work. In twenty-two years, I missed only a handful of days. To keep from missing work, I went to work sick. I had a two-year-old daughter; the only reason I missed a day due to her needs was because she had a surgical procedure. Even then, days after the surgery, when she had a fever at preschool and they called me to come and get her, I picked her up and then dropped her off at someone's house so I could go back to work.

I told myself, "I can do this. I'm a powerhouse. I'm just like the guys."

I was serious about my work, and I was proving it every day. I had the best numbers, I had the best work ethic, and I had the best name in the business. At least, that was my story. On the other hand, I also missed all my sisters' weddings. I missed all the family events that happened in those twenty-two years. When an out-of-town family member came to visit, they knew they needed to come to the dealership if they wanted to see me, because that was where I was all the time.

In the beginning, I worked six days a week, at least ten hours a day. That was just what it took to be in the car business, that was the paradigm. Regardless of what was happening at home, you were expected to be at the dealership. So I was.

Then it happened, the big "aha" that changed everything. My daughter started high school, and I was the one who got educated.

My daughter is a blessing; she certainly was back then, and she's a blessing now. When she was growing up, every event I attended for work, she attended. My place of work was where she grew up. That was where she learned her social skills; that was where she developed her manners. Her first bike was put together by the guys in the automotive shop. They all knew her. She didn't know any different way because I spent all my time at work. That was where life happened, that was just how life was.

One day I dragged myself away from work to attend the freshman parent meeting at the private high school my daughter would be attending. In that meeting, it was made very clear to me that I needed to wake up to the reality that my daughter could be taken by aliens if I wasn't there to prevent it. The aliens they referred to were the alienation of drugs, parties, peer pressure, and teen culture. The conversation that the school administration had with me scared me to death.

It also opened my eyes to the importance of being with my daughter. She was entering high school and my presence in her life was more important than ever. I could no longer expect her to wedge herself into my work schedule; I needed to make time with her a priority if I had any hope of keeping her safe. So, I went back to work and requested to change my schedule to be able to spend more time with her.

My boss looked at me and said, "Your daughter's good, so why worry?" He said things like, "Are you saying I'm not a good father because of the hours I keep? Are you trying to say it's more important for you to spend more time with your daughter than for me to spend with my kids? Or because you're a mother, your kid-time is more important than it is for me as a father?"

I was shocked. I didn't know how to answer him, so I kept quiet. I remembered having had a conversation with the general manager, the man who held the position right under the owner. He'd told me how he didn't see a difference between men and women; he said he always treated them the same.

Remembering this previous conversation while talking with my boss, a shift happened. My true, authentic self woke up, demanding to be heard. My thoughts started coming together.

"There is a difference. I'm not a man. Mothers *are* important in the lives of their children, and I've been missing my daughter's life by working the way I have been." As I listened to him go on about his ideas about work and family, I suddenly knew, "My family is more important than my job!"

Soon after that, I realized two things. First, my boss wasn't going to change his mind or his position. Second, I wasn't experiencing fulfillment in my job in a way that could ever make up for the fulfillment I was missing in being a mother to my daughter. I decided I was quitting the car business.

I started connecting with people I knew in the industry to see where I would go and what might come next. A very prominent woman in the industry recommended that I speak to the owner of the dealership first. She said that if she was the owner and someone of my caliber was leaving, then she'd want the opportunity to speak with me before that happened. I made the request to speak to the owner before I quit.

I was petrified. My self-conversation sounded like, "How can I speak to the owner? I'm nobody. I'm not important. He's going to throw me out and tell me to move on!"

But I was determined. I was a single mother, and I would have done anything at that time to ensure my daughter was raised with everything good I could give her in life. I needed to be there for her as I never had been before.

In my meeting with the owner, I laid all of this out for him. And he said he wanted me to stay. I could change my hours to be with my daughter more.

I was sent back to my boss to complete my scheduling change. My boss made it very clear he didn't agree with the owner's decision. Then he leaned over the desk and spattered me with saliva in his intensity.

"If you think you're going to make as much money as me and work less hours, think again."

I felt it happen right then—he marked me with more than his spattered saliva. With his words, attitude, and intention, he marked me as if I was being branded by the letter "O" for Outsider. Just like Hester Prynne's "A" in *The Scarlet Letter*, I was being called out and marked. I knew my boss would make sure my career was crippled, and he'd make sure everyone knew I'd brought it on myself. My scarlet-letter-sin was wanting to put my daughter before my work.

For several years I continued at the dealership, being reminded of my sins. I'd been experiencing, and working through, tremendous pain for two years from an ovarian cyst. Eventually my physicians determined that a hysterectomy was the only viable course of action. While in surgery, they realized that something else was awry; they diagnosed me with ovarian cancer. I was told I needed to take six weeks off from work after this surgery. In addition, I had to go back into surgery a couple of weeks after my hysterectomy for a hernia repair.

I didn't receive a call, a card, or a flower from anyone at work while I was hospitalized or recovering, despite my stellar career and twenty-two-year employment history.

Within three weeks, I felt my body going through a transformation. I also felt compelled to go to an eWomenNetwork event when an invitation popped up in my email; I felt there was something there that I was to witness. I wasn't even supposed to be driving, so my husband dropped me off. The featured speaker was Diane Easley, the author of *Create the Life You Want*. I was seated at her table. And so began the journey of creating my life.

Just four weeks after my hysterectomy, I went back to work. I justified my decision to cut my recovery time short by going back part time. My second day back, I was called to the main office. I had to climb two flights of stairs to the office meeting room. So soon after my surgery, this climb was exhausting and difficult. Seeing my boss and HR gathered there, waiting for me, I realized I was going to be fired or forced out of my job.

I was told that they "no longer had a need for the position" I occupied in the company. Plus, they had "evidence" I was no longer an effective member of their team. They asked me if I wanted to hear this evidence, and I declined. I knew I hadn't done anything wrong except to put my daughter first. I didn't want to listen to them berate me. I realized that, not only did they no longer want me to work there, but I didn't want to be there, either.

I knew the time had come for me to leave. God had begun preparing me to start my journey when I was off work for those few weeks. It occurred to me that at that moment it was time to rebirth my journey in life. I was done with the system.

Ah, the system.

Our worldwide industrial system was originally created by men, for men. For generations, men left home to go to work and women stayed home to raise children and keep house. In industrialized nations, there were few other choices. There were always exceptions, of course, especially in times of war.

In World War II, for example, able-bodied men went off to fight and women stepped into men's positions to keep the factories and industries operating. Women workers were plugged into a system that had been created for men, and no one questioned it. Money had to be made, and we women did what we had to do.

Women continued to work. We continued to act the way we thought or were told we needed to inside a system that wasn't designed by or for women. Much of this system goes against everything we are as women. Much of this system doesn't recognize or value what we bring to the table as women.

I realize that many businesses are changing to accommodate and incorporate women. But industry wide, it's happening slowly. Although many new businesses are now owned and operated by women, being run in ways that value women as women, many others still try to use the male-oriented model of business operation.

"Women have come a long way." I hear this all the time. And I say, "Yes, we have . . . but what are we coming to?"

Unfortunately, in many of the big companies with big money that exist in an already-created male-dominated system, we women still find ourselves at a disadvantage. To survive, succeed, or even just fit in, we've had to push down our innate traits, values, and abilities: emotion, community, communication, nurturing, win-win team building, cooperative rather than competitive team working, collaboration, and mothering. We pushed down or set aside our natural tendencies to fit into a model of no emotion, only transaction. But we did it, willingly or not, because we had to.

I assert we no longer have to do that. We no longer have to act as men. We no longer need to push down who we are to survive in a system that wasn't created for us. Now's the time for us to be true to ourselves as women—for each of us to be what I call our "True Authentic Self."

I love men. I know that men have abilities we women don't have, as well as ideas and dreams that we don't have. There are many things we can learn from men, but first we need to learn how to be who we are. We are women, not men.

Some say that women are reinventing themselves. Really, we're just learning how to be true to our authentic selves.

Until we women learn to do that, and continue to do it ongoingly, we're stuck with trying to fit into the masculine world of individualism, competition, ego, aggressiveness, machismo, win/lose, and a cutthroat mindset.

Ladies, if a man took on what we do—the household duties, the child rearing duties, the caring for aging parents duties, and the taking care of everyone and everything else duties, along with making sure doctors' visits were scheduled and completed, handling the dry cleaning, shopping for food, remembering birthday gifts for the kids' friends, making sure that everyone was dressed, meeting the kids' teachers, and ensuring that homework was complete—then the work world of today would not exist as it does.

So, I say let's redesign work. Let's change our expectations of the workplace, change the expectations of others in the working world, and change the way we do business. The only thing stopping us is ourselves; we stop ourselves with the stories we carry around about our worthiness. We have a lot of excuses for maintaining a status quo that doesn't work for us. However, we have everything it takes to build our own system/business that works with who we are as women.

Generations of the women-in-bondage theme may have been stored somewhere in our energy, but it's not built into our genes. In the traditional teachings and raising of women, certain expectations have been placed upon us, and for many years we've lived our lives as if this is the only way to go on living. It's not.

Now's the time to step up. It's time to make changes. It's time to answer the call for women to be authentically self-expressed and unapologetically powerful.

It's time for us women to take our positions as leaders in this world.

When I meet women today who claw down the backs of other women, I know they're plugged into the masculine system. I'm sure of this because that's exactly what I did for many years. I had to compete, fight, and claw to survive. I had a daughter to support, and I was the breadwinner. So, I get it. But I've learned there's another way possible.

Deb Anderson, a friend of mine who's a co-author of this book, said, "Men have been conditioned to believe they're entitled to a seat at the table, and women have been conditioned to believe that seating for females is limited. Based on this erroneous assumption, many women think they must fight one another tooth and claw for those few seats. In reality, there are neither limits to the table, nor restrictions to what can be accomplished when fair-minded people of any sex gather around it."

I agree. The only restrictions women have are the ones we put on ourselves with our way of thinking and acting.

If you're a woman still plugged into the male paradigm, then you're doing what you think needs to be done; I understand. There were times that I really liked that false sense of power. I did what I was taught, and I bought into it all. (If you go to school, get good grades, get a good job, work hard, compete, and get to the top, then you'll be set for life.)

What else are you going to do when you have children you're raising, and you need that job? I'm so glad you asked.

Unplug yourself from the masculine system and plug into the feminine system.

It took me many years to learn I needed to do this, but I did. I unplugged from the masculine and plugged into my feminine. We all have both, but one sometimes runs the other. To learn how to do this, I've had help.

I have coaches. I enrolled in training and development courses, and I've spent years playing on the court of life to get a handle on things. What's playing on the court? It's having others challenge your status quo of what you think reality is, challenging you to step into something else you never knew existed, and guiding you in creating something new within that newly found reality. I also found out what had been standing in my way of the success I wanted in life. It turned out that what was in my way was me.

Once I knew my stories and my need to prove myself were running my life, I could now choose. Now that I know how to shift my point of view, I can look at choices from other perspectives or create new choices. I no longer automatically buy into what seems obvious or what I've always done. Instead, I check in with my authentic self.

Now I'm able to look past what I think I see. Believe me when I tell you, it requires a constant awakening to be aware moment by moment of what's really running the show. I have access now to looking past the obvious, seeing what's really so, and correcting my misconceptions … in every minute, every second.

As I started getting in touch with my authentic self, I grew to understand, love, and appreciate my feminine self, and I continue to cultivate it. I now fully comprehend what women can bring to the table, which is hugely missing in today's world.

Men have had theirs; now it's time for women to build ours. It's time for us to design and play our own game.

The internet and COVID have changed the landscape of the business world. I believe this has opened up opportunities for women to recreate our whole world. The pandemic sent us women back home, not just to raise the children and influence their lives, but to develop and run our businesses. So many opportunities have opened up, and so much of what's now available fits women perfectly—we're naturals. Because so much is already changing in business, I believe it's time to take advantage of this timing to make feminine changes in the world, too.

The time of having to fit into an all-masculine world has passed. Little girls have been looking for role models, and now there are more for them to see. We can stop showing them how to fit into a man's mold of success and show them what a successful woman looks like in the world. Let's teach them to be proud of who we are and guide them in building a new world that values the gifts we have as women.

Remember, we give birth. We have a strength no man has. We are mothers, nurturers, team players, lovers, communicators, leaders, supporters, organizers, listeners, community activists, and "just get it done" powerhouses. We don't simply look for the win, we create win-win. We also can learn from and adopt those things from men that add to and round out our experience in business and in the world.

We can have confidence in all we do. We can demand our full worth, not settle, and not let a "no" bother us or stop us from going forward. We can give up worrying about proving ourselves or having to be perfect. But most importantly, we can believe we are worthy. When we believe that, we can figure out everything else.

Before we take all of that on, it's time for us to heal from the inside. It's time for us to trust that God decided we were the bearer of the fruit of the world for a reason. It's time to step out of the restraints of our past. As we grow our feminine world, as we're creating our own, we have the internal power that having our own brings to us; we're showing the world there are many ways to work, not just one.

We can show men, as well as ourselves, that you don't have to work fourteen-hour days to create six- to seven-figure incomes; it can be done with fun, ease, and grace. When we know this ourselves, we will reach over and pull our men to their rightful place at our sides.

The overly masculine way of running things has kept the world out of balance and out of focus; it's up to us women to help us all regain our balance and focus. We can do it by working side-by-side with men to recreate this world. Just like it takes a female and male connection to make electricity flow, it takes female and male energy to make the world work properly. We women are key to this realignment.

Individually, we can't do it alone. One of the truths about the feminine way is that most women work better in groups, collaborating, supporting each other, and sharing our vulnerability with each other. I've created many groups for women, many opportunities to come together and start building ourselves up.

The first step is to work within yourself.

This is something you do as an individual. Reading and sharing this book is a good start. Stretch yourself, find out about yourself, and grow as a person.

Now's the time to get real. Take a good look at your life and square up to where you are, who you're being, what you have around you, and how your relationships are going. Then say, "Okay, this is where I'm at. This is who I'm being. This is what I'm doing. This is what I have." Go through that analysis of your life.

Look at what you've allowed the words in your life to mean to you. Acknowledge how they've influenced you. Notice how these words have determined who you are and what you're doing. See how they've dictated why you're where you are, and decreed what you have, or don't have, in your life. If who you are and where you are, what you're doing, and what you have makes you happy, then your words are serving you. If you're not happy, then get real about the consequences of being shackled to words that don't serve you.

Remember, words are powerful. The words you use or allow into your life determine how well your life works—or doesn't work—because sometimes your words become your shackles. Living shackled means you're using or allowing words into your life that give away your power, keep you from being fully self-expressed, or give permission to yourself and to others to view your shackles as normal.

Also remember, you're a woman, and women are creative. Being creative means you're inherently powerful. You always have the option to choose words that convey your natural, unshackled power.

The second step is to get on the court.

Take what you've read and learned in this book and then put it into action. Work with someone who'll call you on your stories about your life—someone who'll point out those automatic ways you live without realizing it. Perception is reality. What you can see is what you have access to in life. What you don't see, you don't have access to . . . and that invisible thing might be what's blocking you or keeping you from something that you never considered.

The third step is to share.

Be strong enough to be vulnerable. Have conversations. Reconnect with people you've cut out of your life. Forgive. See others as the powerful human beings they are.

As I started sharing my deepest experiences, not sure anyone would ever care about what I had to say, I realized how many other people were having the same experiences. I realized that every time I shared stories of my life, I was releasing others to do the same. Each sharing allowed me to step further away from my made-up meanings and feelings about them to allow me to see the facts of things.

Reaching out to others and sharing the real you will also allow you to see the difference you make for others. Connecting opens up the opportunity for you to see the impact you have on others, then empowers you to teach others to do the same.

The fourth step is to create.

Invent yourself anew. Instead of creating from the past, create from nothing. Creating from nothing means you have no evidence that what you're creating will be anything other than what you say it will be. What you say and the words you use give your creation its power. You can speak something new, and you can invent new things for yourself and others. You can create a new way of being.

Here's an analogy of completing the past so you can create something fresh. Let's say you want to lay down new flooring in your house. You'll want to make sure that the old flooring is all gone first—cleaned up and cleared away—because if you lay down new hardwood on top of the vinyl, tile, or carpet already there, it won't work. The new flooring will not stick tight, the surface will be bumpy, and eventually the new floor will buckle and trip you. New opportunities are just like new floors: make sure the old stuff is cleaned up, cleared away, and completed, first.

Getting a coach helped me get my old self out of my way to create my new self. I found my power. My self-expression now is a powerful attractor that sparks people into action in their lives. Sharing who I am, authentically, has released so many other women. Being authentically self-expressed and unapologetically powerful has encouraged others to discover their own voices and step into their greatness. In turn, their vulnerability and strength has encouraged others. Being coached allowed me to start uncovering the hidden shackles in my life.

I began asking myself and other women questions to allow them to start revealing and releasing their own shackles:

- What thoughts, dreams, and plans are you not allowing yourself to have?
- What old words are holding you back?
- What new words are you not allowing yourself to use, or believe?
- What are you saying, thinking, believing, or doing that stops you or has you getting in your own way?
- What are you not allowing yourself to create?

Here's something else to think about: women are not a minority. Global population numbers show us that there are as many women in the world as men. For the first time in history, women are starting more of the world's entrepreneurial businesses than men, and more women are graduating from medical schools than men. As a result, women who step into their empowering words can literally change the world, not only because the numbers are in our favor, but because of the way we think and because of our natural way of being.

I've created many women's groups focused on making six to seven-figure incomes, and I've had many successes within these groups based on the things I'm sharing with you now. Several women in my groups, even during the years of the pandemic, are on target to hit six figures. They're doing this, not in corporate jobs, but in their own businesses—businesses created to accommodate the raising and homeschooling of their children. They can work their own odd hours with freedom, ease, authenticity, and power.

All of this is accomplished by me getting on the court of life and doing the personal growth work necessary to be free from the stories of who I told myself I was (or wasn't). I worked for my freedom. I freed myself from the shackles that would've stopped me from going forward. I freed myself from the concern of not looking bad in front of others. I freed myself to be who I was meant to be and to do what I was brought here to do . . . to make a difference.

To make a difference for ourselves and others, sometimes all we need is to give ourselves permission. Sometimes granting ourselves permission doesn't occur to us. So, let me get you started by giving you permission to make a difference.

You have my permission to live your highest and most powerful life. This is what I want for you, my sister. Let's live our highest and most powerful lives together.

Give yourself permission to share what you've learned in this book.

Give yourself permission to be curious and hungry for more of this kind of information and encouragement.

Start your own Empowering Women with Words group. Get a group of women together, in person or online, maybe once a week or twice a month, to read and talk about each chapter in this book. (See contact details at the end of my bio for this chapter.)

Empower other women. When we do that, when we create a space for women to help women . . . then we all rise.

Collaborate with other women. Do something cooperatively or collaboratively, just as we writers have done. Band together with other women to be community activists. Join your voices together to become a force to be reckoned with.

Find your own words of power and have conversations that really matter. Be strong enough to be vulnerable and share your life lessons with others. As Sandra Yancey said in the foreword to this book, "Let your mess inform your message."

Create our women's world. Most importantly, give yourself permission to create. Create what calls to you, personally. Create a new world for our sons and daughters and show the younger generation that both men and women have value, and they both bring something wonderful and different to the table. Show them it can be done with freedom and ease.

But first, let's do it for ourselves.

Creating something new is giving birth to it, my sister. Creating is what we women do.

RHONDA PEOPLES has worn a lot of big hats without having gotten a big head about it. Ranging from flashy and stylish to gritty and functional, her emerging favorites include team leader, inspirational speaker, and innovative business developer.

Rhonda spent her early career working hard, competing with men, and proving her worth before discovering it might be not the only, or even the best way to do things. This created a fire in her belly to reach out to other women. She shares how women can create new paths for themselves individually and collaboratively. She leads the way by demonstrating innovative trailblazing.

Rhonda teamed with Deb Anderson to generate the first *Empowering Women with Words* collaborative book. They invited women in their circle of acquaintance to join them in this endeavor; all shared their personal stories, life lessons, passions, and insights. Together, this group of remarkable women founded the Empowering Women Alliance.

Contact Rhonda for speaking engagements, coaching, or training:

> LinkedIn: Rhonda Peoples
> Email: rhonda@rhondapeoples.com

Find out more about the Empowering Women Alliance and the Empowering Women with Words book series, inspiring women to be authentically self-expressed and unapologetically powerful:

> EmpoweringWomenAlliance.com

AN EMPOWERING INVITATION

The authors' intent in writing and publishing this book is to make a positive difference in the lives of women. Each chapter is meant to be thought provoking, talked about, and shared. During their collaboration, each writer discovered her authentic voice and learned to claim her personal power without apology.

The authors hope you will choose to share with other women your empowering, enlightening, inspiring, uplifting, or encouraging experience of reading this book.

A great way to do this is by starting or joining an Empowering Women With Words group. In these intimate gatherings, women come together in person or online to share insights and discuss each chapter. The authors provide a supportive, group format for individual self-expression that honors every contribution to the conversation. They also offer exciting ideas and opportunities for other collaborative writing projects.

Express yourself, claim your power, and share an innovative, difference-making experience by creating or participating in an Empowering Women With Words group.

Find details and information about discussion questions at:

EmpoweringWomenAlliance.com